The House of Shekinah:
A Struggle to Find the
Visible Presence of God

The House of Shekinah: A Struggle to Find the Visible Presence of God

OUR STORY

Ruth Elizabeth (Heighton) Gibbs

ISBN: 1517367883
ISBN 13: 9781517367886
Library of Congress Control Number: 2016904454
CreateSpace Independent Publishing Platform
North Charleston, South Carolina

Contents

Preface · vii

Endorsements · ix

Chapter 1   Where It All Began · 1

Chapter 2   One Redhead and a Campus Full of Boys · · · · · · · · · · · · · · 16

Chapter 3   I Thought It Would Be Perfect · · · · · · · · · · · · · · · · · · · 20

Chapter 4   Together at Last · 25

Chapter 5   It Can't Be · 28

Chapter 6   A Journey North · 35

Chapter 7   Daddy, I Want to Go Home · 40

Chapter 8   The Good Life...Our Own Fairy Tale · · · · · · · · · · · · · · · · 47

Chapter 9   Camelot · 60

Chapter 10 Seduced by the Dark Side of the Force · · · · · · · · · · · · · · · 80

Chapter 11 Some Breaks in the Fog · 94

Chapter 12 House of Shekinah · 123

Chapter 13 So Many Good Decisions · 138

Chapter 14 Room 101 · 148

Chapter 15 Unthinkable · 153

Chapter 16 Interlude of Miracles · 178

Chapter 17 We Did Follow the Yellow Brick Road · · · · · · · · · · · · · · · · 187

Chapter 18 Lord, You Stretch the Shoes · 196

Chapter 19 Take Me Home · 201

Chapter 20 Yes, Chicken Little, the Sky Has Fallen · · · · · · · · · · · · · · · · 213

Chapter 21 Barnyard Care · 224

Chapter 22 Grief Is a Long Journey · 232

Chapter 23 Tidal Wave of Grief · 236

Chapter 24 Life Experience Changes Theology · · · · · · · · · · · · · · · · · · 246

Chapter 25 Salt or Healing Balm: A More Excellent Way · · · · · · · · · · · · 253

Postscript Kyrie Eleison—Lord, Have Mercy · · · · · · · · · · · 257

Epilogue · 263

Glossary · 267

Bibliography · 271

Preface

As a daughter, sister, wife, mother, grandmother, aunt, friend, and daughter of God, I want to open the door of my heart so that you might peak in. We are all capable of putting on masks to cover the pains and less-than-perfect experiences of our lives. But it is these very experiences that mold us into the human beings we are or are becoming. I have chosen to open the book of our lives without a mask.

It is my belief that all humans are omnibuses of experiences and genetics. As I take you down my personal life path and the life paths of our eight children that truth will ever be apparent. The pages of this book represent our story. It is a testament to the effects that a myriad of factors have on an individual: early imprinting, a generational mind-set, church affiliations, our own choices, the choices of others, and the words of those who meant well (but unknowingly pierced our hearts). It is a testament to our daughter Teresa's strength of character and will to fight off death.

Furthermore, this story is about love between two people: their shared passion for God, their commitment to polish jewels for the Kingdom of God, and the effect of the omnibus in life—over which we do not always have control.

I desire and invite you to walk with me through a fairy-tale existence, tragedy, loss of faith, renewed redemption, and healing. After the smoke of battle clears, we remain standing tall. Please take the journey with me.

Endorsements

Dr. Cecilia Ranger, educational advisor and friend

"Once upon a time" a certain energetic, enthusiastic, eager redhead walked into my office when I was serving as Chair of a Religion and Philosophy Department at Marylhurst University in Oregon. Though it is possible that I favor red-heads, for my father was one, Ruth Gibbs, B.A., became my favorite student. She shared that she had raised seven children and added a son from India, who excelled in their academic work, assisted her husband to achieve his Masters in Sociology, and that she too wanted to be an outstanding graduate student. We made a deal: She would submit her papers to me ahead of every deadline; I would edit them; she would produce A quality papers and graduate with an A or A- Average. And, so it was!

That may be a paradigm of the story she tells in twenty-five chapters of *House of Shekinah*. Ruth knew her gifts and goals, often set them aside for years to assist others in achieving theirs, and then effectively moved in the direction that the Spirit of Shekinah had led her all along. This book leads us to that House, opens the door, walks us into rooms of suffering and joy, and allows us to sit down at the table with her to enjoy the fruits of a life well-lived.

Cecilia A. Ranger, SNJM, PhD
Former Chair, Religion and Philosophy, Marylhurst University, Oregon
Currently, Adjunct Professor, several universities in Washington, Oregon, California

Reverend Jack Prentiss Hansen, pastor, friend, Doctor of Ministry

There are few people willing to be as honestly transparent as Ruth Gibbs in sharing the years of their personal family life. Many readers will identify with the ongoing Gibbs' adventure with joy and heartbreak. There are very few books like this one to awaken us to what it means to be a family.

Jack P. Hansen, Pastor, D. Min.

Priscilla Thomas, personal friend

Don and I attended Northwest Christian University together in the late 1940's. Later on, my husband, Durwood and I, became fast friends with the whole Gibbs family, spending many celebrant occasion together. It was when their oldest daughter was stricken with leukemia that it was our privilege to journey with them through a very dark and devastating time. They have weathered the storm and have been an example of true family love.

Don Ralph Gibbs, oldest son of Don and Ruth Gibbs

Courageous people, organizations, and even countries have been compared to the mythical Phoenix, rising from the ashes of their destruction when they emerge from catastrophic events. Likewise, in the pages that follow, you will find a story of innocence, love, combat, faith, obedience, and transformation. It is the journey of two modern champions of faith as they emerge from their fiery furnace of life in the 20th and 21st centuries. As one of the seven children that shared their journey, I can assure you that you will laugh, cry, grieve, rejoice, and be overcome by great anger at the cruelty of believers and family. Perhaps, you may see your own journey in that of Don and Ruth Gibbs.

While there are many life-lessons to be gleaned from this Love Story, the one that resonates most with me is the impact of something I call "Disney Theology." I was born in the shadow of California Disneyland and, during my youth, watched every Disney movie ever made. In doing so, I/we came to believe that as long as we followed Biblical principles, even if we encountered trials, we would always have a happy Cinderella ending. While this Walt Disney "Theology" is not scriptural, such was our belief in the positive outcomes of walking with Jesus.

When a devastating life event occurred, such as the untimely and very painful death of a daughter and sister, there are unintended consequences for the "Disney" believer.

In summary, this "Tale of Two Believers" and their personal Fiery Furnace is my story too. It does have a happy ending.

With great gratitude and affection for sharing the ride with me,

Signed, One of your sons,

D. Ralph Gibbs, Lt Colnel, B.S, M.S Director of Aviation & Assistant

Professor
Eastern Kentucky University Aviation
Home of the "1000-Hour Power" Colonels
(859) 622-1014
http://aviation.eku.edu

Jason Taylor Deissl-Gibbs, B.S., M.B.A., M.S, youngest son

This book takes an authentic look at the personal costs of being brutally confronted with deep-seated fear and loss for anyone on a spiritual journey. Regardless of one's faith or beliefs, it is not difficult to find someone who has been affected in a negative way by supposed followers of an organized religion during a time of difficulty. Through the author's retelling of her own life story she addresses this religious naiveté head on and leads the reader down a path that ultimately embraces the impermanence of life and the discovery of the redemption and presence of God that we can all find through true community with each other.

Abraham Philip (Raju), foster son, Ph.D.

The British journalist Malcom Muggeridge, who was influenced by Mother Teresa in coming to Christ, wrote, *"Contrary to what might be expected, I look back on experiences that at the time seemed especially desolating and painful. I now look back upon them with particular satisfaction. Indeed, I can say with complete truthfulness that everything I have learned in my seventy-five years in this world, everything that has truly enhanced and enlightened my existence, has been through affliction and not through happiness, whether pursued or attained."*

In her book, House of Shekinah: A struggle to find the visible presence of God, Ruth Elizabeth Gibbs echoes Muggeridge's observation that our existence is indeed "enhanced and enlightened" through affliction. She takes us on a remarkable journey through the canyons of her life experiences and shows us that we can trust God to dispense His redemptive and healing grace in our suffering and pain. Though Ruth walked through the valley of suffering—death of a child due to cancer and financial reversals—she was not alone. God was with her in her trials, and He brought her to a broad place (Ps. 118:5). In the House of Shekinah, Ruth clears the blinding fog of "health and wealth" theology and helps us to see that suffering is God's instrument to make us more like Christ.

I know that the story of Ruth Gibbs is true because I am a part of her life story. I came to know Ruth and her husband, Don, when I came to the United States at the age of eighteen to pursue my education. The moment I met them, there was an inseparable bond between us, which continues to the present day. Ruth and Don embraced me as one of their own children. Through the years, I have witnessed first-hand the testing of her faith and the endurance which enables her to say, "But He knows the way that I take; *when* He has tested me, I shall come forth as gold" (Job 23:10). Her legacy of love, faith, and hope continues to glow "like the shining sun that shines ever brighter unto the perfect day" (Pr. 4:18).

Rev. Abraham Philip, PhD
President, Proclamation Ministries
Newark, Delaware.

CHAPTER 1

Where It All Began

My Church

It was on a snowy Christmas Eve in 1932, in a small Eastern Washington community of six thousand that I was born with a love for life. And other than when I had whooping cough in the first three months of life, I was happy and contented—or at least so friends and family tell me. My early beginnings were in the Baptist church and a little mission church, both containing very loving folk. Both of my parents were members of the Baptist church, which meant any children born to that union were put on what is called the Cradle Roll. The church committed to following up with these children on the roll to make sure they were nurtured and instructed in the ways of the Lord.

When I was around two years of age, my mother became acquainted with an osteopath who belonged to an Advent Christian church. He convinced her to come to his little mission church. I do not know why both my parents began going to this little mission church, for my mother's friends were in the Baptist church. Even though I have nothing but positive memories of going to this church, some of the church's theology added to my greatest phobia in life: soul sleeping. This philosophy states that rather than going to heaven at death, you lie in the grave unknowing until Christ returns at the Last Day. I eventually developed some deep-seated emotional turmoil from the continual talk of death—truly a conundrum of troubling messages! I do not believe death should be the prominent discussion for young children. This seemed to be the consuming talk for those being indoctrinated into this Advent Christian church. This philosophy was to be blaring throughout my life.

However, the little mission church had a warm atmosphere, and there were often guest speakers. On one Sunday evening, as the guest pastor asked everyone to stand for the last hymn, he asked anyone who wanted to love and follow the Jesus he preached about to simply raise his or her hand. From the security of my father's arms, I raised my two-year-old hand. No one told me I should; I just knew I loved the Jesus I had heard about from my mother.

That is a happy memory of my father, but my other childhood memories are very limited regarding his involvement with his family. I am not sure when he stopped going to church or totally withdrew from his family, but my memory gives me ancient glimpses of him singing in a church choir with a fine voice. In my earliest memories, I know he played card games with my older sister and me on cold winter nights and played his harmonica to entertain us. Those are good memories, but the unpleasant memories are more vivid. I remember him complaining about women who took leadership or women who dressed fashionably. He thought women and children should have two outfits: one for dress and one for play and work. He believed women as well as children should be seen and not heard. It was a man's world in his era. His complaints did not sway me; I loved church in spite of his complaints—including the women in leadership who were fashionably dressed!

I loved being coached to perform in church. I would be placed on a table in front of the congregation, so I could be seen singing "Zacchaeus Was a Wee Little Man" or "This Little Light of Mine," all the while delighting in the oohs and aahs! I did love the attention from those loving people. That was where my desire for the spotlight and leadership took root. This was where the desire to be involved in all that life had to offer began in my limited understanding. At that time I truly was undaunted by negatives.

Even before I entered first grade and on into the primary grades, it was not uncommon to see me on my knees at a Wednesday night prayer meeting. At that time only my mother attended church, driving us often to the little mission church east of Lewiston, Idaho. The worst part of going to church at that time was that as my sister and I grew taller, we had to ride in the back of a pickup truck. It bothered me more than it seemed to bother my older sister. I tried to hide from the glares of following car passengers. It was twenty minutes of pure agony for me—the time it took us to get to that little mission church.

On those prayer meeting nights, though I was dutifully kneeling in supposed prayer, my mind was racing with goals and dreams. Others were praying, but I did not bother to listen; my imagination was running wild with my own dreams. I was usually in church at least four times a week, including Sunday morning and evening worship, prayer meetings, and, of course, women's missionary meeting… or was that *gossip meeting*? Even though I spent much of the week at church, it was never enough. I lined up little chairs and set my dolls upright to participate in a living-room church of my own. I was sure my dolls absorbed it all, and so did I. I was the pastor, song leader, Sunday school teacher, and mommy to those dollies.

As time went on, my Sunday school experience remained positive, but the preaching of "thou shalt not" and my home life governed by my father's harsh view on women and children created a great chasm of disparity. This early conditioning or imprinting presented me with the ironic realization that many things in life are a comingling of good and bad. It prepared me for a lifelong battle of filtering through erroneous ideas. It forced me to continually embellish the positive and discard the shackles of the negative.

My Home

My first and only home growing up was a humbly built two-story house with a basement—much of it unfinished. This was 1932, soon after the devastation of the Depression. My father was a very frugal and closed-minded man who believed any roof over one's head was adequate living. He had saved a great deal of money since high-school graduation by being so frugal, but he had lost much money in the 1929 financial crash. In retrospect I perceive that during that time, he became a very self-centered man. He prided himself on the fact that he was a World War I veteran, and after years of being on his own, he was not ready to take on the responsibilities of family life.

My sister and I slept in the upstairs bedroom. To get there you had to go outside the kitchen, into the screened porch, and climb the enclosed stairway up a very dark and spooky passage leading to the dimly lit upstairs, which was more like an attic than a bedroom. When we were quite young, flashlights were the only source of light in that domain.

Later, my father built an outhouse that was more elaborate than the house. He called it the shower house and not the outhouse! It had a hot-water tank on the roof for showers in the summer. It had a two-hole toilet and Montgomery Ward catalog pages for toilet tissue. We had a white chamber pot for nighttime, which had to be emptied each morning.

My dad had built the house using lumber he had acquired by merely hauling it away from discarded piles of others. The lumber was left from barns and houses that were dilapidated, or there was even new lumber left over from contractors. Most all were happy to have it hauled away. However, the shower house was built with new lumber, as was a classy barn that was built later on. This greatly disturbed my mother, who very much wanted a classy life and a classy house to go along with it.

My parents' union was already plagued with misunderstanding and heartbreak when I was born. The age difference between my parents may have played a significant role (my father was thirteen years older and had been in the military and on his own since high school), or it may have been the false expectations they both had entering into marriage. Perhaps a man of thirty-three marrying a young high school graduate of twenty was a recipe for disaster!

My mother had spent many years crippled and in a wheelchair, thus missing some school years in school, which put her behind her contemporaries. Her brother had thrown her across a creek when she was quite young. He had not intended to injure her, but he had. Her family opted not to take her to a doctor or seek help other than providing a wheelchair. I am sure that is where some of her self-pity and need to be cared for began. She was a timid and compliant child, the youngest, a twin in a family of ten children. Even with this handicap, she was very studious, becoming the valedictorian at graduation. I believe, from her own words, she had envisioned greatness and love. From many stories I heard later on, this truly was a generation of dysfunction. It was an era when men were the lords of their families and a bit—or even thoroughly—sadistic! Most husbands and wives did not have cherished walking-side-by-side relationships.

Whatever the causal factors were, I determined at a very young age that my life and future would be different. I was a strong-willed child, beyond my years in perception of what was good and noble as well as what was right and wrong. My older sister has told me I wrote an essay when only in grade school on the perfect family, which sent my mother into a fit of tears. I do not remember this, but I did have ideals of the perfect family. What does a child know of breaking the cycle of a broken home? But I did have a head full of dreams and goals for my life. I was an idealist and knew I did not want my grown-up life to be the same as I witnessed in the grown-ups around me. Children do not understand the dynamics of a dysfunctional home. They can only react to given stimuli, whether they are positive or negative. Children should not pay the price of generational dysfunction, though they do. It has taken me a lifetime to overcome that stimulus.

My Father's Influence

By this point in my few years of life, my father was slowly becoming a nonexistent commodity. I have a vivid recollection from when I was three or four of my father coming in from outdoors. He was a manager at Safeway at this time. He usually did outdoor chores when he arrived home, before even coming into the house. It was his custom to work until dark, not considering when my mother would have the evening meal prepared. He was in his thirties and had never had to answer to anyone else's needs.

It was dark and cold, so I am assuming it was wintertime. When he finally did come in, there was only a dimly lit kerosene lamp burning in the corner of the small kitchen, right next to the wood-burning stove. Since there was no indoor plumbing, he would wash his hands in a washbasin of cold water. It sat on a stool near the kerosene lamp. After leaving very dirty water, he instructed me to wash my hands. I refused. From birth on, I think, I had a fastidious belief in being clean, not wanting to get any part of me dirty!

Continued demands and continued refusals brought on a whipping with a belt...and still I refused to put my hands in that dirty water. The stinging of the belt and the forming welts did not alter my refusal to put my young hands in that grossly dirty water. Sobs—probably more like screams—filled the house. Finally my mother rocked me to sleep. This incident left me with a feeling of repulsion for the man called my father, who wanted me to wash in his dirty water. I had already eaten and had clean hands with no need for washing. But even so, if a child needs his or her hands washed, should not the child's hands be washed in the clean water first?

Events like this were confusing to a small child. Compliance (even against one's will) was all that was acceptable. That event was imprinted on my life as a defining moment. In my mind, at that very early age, I determined to walk on a higher plain. Maybe I was stubborn and determined, but this trait served me well in later years.

At that young age, I knew I was different from my family. My older sister said she was sure a stork had dropped me because of the stark difference. I was not compliant. Perhaps that mind-set did save me from the unsupervised boys of the neighborhood. And it most definitely served me well in steering clear of the dirty old men in the community, who gladly would have taken advantage of a compliant, young child. The families in the area were unaware of this type of behavior and would have been shocked that such deviousness was lurking in the supposedly God-fearing community.

In the ensuing years, it seemed my father was always angry, often stating he wished he had not married and singing "Waiting for Ships That Never Come In." He became more and more distant. He frequently took off, and his where-abouts were unknown. He no longer played games on cold winter nights, no longer played his harmonica, and in general spent his evenings working or fish-ing until dark. He was a selfish, self-centered male who thought women were there to serve his every need. He did not know how to be a leader, nurturer, and shareholder in the development of family togetherness.

Out of this setting, I listened and looked to other adults for nurturing and guidance. In spite of this home life scenario, I always felt I was a little special because I was born on Jesus's birthday and had red hair. It is odd the things that can identify one's self-concept.

My Mother's Influence

In spite of the home dynamics, my mother remained friends with some of the people from the Baptist church where she had attended for many years. The Perkins, an older couple, had two daughters in their twenties, and they—as well as their father, Dad Perkins—took me on as a project of love. Dad Perkins gave me all the male love I lacked from my own father.

In the years before I entered first grade, my mother would read Bible stories to me from *Hurlbut's Story of the Bible*. I wanted to hear the stories over and over. I especially loved the story of Solomon and the two women who came to him. Each of the women claimed the one living child was hers. One mother had rolled onto her child during the night, smothering it. She then placed her dead child next to the other woman and took that woman's live child. These two women went to King Solomon to ask him to solve the dilemma.

Solomon was only twenty at the time. He declared that the remaining child would be cut in two and half given to each of them. On hearing this, the real mother said, "Give the child to the other woman." Thus Solomon returned the child to the rightful mother. I began, at that very point, praying for wisdom for my life, even though I was not yet in school. My heart was very tender to the teachings I learned from my mother.

My World

As I became older and roamed the large acreage surrounding my home—along with my little collie, Laddie, who was always my playmate—it became my own little world. There was the frame of an old Model T sitting at the end of our four-acre place. I would crawl up on that old car, get in the driver's seat, and go on many an adventure. From this broken-down inner skeleton of an old Model T, in the silence of the country, after hours of imagined adventures, I could be summoned with calls or whistles. No one in that era feared for the safety of children roaming the countryside.

My imagination always took me beyond the trappings, and I lived in a fantasy world with only old-fashioned toys such as stilts to maneuver, grape arbors to climb, cliffs and a nearby riverbed to collect rocks from, and a tire swing to send me flying through the air. When I was not involved in physical activity, I could be found nursing a runt piglet rejected by its mother at birth. I would take it into the kitchen and sit by the old wood stove, wrapping it in a baby blanket to keep it warm while feeding it with a baby bottle. Such was my life on a farm.

These activities—which also included riding a bicycle—provided more physical activity and entertainment than some city-born children experience. There were few other children living that far out in the country, but the few found great fun in playing kick the can or other games! A day full of playing brought peaceful nights tucked into a bed with clean, line-dried sheets. Nights were peaceful until a later date.

I loved attending vacation Bible school in the summer. I remember one particular program where we were to act out the Bible story recorded in Matthew 25:1–13 of the five virgins who had their lamps full and the five foolish virgins who were not prepared for the master's return. I remember thinking and praying that I always wanted my lamp full, to be ready for the Lord's appearing.

Though my relationships were rich with many examples of wholesome living, I wanted so much more in life than what this little acreage allowed. Though in reflection, from this vantage point in life, I realize how rich my early life was in spite of the family dysfunction. My involvement in the church community continued, and I was blessed by powerful speakers who ignited the desires of my heart along with speakers who put fear in my heart. In spite of the fear that many speakers used to control behavior, my heart was receptive to the teachings I absorbed into my life.

Missionaries (Worthiness versus Beauty)

I was in awe of missionaries who came from India and China to preach in our little mission church. On one occasion missionaries from India came and brought their young Indian foster daughter, Belle Kari, with them. I was very young and impressionable, and I loved beauty.

Belle Kari was probably seventeen or eighteen years of age. She instantly became my idol, and when she slipped a narrow, gold glass bangle bracelet on my wrist, I was as smitten as though God himself had touched me. Her beauty—with her dark-olive skin and flashing white teeth—was overpowering to my young, idealist desires. Right there and then, I fell in love with the Indian culture. I would go to India to be a missionary—that was if I could become holy enough, for already the concept of worthiness was being imprinted on my heart. I was smitten with the idea of adventure that would take me beyond the Clarkston hills that enclosed this small community. However, because of my fundamentalist teachings, I probably could not be a missionary. I knew I did not qualify according to the fundamentalist standards. I would have to work on holiness. I was taught that Christian workers had to be plain and saintly, without outward adornment.

My Sunday school experience remained positive; it was the preaching of "thou shalt not" and my home life that created a great chasm of disparity, a cognitive dissonance embedded within my own spirituality. This early conditioning has resulted in a lifelong battle of filtering through erroneous ideas, embellishing the positive, and discarding the shackles of the negative. I wanted to be beautiful, sing, and wear makeup. My mother's fundamentalist involvement, I believed, had warped her own beliefs. She never cut her hair, wore absolutely no makeup, and wore only clothing that covered her full body. So I heard about being unadorned both in the home and at church. Women who were adorned were considered "women of the street." Though it was never explained what a "woman of the street" was, the young people knew it wasn't what our elders wanted for us. This teaching created a dilemma in my mind of worthiness versus a gifting or calling to ministry. I was so young and yet so deceived by imprinting!

We had prophetic evangelists who came and showed their slides of future happenings. This put both fear and faith in my heart. It seemed these missionaries and evangelists took a special liking to me. They said my interest went beyond my young years. So I wrestled with being inspired but conflicted about worthiness. Most guest speakers brought special guest musicians and singers with them, and they opened my heart to the world of gospel music. These gifted singers and musicians left me inspired—especially the singers who wore lipstick, which was forbidden in my home.

Love of Children

As I grew into the middle school years, radio was our main entertainment in the winter months. There were some grand programs to listen to. Henry Aldridge of *Oh, Henry!* was one of my favorites. However, my mother thought I spent too much time with my ear glued to the radio, so I started reading books. I was allowed to read the Nancy Drew mysteries and the Bobbsey Twins series. I also memorized full chapters of the Bible.

But my favorite books were the Bobbsey Twins series. In one adventure an abandoned baby was left on the twins' doorstep. Reading this filled me with an unusual desire, and I found myself praying, "Dear Jesus, would you leave a little bundle on my doorstep someday?" My mother was friends with a young couple who had four children, ages two, three, four, and five. I loved to go help with those little ones. The seed was sown for my own future and love of children. If I couldn't play with live babies, I would play with my dollies and baby paper dolls. My older sister would play with me, but she preferred the paper dolls of Sonja Henie, the famous Norwegian figure skater. Interestingly, to this day she is enamored with ice skaters.

Fear of Death

Another defining event happened when I was six years old. It was early fall, and my baby sister had just been born a few days earlier. My mother was with a friend, sorting grapes in a big galvanized washtub. It was dusk, but we were all in the kitchen with the dimly lit kerosene lamp.

My maternal grandmother came breathlessly into this setting and said, "Poppy just got up to turn off the radio and slumped over onto the floor." I learned later that my grandfather had been spitting blood into a bucket and was told he only had six months to live. He died from cirrhosis of the liver. My mother walked back to their house, which was approximately one thousand feet down the road, on the adjacent property. I am not sure how they alerted the local undertaker to pick up my grandfather. I do not remember where my grandmother stayed that night, but the friend helping my mother with the grapes stayed with my two sisters and me while my mother dealt with this unhappy event.

It was September, and in a few months I would be seven years old. I had started first grade, had a new baby sister, and experienced a family death. This was quite a lot for a six-year-old to handle. When my mother left, in the dusk of that evening, both my older sister and I went out on the porch to climb those stairs to the darkened two upstairs rooms. I remember it being so creepy that I clung to my sister. This little room, more like an anteroom, was at the top of the stairs, just before you entered the one small bedroom. This was the room where all the stuff was stored that would not fit in the rest of the house. There was only one window in that room. Underneath the small window, a travel trunk sat. I climbed up on that trunk and peered out, trying to see this unhappy event unfold. I was terrified and tried to imagine what was going on even though I could see nothing.

The next day relatives began arriving at our small, overcrowded house. As they came and the funeral took place in a local mortuary, my phobias began to manifest. There were tears as relatives looked down at my grandfather as he lay in his casket. Tears of grief or relief, I will never know, for my grandfather had been a vindictive, sadistic, and domineering man. I had experienced some of his sadistic behavior, as he would chase me home and say my mother was waiting to beat me. He probably was drunk from drinking wood alcohol most of the time, so I am told!

He had held all of his children in terror of his violent temper. His boys had left home in their early teenage years. My mother said he had caught her looking through a catalog. As the page stopped at men's underwear, her father beat her and accused her of looking at undressed men. Free Methodist training was their involvement with religion. The Free Methodists were an extremely judgmental, restrictive, and unloving community. When my mother chose to marry at age twenty, she cut her long hair into a bob, and consequentially her father disowned her. It seemed everything was a sinful act.

My grandfather's funeral was the beginning of my defining fear of death. The mortuary, called Merchants, had a dome-centered door, and if I were driven past this entrance or even near the street I would scream out in terror. This happened to be the main street of Clarkston, which made it pretty hard to avoid.

From that point on I had nightmares of caskets surrounding me. I feared going to bed at night because of the imagined caskets filling my upstairs bedroom, which—as I have mentioned—was a little spooky even without caskets crowding it. I dreaded nighttime. Death and funerals caused me great stress. My father forbade us from having any kind of night-light on, be it flashlight, kerosene lamp, or, later, electricity because it would cost too much money. Statements my mother made later enhanced this phobia. She seemed either to have had many older friends who died, or she had an unhealthy obsession with funerals. She would take me to them, and as we rode behind the hearses, she would say, "Do you see her coffin?" I understood it to mean, "Do you see her coughing?" Another statement she made was, "They could almost sit up." Or when my mother would take me—with my Dy-Dee doll—to Women's Missionary Society quilting and gossip sessions, I would hear such things as, "Wouldn't that just make Mr. Burlingame turn over in his grave?" Supposedly his wife was now having various affairs. Whatever that was, I did not know!

For an impressionable young child with a vivid imagination, these images and quotes caused me great trauma throughout life. Also, it was an era of older people taking delight in sharing stories of the morbid and macabre. *The Three Faces of Eve* became my own story, though I did not have to kiss my dead grandfather, nor did I develop multiple personalities. It took some time to tuck these happenings into my subconscious!

Becoming a Young Adult

When I was in the fifth grade, my father went to Alaska to work on the ALCAN Highway. He was gone for three years. I do not remember much about that time except that when he came home, he was more distant than ever. I was not excited to see him, for I remembered how my mother had struggled putting in a large garden and canning the produce from that garden. She had also raised chickens. My mother would gather ten chickens or so, take a hatchet, and cut their heads off on the chopping block; let them flop around in the yard until they lay still; put them in boiling water, pluck their feathers, and finally butcher them to take to a local store's rental freezer. We ate well—as did the neighborhood, for it seemed my mother fed them all. She was always delivering produce, eggs, and meat to neighbors close and even in town.

During that time one of my responsibilities was to milk the cow and feed the rabbits. The work did not hurt me, but the two-mile walk to school after the morning chores, carrying my trumpet, would give me ammunition later in life to taunt my children about how easy they had it.

We remained very active in the local Advent Christian church, which I loved. In all the experiences of life, I remained in love with Jesus and in love with so many people who crossed the pages of my young life. But I recall how I cringed with guilt in the presence of a visiting holy, pious, white-haired, super-religious evangelist married to a plain and holy, equally pious woman. He came to my church to preach a holiness gospel of don'ts. "Girls, do not adorn your outward appearance with styled hair, earrings, or lipstick—only prostitutes do that—or expose any part of your body. Do not attend movies, dance, play cards, hold hands with the opposite sex, swim together in the same pool or river, or keep company with those who do."

Guilt mounted in my heart, for I did it all! I also snuck out to go to dances and movies and even ice-skated cheek to cheek when the river below our house was frozen over. In this man's presence, I cringed and felt even more alienated from God, and the disparity between my desire to serve God and my feelings of unworthiness grew even wider. I still wanted to praise Jesus in song amid my raging teenage years of exploding-and-developing personality.

With no father figure in my life, the evangelist's theology and words only added more confusion and damage to the innocent desire of my heart. He would have had more influence if he had just slipped his arm around this young girl, affirming her search for the real God of the ages. Compounded with this religion of don'ts was the doctrine of soul sleeping. The members became quite eloquent in quoting scripture to give their doctrinal belief credence. I believe death and dying are scary enough subjects, but to build a denomination on them—to teach a child in the formative years that soul sleeping is a precious doctrine—has life-long implications. It was freeing when, later in life, I learned the truth about these super spirituals' troubled personal lives, but it was also infuriating to have been subjected to such control tactics. That being said, some of the leaders, of that denomination, were great spiritual models to follow and I am grateful for their influence.

In spite of the dysfunction and phobias, my early life was good and happy—mostly because I was a happy child and a bubbly teenager and even grew into a happy young woman living a life filled with activities. I was a magnet for friends in school and at church. In school I took up the trumpet and French horn. My happiest times were performing in band or choir. My mother struggled to pay for voice lessons. She would sell eggs and chickens to be able to afford those lessons. (The feeling was there once again: I loved the recognition of the audience when I performed.)

My dream to change the cycle of a broken home was the focus of my existence. I took refuge in church fellowship, many school friends, a head full of dreams, and my determination to live out that ideal. Even the harsh fundamentalism did not deter me from my goals. When in an evening evangelical service an older, dear pious lady leaned forward and whispered to me that I should go forward and confess to the Lord the sinfulness of wearing earrings, I was confused, but I did not go forward nor give up my earrings! The belief that Jesus might come and find you in a movie or dance hall, banishing you forever from his love and heaven to come, was not something a young, gregarious teenager wanted to hear. But even though it did cause much guilt, I set the guilt aside and continued my charmed life. I knew I wanted to be a disciple of Christ with all my heart and intended to do some kind of Christian ministry when I grew up. Also, so help me God, I did not want to carry on the critical spirit of those missionary ladies and pious preachers. If I could become good enough!

On one occasion, when my mother was in the hospital, some of the church elders called on her. I was there, and they asked me to lay hands on my mother, which I fearfully did. A strange sensation went through me. My mother said she felt a surprising power go through her body as well. I pondered this experience and wondered if God had granted the desire of my heart to be used by him with a healing ministry, physically and emotionally. How could this be when it appeared I was too adorned with outer beauty, according to the old ladies of the church?

As a gregarious teenager, friends were very important to me. I threw parties for my friends; I was the only one sober on many occasions and looked after their welfare. I always had girlfriends spend the night. My youth group filled many hours. I began singing in a quartet that sang at the Saturday night Youth for Christ meetings. Local pastors were in charge of these meetings, where they also showed videos of the young Billy Graham. I loved being involved in the youth work of the community.

Another defining event in my life came when the bass singer in our quartet was drowned in the Sandy River in Oregon, where our church held a yearly camp meeting. This fine young man stayed after the camp meeting was over to clean up the grounds. He decided to go swimming after his work was done. The

Sandy River is known for its changes in the depth of the water that can happen at any given time. He stepped into an area that was over his head, and—not knowing how to swim—he drowned and was not discovered until the next day. I was devastated, and this renewed my fear of dying.

However, our quartet—now a trio—was asked to sing at his funeral. I agreed to sing only if I did not have to be anywhere near the casket. It was agreed that we would sing in the curtained room near the back. Besides, I was in love with the tenor, and I loved to sing, so I set my phobias aside! It was difficult, but in spite of my phobias, it gave me joy to be in this kind of ministry. I was too gregarious to be sad for long.

When I turned sixteen, the church youth gave me a surprise birthday party. It was a perfume party. My friends all knew perfume was my trademark. I lived on a farm, around pigs, cows, goats, chickens, and manure piles, and I wanted to have a classier identity. I dressed to the hilt, always wore makeup and perfume, and wanted to be as beautiful and perfect as I might. I was forever trying to improve and work with the gifts God had given me. How happy, rich, and blessed I felt.

My older sister had married at sixteen, after a severe beating from the man called our father. My mother, not wanting me to depart early as well, let me do just about anything I desired, including wearing a wardrobe to make any teenage girl the envy of her classmates. This was in the era when credit cards came into being. I am sure my mother was first in line to sign up. And as money became more plentiful, she became a true shopaholic!

My classmates and I had much fun and laughter together. But they too learned of my phobia of death and would take delight in trying to take me to the cemetery late at night. I would scream in terror even though I was old enough to know better. That phobia was deeply imprinted!

Ready for the Road Ahead

I do not want to leave the reader thinking I had a horrible and dysfunctional time growing up. Let me restate that I truly believe one can learn from negative experiences by sorting out the bad and retaining the good. In spite of his harshness and distance, I did learn important traits from my father—a thing like honesty, hard work, freedom from addictive vices, and that everything has a place.

From my mother I learned by observing the situations and events that motivated and afflicted her. I wrote a poem later in life that captured these lessons:

Tribute to My Mother

Out of your broken dreams, I was inspired to hold on to my dreams.
Whereas your powerful intellect was crushed and impaired by insurmountable roadblocks, I caught the challenge of winging upon mountains of achievement.

Your desire for travel and adventure
made me determined to experience travel and adventure of my own.

You ministered to those around you in need,
A trait I continue with gratitude to you.

Your disgust for men only made me cherish them more deeply.

You wallowing in self-pity for the pit into which you were cast,
Caused me to climb to great heights of positive living.

In your impaired way, you did love the Lord with all your heart,
For that I am eternally grateful and have held on to it tenaciously.

All your brokenness caused you to leave this earth far too soon,
I pray you are now able to achieve all your greatest dreams and more.

So it was, with a head full of dreams and goals and the lessons I had gleaned from my early years, I was ready to take on the world. Or so I thought!

CHAPTER 2

One Redhead and a Campus Full of Boys

A New Life Begins

With fear and excitement, I graduated. I was so sad to leave my friends, but I was excited to leave home and experience the world. I always felt trapped in the valley of Clarkston, Washington. Hills surrounded this small community, and I knew there must be excitement and adventure beyond those hills. So, the fall after graduation from high school, I headed for Northwest Christian University in Eugene, Oregon, to acquire a degree in psychology.

I was an idealist determined to save the youth of the world with my ideals and faith. I went off to college to become a youth worker. At that point I thought I wanted to work with troubled youth—those who had grown up in the same dysfunction I had. Though there were colleges nearby, such as Washington State University and University of Idaho, I wanted the adventure of going far away from Clarkston. I wanted to experience life on my own, away from the naysayers!

A dear friend and I had been exploring colleges located some distance away when a quartet came to the Clarkston Christian Church to promote their Christian college in Eugene, Oregon. These four young guys were so handsome that our decision to go to that school was sealed then and there. Most girls' motivations in the '50s were to attend college and receive MRS degrees. To be unengaged or unmarried at twenty was considered almost immoral. To be passed over, with spinsterhood as the only option, was unthinkable. (Thank goodness for the feminists.) I left a boyfriend at home—the tenor, who was still a senior in high school, class president, and a hunk—although gossip suggested he had already moved ahead in his search for female admiration. He later told my sister he had everything in life but me…too bad!

I entered college with the desire and imagined wisdom to conquer the world. In spite of this lofty ambition, I was a freshman, a flirt, and in love with life, and though I was still in love with the boy back home (I thought), the boys on campus sought me out. One of my roommates—also a freshman—and I were voted the most desirable freshman girls on campus by two boys' dorms.

I was free to explore with no one looking over my shoulder. I had been mischievous as a child, and I was no less so now. So college was one big party with the boys on campus, who took a special interest in this new redheaded freshman. In this new era of freedom, my grades became a low priority. I flitted from boy to boy and adventure to adventure, loving this newfound freedom. Weekends found me going along with a team to small churches to sing and give what was called a testimony. My testimony was weak, but I loved the singing with a passion.

I was fickle in my new relationships. However, in my speech class there was a senior—rather arrogant, I thought—who had the most beautiful blue eyes and who drove the biggest, blackest Oldsmobile I had ever seen! When each class member was to give an extemporaneous speech, he chose to talk about his Oldsmobile. We fellow classmates were to critique each other. In my own arrogance, I pointed out his arrogance in owning such an automobile. He seemed a little taken aback by my daring; however, when it was spring, I asked him to a house party we were having at Rheme Hall, where I lived, and he accepted the invitation.

After that he never ceased his pursuit. He was forever knocking at my dorm door to see if I was around. He did not like my fickle ways! It was later, during the college Senior Sneak that I really thought seriously about being Don's life companion. He was so warm and comfortable to be with. While we were in the swimming pool, he lifted a little two-year-old boy up and tousled his hair with such gentleness. I was impressed, especially since I had not shared with him my insatiable love of children. And so it was, by the end of my freshmen year that this pushy senior (who was studying for the ministry) won me over with promises and a head full of dreams of his own.

My Faith and Children

Already I had formed some definite ideas about child-rearing. I wanted to raise all my children for the Kingdom of God. My catchphrase became—even before my own children came—"Polish jewels for the Kingdom of God."

I believed a newborn baby was an empty slate, carrying no emotional characteristics of his ancestors. All it would take was pouring in love and affirmation to produce a mentally healthy child. His parents and those socializing him would mold him into a productive human being. (That theory, I found through raising children, is not necessarily accurate! Over the years I have learned it is both nature and nurture. We all are omnibuses of generations of genes. Babies already have some inbred characteristics that define who they are to become.)

I believed that from infancy, a child should be treated as thinking individual and that his or her rights should be respected. I declared that no child of mine would be indulged, manipulated, or treated as an object. These beliefs have weathered time and have proven to be valid. Actually I took all of these ideas to my child psychology class; the class only confirmed my beliefs. I loved my teacher, and she loved my wisdom about child-rearing, so she said.

I further believed that a child must grow up in an atmosphere of love if a well-balanced personality is to be achieved. And, above all, the parents must love each other in order for the child's healthy psyche to develop. Indeed, from my perspective that would be the greatest legacy of all: to have parents who love and adore each other.

My ideas about child-rearing were well formed in my mind before I even thought of marriage. I had hoped that a degree in child psychology would assist me in youth work. I saw the poem "Children Learn What They Live" in some book I read for a child psychology class, and it would hang on every wall in as many homes as Don and I resided! A poem written by Dorothy Law Nolte:

> If a child lives with criticism, he learns to condemn.
> If a child lives with hostility, he learns to fight.
> If a child lives with ridicule, he learns to be shy.
> If a child lives with shame, he learns to feel guilty.
> If a child lives with tolerance, he learns to be patient.
> If a child lives with encouragement, he learns confidence.
> If a child lives with praise, he learns to appreciate.
> If a child lives with fairness, he learns justice.
> If a child lives with security, he learns to have faith.
> If a child lives with approval, he learns to like himself.
> If a child lives with acceptance and friend-
> ship, he learns to find love in the world.

A Challenge of My Beliefs

I had so many lofty ideas of how I would change my own family history, and in this strange new world at Northwest Christian University in Eugene, Oregon, I felt lost at times, fearing I would lose my course and not keep my dreams alive. I was to hear another denominational set of rules and creeds that stated if you did not obey these rules, you would be lost—such as water baptism was a must for salvation. I absorbed the denominational theology I heard in Bible classes.

I tired of dating and was not sure what I wanted in life. Maybe I was not as into my studies as I should have been. In that era there was not a push for girls to find vocations outside of marriage. If they entered any vocation, it should be in the field of nursing or teaching. At best a woman was to support her husband's aspirations and help him to become a success, minimizing her own need for excelling in any chosen vocation. I just knew I wanted to be in ministry of some kind, preferably with young people. As I wrestled with my dreams, Don kept up his marriage campaign.

It was nearly the end of my freshman year at school, and I needed to make some decisions about whether to return to Northwest Christian University or go to Biola in Southern California. One of my dear girlfriends, Martha Blackwell, had gone there and wanted me to join her. She raved about the school and the sunshine. In Eugene it rained all the time, and I did miss my friends from my church as well as friends from high school. What to do? Maybe I was being catapulted into growing up! I needed to make some decisions about where I should continue my education and what to do about this pushy senior.

CHAPTER 3

I Thought It Would Be Perfect

> This explains why a man leaves his father and mother and
> is joined to his wife, and the two are united into one.
> —Gn 2:24, NLT

Not Quite Camelot

It was July 26, 1952, and my goals and career ambitions had shifted. I entered into marriage that day, declaring that this was to be my first mission in life—a new fairy-tale existence. I was only nineteen, and Don was twenty-three—mere children, from a later perspective.

The wedding was a gala affair in Clarkston, Washington, my hometown. At our wedding we had my high-school friends playing the organ and singing "My Hero" and "I Love You Truly." A college friend—soon to be my dear friend Bebe's husband—sang "Together with Jesus." Bebe was my friend who had gone to Northwest Christian University with me. However, none of Don's family appeared at our wedding. Their excuse was that they wanted to save money to care for us when we went back home! Little did I understand their bid for control at that time. My head was full only of love and spiritual dreams for our future.

After a couple of days on the road, going to Multnomah Falls and spending time in a lovely hotel, we arrived back in Roseburg, and we opted to stay in a motel until our apartment was ready. Don's parents threw a fit and said we should stay with them. It was agreed that we would stay in an apartment over his parents' garage until Don finished his commitment to his church. His parents were livid that we would go to a motel rather than stay with them until the apartment over their garage was ready. As a young couple in love, we wanted privacy.

This was not the fairy-tale beginning I had wanted, for Don's parents were controlling and criticized his every move. They had put doubts in his mind concerning whether I would be a good minister's wife…maybe not holy enough, as defined by the clan! There was that pious thinking again.

Even with my lofty ideals, goals, and dreams, we fumbled around the first months of our marriage. Don needed to finish his summer appointment as parish minister at his home church. We would take a honeymoon on our way to Butler, in Indianapolis, where he would do graduate work. That was the plan.

A few weeks into our marriage, Don also accepted an appointment to be a leader at a youth camp. It was not his idea but that of his parents, his aunt, and a church evangelist who was visiting at the time. This certainly was not my idea of newlywed activity, even though my heart's wish was to be in ministry. It seemed to me that this should have been a joint decision.

We could not stay together at camp, and I was put in a dormitory with young girls—not given any kind of role in the camp ministry. In my own home church and summer camps, I had been a leader and extremely active. This was a strange shift of events. I was very unhappy and disillusioned in such a setting as a newly married couple. Don's parents, his aunt, and the evangelist had manipulated him by saying he should put the work of the Lord before marriage. What a damnable statement to make to a young married person. But it seemed everyone had an opinion of what Don should do and how he should do it.

We ate dinner with Don's family, and his father railed against church people until late in the evening. I had not experienced this attitude while on the college campus. In my opinion we were not obeying the commandment that is recorded in Genesis 2:24, to leave mother and father and cling only to one's spouse. Don's parents continued to tell him what he could and could not do. I had questions and many tears during those remaining weeks of the summer, which seemed an eternity at the time.

Getting the Dream Back on Track

After one of the long harangues about church members around the dinner table from Don's father, I held my tongue. When we finally got to the apartment, I told Don it was not my experience to hear such demeaning gossip around the dinner table, and that was not how I viewed church members. (In my own home, my mother usually had the pastor and other church members over for dinner each Sunday.)

It seemed we were being pulled from every direction, and it would have been much better for us as a newly married couple to take a honeymoon and seal our marriage before being thrust into his parents' demands. All the while my Advent Christian church friends were coaxing me to invite Don to my childhood church. I was conflicted by a lifestyle I did not want. I did not understand it.

Not only were Don's parents instructing Don, but they began planning how I should spend my money. We had been given a love gift of money, and I bought matching shirts for Don and me—that sent them into a tailspin! They stated they would purchase a large house where we could all live together. That way they could take care of us. I had never observed this phenomenon before. Before our wedding Don's parents had asked us to be married together with his brother and fiancée in their home church, in a double ceremony…away from my friends. Not in a million years!

I was still not compliant, and so the conflict began. Though I did not say anything to Don's parents in a disrespectful way, I persisted in reaching toward my own dreams and goals.

My Advent friends were still calling to see how I was doing and kept up their campaign to get Don into their denomination. My friends loved him and thought he would be a grand asset. The Advent Christian church had their denomination school in Boston. I think Don knew he'd better get me out from under his parents' control or he would lose me, so in September he and I did go back to Boston for a short time, and it was probably that trip that saved the marriage. I was pregnant and very unhappy about Don's relatives controlling our every move. In contrast, to take off to a different city (Boston) alone seemed to buoy my fairy-tale mind-set.

We stayed in Boston for four short months. When some of the powers in the Advent Christian church offered Don a small church in Colton, California, we jumped at the offer to get out of the cold city of Boston. We had rented an apartment in a dingy section of Boston (Brookline). It had sewer pipes running through our small kitchen; it was drab, with used furniture and an entrance through a dark, cold stairway up to the third-floor apartment. However, there was much love within those walls, and our time there cemented our marriage.

We both worked at a local grocery market to survive. But in a February blizzard (more like a whiteout), we took off for our new adventure in Colton. We followed large food and transport trucks in order to stay on the highway.

On our way to California, we planned to stop and see our families. My family greeted us with a baby shower for the upcoming event and provided us with dinners of sumptuous foods. I was glad to be home…so glad to see my two sisters. But it was a different story when we arrived to visit Don's family. It was traumatic. They had written letters while we were in Boston lambasting me for coercing Don into making the decisions to go to Boston and take the Colton church. Indeed they were furious and said they would buy him a station wagon if he would just take a church that was open a few miles down the road from them. But, to my delight, Don's mind was set, and we continued on down the highway to California.

I was so filled with love as we stopped at warm, friendly restaurants—a new experience in this sunny state called California. The small, loving church we found in Colton warmly welcomed us. Life was good there as we awaited our firstborn. We were both very young and inexperienced at leading a church and being parents. We did our best and grew deeply in love out of reach of Don's demanding parents, who were still dangling carrots for their firstborn son. When he did not comply with their wishes, they would verbally chastise him.

My Husband's Imprinting

As a young boy, Don's mother had literally taken over his life, doing everything for him, controlling his every move and his money, and even preventing him from joining the military by some manipulative move with the recruiting office. She bribed him with material items and empty promises, impairing him in many areas. The following is a quote from Don concerning this bondage:

My social and cultural background is one of desperation. Basically I came from a lower middle-class background where my father was a dentist in a small backwoods community. My father was not the man of the house; my mother was the dominant personality. I rebelled against this type of arrangement from the onset but found there was little I could do to change it.

My method of adapting was to shut myself off. This early development caused many problems in having open relationships as an adult. My parents used me as an emotional tool for their own gratification. It was a great hindrance in accomplishing my own potential as a teenager and caused a great lack of self-confidence. It has taken years to undo the damage.

Don was a brilliant young man, but he did not have the support from his mother and father that he should have. He had his pilot's license at the age of sixteen and aspired to follow an uncle in military aeronautics. His father called it an "air coffin" and badgered him about his every effort to break free to follow his own dreams. His father was an avid fisherman, and when taking his son fishing, he lambasted Don for being unable to put the gaffing hook into the fish correctly in order to secure the fish. In anger he invited other young neighborhood boys to join him rather than his son. Put-downs were never ending in this young growing boy's life. That imprinting stayed with Don for years.

His father, being a small-town dentist, thought his son should follow in his career whether Don wanted to or not. He was a closed-minded man with a negative outlook on every aspect of life. It seemed he hated all church members and workers—not a very good legacy for young children. This was difficult for me to comprehend, as I had known much love both in and out of the church setting. It seemed no one tried to talk me into any career...or maybe they were content to observe me living the noncompliant dreams of my own. My mother just wanted me to follow my dream of working in some kind of ministry.

To be somewhat forgiving of Don's parents' parenting skills, they were steeped in their own cultural upbringing and were not able to advance or see beyond that. I learned that Don's father had wanted to be a railroad worker, but instead he followed the career choice his relatives wanted for him. So it was a generational issue. Indeed it was a teaching tool for me. I learned that a child must follow his own gifting and heart's desire to be successful and contented with his vocation. I just wanted my children to follow their passions, and if their skills allowed them only to be ditch diggers, so be it. Be the best!

Yes, you can learn from negatives! A dear friend tried to abate my hurt by telling me this little poem: "A daughter is a daughter for life, but a son is a son until he takes a wife." I am sure Don's parents were fearful of losing their hold on their firstborn son.

CHAPTER 4

Together at Last

All experience is a torch to light the way of each new challenge.
—UNKNOWN

With the physical distance between us and Don's demanding parents—and the fact that we had to depend on each other in this sunny paradise—our bond to each other became tighter than ever. I was so in love, I said heaven could not be any better than this. I was full of joy and excitement for the future and full of expectation for this child growing within me. Don and I knelt by our bedside at night and prayed for our small church, and we prayed our lives would be filled with holiness. Such was our innocence of belief in the goodness of life. If we would live a godly life, surely no evil would come near us.

A New Life Brings a New Life

We had only just arrived in California and started our new life with loving and supportive people who would do anything for their young pastor and wife. So innocent we were. How could we know what it meant to have a child, bring a new life into the world, and become a family? But at the tender age of twenty, early on a Monday evening, I was stricken with the most painful contractions I could imagine. Don took me to St. Joseph's in San Bernardino, about five miles across town. Our firstborn son, Donald Ralph, came into this world at seven thirty Tuesday evening, after approximately twenty-four hours of labor.

I had a spinal, and I was fully awake when he was born. They laid this little blond, blue-eyed cherub on my stomach, all purple and bloody, but I thought he was the most beautiful sight I had ever seen. I was engulfed in a love I had never experienced, and I found myself praying a different kind of prayer, with a dream to polish this God-given jewel for the Kingdom of God. And that became the passion of my calling. I saw my calling as a mother to be the highest possible calling in life and made no apologies for my belief. I believed our lives would become a fairy-tale existence, and I truly believed we had a sure formula for polishing jewels.

The house we took this bundle home to was an old house behind the church, with a cement patio joining our house and the back door of the church. Across the street, it was said, there was a red-light district. There was a Peeping Tom who looked in our bedroom window one evening while Don was out. I quickly gathered my little son up, headed for the bathroom, and locked the door. We took a hot bath until Don arrived home later that evening!

I never felt safe in that house. We were living in an era when people did not lock doors and even left keys in their cars, but we kept the doors to our house and car locked and the blinds drawn! We had many bums come to the door for handouts. We felt surely the house had been marked to alert them that this was a good place to try! We would empty our pockets of any small change or give them loaves of bread. In that era we did not see any street-corner panhandlers; they were more aggressive and came to homes.

Life in a Small Church

The church family truly looked after us. If we visited their homes—baby in tow at their request—they would prepare sumptuous meals and share stories of their lives. One dear couple—not very old, I thought—shared that they had lost their only child, a daughter, to death. The daughter had been a young teenager. Oh, the pain! How could anyone endure such a loss? I certainly could not have endured such an event. The mother said her hair had turned white overnight. This put a great pain in my heart, and I found myself praying that nothing so tragic would ever befall our family…such was my terror of losing a child.

However, I felt more bonded to the generation older than the thirty-year-olds, whose wives insisted on telling Don all their marital problems for hours on end. (When, years later, I served on a sexual-misconduct team for the Presbyterian Church, I remembered the attempts these unhappy women made to attract a young pastor.) It was not that I did not want Don to minister to these young women, but what they had to say should have been said to a woman instead of to a young pastor. Both young men and young women are vulnerable to flattery from the opposite sex. When young, unhappy women with troubled marriages see a happily married man, a man of the cloth, they begin to enviously fantasize. There was inadequate ministerial training in those days, and perhaps this was the reason for many of the inappropriate sexual liaisons in the church as well as in other outreach organizations.

Life in Paradise

Saturday evenings found me polishing baby shoes, cleaning house, moving furniture for a new look, and laying out what we would wear for church the next day. If someone would hold my baby while at church, I would sing solos or play my trumpet. Our services were always full, and I believed it was because of my young husband's dynamic preaching. If our pianist was missing for the evening services, I often played the piano.

Life was good, and I was so very happy in our new paradise! We ate Sunday chicken dinner at the local diner and paid $1.50. We would take along Gerber baby food to feed our baby. People oohed and aahed at our darling little bundle in his yellow crocheted cap and cowboy booties. Later we would take the baby-food jars out for target practice with Don's guns. He was somewhat surprised that I was such a sharpshooter, but I was determined to share his sports and interests.

Our only other vice and form of entertainment was watching TV. We were able to purchase a new black-and-white TV for fifty dollars, and this was our only expensive possession. Too often we would watch TV late into the night, so enthralled were we with this invention. We'd had only radio growing up, and movies were frowned on.

Day trips also became a form of entertainment for us as we took our firstborn son, Donald Ralph, all over Southern California. On one occasion we climbed into our car and headed for Mexico—the first excursion with our newborn, when he was less than two weeks old. I had determined that having a child so soon would not tie us down, and all activities would become family affairs. And so we enjoyed many trips through the fragrant orange groves, windows down, the air filled with beauty, baby in my arms...no seat belts required! Yes, life was good! Since we had not taken an official honeymoon, my philosophy was that all of life would be a honeymoon...and so it seemed.

CHAPTER 5

It Can't Be

> Experience is not what happens to you; it is
> what you do with what happens to you.
> —Aldous Huxley

> The greater the difficulty, the more glory in surmounting it.
> Skillful pilots gain their reputation from storms and tempests.
> —Epictetus

The Unexpected

Pregnant! That word hung in the air as I sat in the doctor's office in stunned silence. With a five-month-old baby at home, I could barely comprehend his words. I said, "I'm sorry, Doctor, it just can't be." I had been having some odd stomach pain and passing out. Finally, at Don's insistence, I had gone to see Dr. Smith. He had been my doctor at the birth of our first child only five months before. His mother was a member of our church and such a lovely lady. She treated me like a beloved daughter. The doctor felt more like a father than a doctor; he was so tender with me. I had not experienced that kind of care from my own father.

At that time doctors were family doctors and not specialists. Dr. Smith made a smart remark about some women getting pregnant if their husbands hung their trousers on the bedpost. "Not very funny," I thought.

I was very much affected by people's opinions and concerned with pleasing relatives and being a good wife, mother, and minister's wife…and the list went on. Don was not only struggling financially as a young minister—earning a mere $2,000 a year, plus housing—but he was struggling to find his own identity. It seemed the opinions of his conservative clan were ever lurking over our shoulders. I so wanted Don's relatives to regard me as a charming young woman— something I'd had with other people while growing up…but it was never to be. It seemed Don's parents thought no one was quite good enough for their son. Since they had controlled his life for twenty-three years, I wondered what they would have to say when they heard the news. In stunned silence I walked out of the doctor's office.

In tears I walked the five blocks to our house, pondering so much in my heart. Had I not said my new passion was to polish jewels for the Kingdom of God? Emotions bombarded my heart as my thoughts traveled back to how it had felt to be a freshman in college, free and gregarious, set on a psychology career and a ministry in music or psychology. Don had been so determined to marry me since he'd planned to leave for graduate school in the fall. He had changed his mind and decided to serve in a couple of small churches for practical experience before going on to graduate school.

So there we were in a small church in Southern California, a most beautiful, sunny location, orange blossoms filling the air with their fragrance. Our firstborn son had arrived barely nine months and two days after our marriage. That had taken adjustment—from being a nineteen-year-old college freshman to a responsible adult—and now this! I had always loved babies and small children and had often jested that I wanted twelve…but this was ridiculous. Where would the money come from? Small churches paid very little salaries, and it was already almost impossible to cover all our needs. What would people say when they saw me carrying one baby and pregnant with another? At twenty-one, I was still very concerned about my appearance and the comments from Don's clannish family.

I recalled how Don, one of two much indulged boys, had rarely been allowed to make any decisions of his own. He was controlled and manipulated by materialism, and even now his family was coercing him back to the family confines with promises of material objects and verbal chastisement when he did not comply. My own mother wanted to spend months at a time with us, escaping her own unhappy environment, showering us with gifts, hoping to gain the love she lacked. It was truly a dilemma for this young, idealistic couple.

In my Bible class at Northwest Christian University, I had learned that a family cycle is rarely broken. Sociologists have observed that generally the same lifestyle, good or bad, will be carried on from generation to generation. The instructor declared that the sins of the fathers shall visit the third and fourth generations. Even if that were true, Don and I were determined to change the course of that generational lifestyle on both sides.

With all these thoughts going round and round in my head, I had been unaware of the five blocks I had automatically and unthinkingly walked. I was now at our door and had to break this latest news to Don. The words stuck in my throat, but he did not seem nearly as distraught as I had feared. Amid my tears and his kisses, he merely stated, "A boy for me, and a girl for you!"

We drove down to San Diego to attend a church retreat on February 21, 1954. We were not expecting our newest arrival for some time, but we did not really have an exact due date. We went with another couple, leaving our baby with an older couple who planned to keep him overnight and take him to church the next morning. It was a good day, and after we arrived home late, we tumbled into bed, tired but happy. Our sleep was soon interrupted when I started having intense pains that surely said it was time. Don made a hasty call to the doctor and said he would call the elderly couple to tell them I was in the hospital. Then off we went across town.

After traveling at top speed across town, we arrived at the same hospital where only nine months and three weeks earlier, our son had been born. No labor rooms were available, and I was bedded down in the hallway, with Don cracking the same jokes as he had nine months before. After taking some drugs (maybe too many), I floated off into a nebulous realm of pain and semi consciousness. At 10:30 a.m. on Sunday, Don left me to fulfill his responsibilities to the congregation he was serving. I was in too much distress to know he even left.

But at 1:04 p.m. our seven-pound, twelve-ounce miracle baby girl arrived after a breech birth. As I was being wheeled down the hall, Don met us. I was very groggy, but I managed a weak "it's a girl," to which the doctor—a father of four sons—added, "Some guys have all the luck!" Don beamed. However, I was to learn that due to too many labor patients, there had been an oversight, and I had been given too many shots of Demerol. Our baby daughter had to be put in an incubator for eight hours to help her wake up…because she too suffered from the overdose.

I was still very groggy when they asked me her name, and I said, "Teresa Lynn." But I later told the registration nurse that her name was Teresa Lois, and that was what was recorded. Teresa eventually preferred Teresa Lynn, and that is how she later signed her name.

Blessings and New Beginnings

All of my apprehension about caring for two babies melted away when I held this beautiful miracle of God…this little creation with an inch of black hair and one-eighth-inch fingernails. Yes, I did feel a little special. We had a perfect family…God was good…really good! My smugness was disarmed, and reality hit when I was wheeled out, baby in arms. The nurse casually said, "I'll see you in nine months." It was a good laugh for everyone but me, who had been pregnant for nearly eighteen months. I breathed a silent prayer: "Lord, maybe I don't want twelve children…not just now!"

As a teenager I had worked for a Catholic family. I worked for them at the time of the birth of their fifth child, and they needed assistance. Their oldest was only six. All five children had been named for Catholic saints. I was impressed. I loved the names: Mary, Elizabeth, Teresa…*Teresa*…What a lovely name. I made the decision then that I too would name a daughter after St. Teresa. And now we had that beautiful daughter!

I was familiar with many of the Catholic saints, but I had never heard of St. Teresa, nor did I know there were two saints by this name who had lived three hundred years apart. The later St. Teresa was also referred to as "little flower of Jesus." Her life was incredibly simple and profound. Her intense love of Jesus is noted in her autobiography. Her desire to be a nun was granted when she was only fifteen. Her devotion has impressed the world. Perhaps, had I known more of this great saint, our daughter would have been named Jane!

Teresa, in Greek, means "desirable" and "full of virtue." So it was that this most unexpected bundle arrived to be destined for or endowed with all of these attributes. One so unique must surely deserve to be named for a saint!

After a week we took Terri, as we had nicknamed our daughter, to the doctor for her checkup. The doctor gave her gamma globulin. He did not really explain to me—one way too young to be a mother of two—why! Terri seemed to cry constantly and needed to be continually held close to my heart. For Don and me, the nights and days ran together. Only Donnie, our son, was unaffected by this new scheduling. By day he scampered about in his Kiddy Kar stroller, charmed by his new little sister. By night he slept soundly, while, with drooping heads and glassy eyes, Don and I took turns feeding Terri hourly and rocking and cuddling her close. I say "we," but it soon became me, as Don contracted the mumps when she was less than two weeks old. So weary from the birth of a new baby, and bewildered, I began nursing duty for two babies and one grown man around the clock. But I did survive this small interlude into an otherwise delightful beginning.

Donnie discarded his teddy bear for his new little sister, such was his delight in her. He was pleased that she was awake more than she slept. He kept peering into her rickety bassinet we had borrowed. It was not very sturdy from years of use. One day he stretched tall in his Kiddy Kar, tugging with his chubby little hands, to get a closer look at this wonder, causing a crashing bundle screaming to the floor. They both were terrified, but this was to set a precedent. As Donnie started talking and Terri graduated to a crib, he would peer into her crib and say, "Wake up, Terri, I wanna play wish you."

A four-thousand-mile trip when Terri was four weeks old did not help to ease the hyper temperament. The continual change in tap water on the road and strange places only aggravated the chronic colic. Then again, it may not have had anything to do with the colic. But in keeping with our philosophy that children would not tie us down but share in the adventures of travel and expanded living, our determination was not subdued by colic…we just slept less.

Soon Teresa adapted to us (or was it vice versa?), and she became a charmer to all, full of giggles and delight. She was rolling completely over at three and one-half months, sitting unaided at five and one-half months, crawling and pulling herself erect at seven months and, more surprising to us, walking at eight and one-half months. Was it superior development or a desire to keep pace with her big brother? Whatever it was, we noted something unusual about this child, pondering it only in our hearts.

As a toddler Terri did outgrow her colicky beginnings, and these two darling children were the delight of my life. I was to learn that a disciplined child is a happy child. Don's philosophy was to start discipline at birth until three, and then no further discipline would be necessary…or was it that he had grown up in a home with a father and two grandfathers who were abusive in their treatment of others, children especially? I did not share this severity in discipline but never contradicted their father. I just tried to temper this with love and tenderness…maybe a good blend for all children. But for me, I preferred tenderness!

There was a gentleman at church who was quite severe. (I call him a gentleman to be gracious, but he was an idiot.) He would unmercifully spank his children before church to make sure they behaved in service. He had two of the most darling little girls who, I am sure, grew up with severe mental problems because of this brute! When Don saw the severe abuse this father heaped on his two darling girls, it did cause him to become a little gentler with his own two darlings.

Along with Teresa's beguiling charm, she displayed a feisty temper. We cited this poem often:

> There was a little girl who had a little curl.
> That curl was right in the middle of her forehead.
> And when she was good, she was very, very good.
> But when she was bad, she was horrid!

We often called her wickie woo, for she had such a short fuse. But she would quickly go from anger to giggles.

This delicate flower of God's creation seemed to require much discipline but also needed to bask in the sunshine of our deep love. Terri had some physical hurdles. A hernia had developed from her colicky crying. When the children had hard measles, it seemed Terri had them much more severely than Donnie. She developed a heart murmur…was that from crying as well?

However, in spite of these things, sleep became possible once again for us—though Terri was to develop an *"early to rise"* habit that would follow her into adulthood. There were never enough hours for her joyful frolicking. She and her brother were inseparable. Holding hands always, they were off to another adventure: Donnie riding Terri on the back of his trike or pulling her in his wagon. We allowed bathtub bubbles to overflow onto the bathroom floor, such were the giggles and delight before bedtime. Memories of those precious moments linger.

I kept these two jewels immaculate—such was my fetish for cleanliness—always making it difficult for people not to treat them as adorable objects. Bows were always tied to that curl in the middle of Terri's forehead! When people oohed and aahed, we determined and insisted the children not be treated as cute objects but as unique individuals…beautiful children of God.

I managed to keep the children bathed and dressed like angels, and I kept their little shoes polished. I also mowed the lawn, did the laundry, and was a minister's wife besides—a role I loved but knew little about. Most of all I wanted to be Don's perfect wife, mistress, and lover. All the while it took both of us to care for these two almost twins. This was to become our lifestyle—a joint effort. I shared his workload, and he shared mine. Hence it became *our* workload, or a better expression would be *our joint commission.*

Old Phobias Lurking

I loved every aspect of our ministry, except when I was asked to sing for funerals. Here again my phobia about death raised its ugly head. When I sang for funerals, my fear of anything associated with death and dying became overwhelming. At one service for a young woman, I sang from a loft above the sanctuary. The only view was looking down on the open casket. I did get through the song, and people said I sounded like an angel, but it took every ounce of determination I had to do so. I had trouble sleeping for some time…but Don let me keep a night-light burning! I knew, as a minister's wife, that I would often face death, but I knew I could never deal with losing my children or husband.

The School of Life

We learned so much about life and about people's diverse living philosophies while serving our small congregation. I believe I learned to allow people to be who they were without prejudice. I did struggle a bit in one area. My home had to be immaculate. Maybe it was obsessive-compulsive disorder, but I would have been happy if everyone had that disorder. As a pastor and his wife, we were invited into many homes of pure squalor. If we were invited to dinner, I could only gag my way through the meal and disinfect my babies when we returned home! I received quite an education in self-control, including keeping my mouth shut!

I certainly was being taught in a school of learning that I had not intended to enroll, but there I was. I could adapt and learn, or I could live in total denial of my surroundings.

CHAPTER 6

A Journey North

> I think and think for months and years. Ninety-
> nine times, the conclusion is false.
> The hundredth time, I am right.
> —ALBERT EINSTEIN

On the Move Again

We had concluded three years in this paradise. It was a good life, but we both missed the seasons, so when a call came to take a church in the Pacific Northwest, we remembered only the good memories and made preparations to make the move.

It seemed we always made our moves in the dead of winter. When we arrived in Spokane, Washington, it was cold and snowy, unlike the sunny weather we had left…what were we thinking? But we moved into a lovely little home and began a ministry to varied ages within the church, for this was a church full of young married couples, teenagers, and middle-aged people. It was a well-blended generational church. There was an instant love between this congregation and Don and I. The church was full, with a nursery overflowing with young children. However, the former pastor was in the congregation, and it did not please him to see how the church was growing seemingly because of a young, dynamic pastor who seemed to draw crowds.

I tried to set the rumbles aside, for I knew this former pastor and knew he was reported to be a troublemaker. But what could he do to hurt Don with the whole church loving him? I was too involved with my cherubs to be bothered much, but Don was experiencing the same type of control that had been so pervasive in his past. He became depressed and began talking about continuing his education back at Butler University, which had been the initial plan. He did his best to appease the former pastor, who thought Don was not Advent Christian enough in presenting the denomination's tenets of faith. He thought that too many teenagers and young married couples were accepting Christ without allegiance to the denomination. Even though Don was distressed, we would hang on for a few months.

The Joy of Children

When Teresa was eighteen months old, I decided it was time for her first permanent. She was used to my daily ritual of fixing various hairstyles, but she was unprepared for the ensuing process of smelly solution and tight curlers that pulled the eyes and neck to the crown of the head. Through many tears emerged a beautiful little flower with fluffy artificial curls and a very tender scalp.

At the annual Christmas pageant, Terri—now twenty-one months—appeared as the angel, with silver wings and a halo. This little angel stood with folded hands and, during the prayerful musical praises, looking intently at the audience, who were absorbed in this precious girl. I thought, "We brought this angel into the world, and what a grand future she will have." She continued smiling and grinning, totally aware that she had a captive audience. Her delight in entertaining and relating to people became more and more apparent. Donnie—who was a shepherd boy in his little bathrobe—evoked oohs and aahs from all in attendance, but he did not bask in the attention, as did Terri.

This was one of Terri's endearing moments, and we experienced many of those on a daily basis. However, there were also less endearing times, like when she stuffed a bean up her nose just to see what it was like, which sent us scurrying for a nose syringe to suck it out. The delight and anguish these two children caused kept us continually on our toes, never knowing what to expect from them.

Conformity Again

The former pastor's angst at Don's success, as well as Don's having a restless heart, made Don think more about his desire for further education. The elders of the religious system we were in held to doctrine tenaciously and insisted that for anyone to be a part of this religious system, he or she must embrace the doctrine. It was mandatory. (It is no surprise to me that this denomination is almost extinct and unknown by most.)

Hand in hand with the soul-sleeping doctrine was the expectation of the immediate return of Christ. Any future plans were discouraged. One was to be consumed with readiness for Christ's immediate return. To be concerned with future educational plans, leisure activities, or any other life pursuits meant being left behind to burn up with the earth—a crippling and diabolical theology to an impressionable young mind. However, in some religious systems the founders use scriptural references to build their doctrines and control methods. The leaders were quite eloquent when quoting scripture to give their doctrinal beliefs credence.

Don found this system to be most confining, and to escape he finally succumbed to his parents' haranguing and took his wife and two children home to live in their garage while he secured the means to go back to Butler University (his original plan). This was certainly not a good solution to the problem, but being under his parents' roof made him more determined than ever to break the bands that controlled his life. The interference never let up, and eventually my tears and our general discontent with in-law demands resulted in our serving at a little church in Orofino, Idaho, for a few months until it was time to make the trip east.

We had so much to learn. It seemed like we were two kids trying to find our way in life and to carve out our own destiny. I believe our own generation, even with our me-ism, has more regard for personal boundaries than the prior generation. The scripture "a man shall leave his mother and father and cleave only to his wife" was unheeded in our case. I wish that principle had been emphasized in our childhoods. It would have saved so much anguish!

Together Again

It was pure happiness to be alone with my beloved husband and small family again. We spent the summer months of 1956 in the wilds of Orofino, Idaho, a small town in the mountains up the Snake River. It was a small Disciples of Christ church, full of loving people who thought we were the perfect little family. We had such fun with our children, often bundling them up in their jammies and going to the outdoor movie theater for a night of cuddling up in the front seat of the car watching movies—which cost one dollar per carload. Another baby was on its way, surely a boy. We were having so much fun, and, with a trip east coming up, I did not even bother with going to a doctor.

We spent time building bonfires on the river beach and roasting wieners and marshmallows and, of course, going to those drive-in movies, where we took homemade popcorn and warm blankets. If Don and I wanted time together as a couple, Terri, our social bug, would willingly stay with a dear childless couple we knew. They so loved our little children and begged to have them overnight anytime the children desired. However, we didn't take advantage of their generous offer because Donnie would join the couple with Terri, but we would have to go pick him up at nightfall. This lovely couple so wanted children and it brought them great joy in loving our two angels. Louise, the wife, was so dear to us that we named our next child Louise…not Louis!

Anxieties of Parenthood and Loving People

On one summer day in Orofino, Donnie and Terri were playing on the back steps while I was working in the kitchen four feet away. Don was in the church office, which was connected to the side of the manse. I checked on the two little ones periodically, but at one point Terri was nowhere to be seen. Donnie said she had just gone around the house. When I couldn't find her, I became hysterical and searched the neighborhood with Don and the neighbors.

After what seemed to be hours but was probably more like half an hour, Don noticed the church bathroom door ajar. The bathroom entrances in this old church were outside at the rear of the church. Don bolted for that door and was so relieved to spot Terri, our fearless little angel, asleep on the bathroom floor. There was barely room to turn around, but Don scooped her up and called the neighborhood search off. Still sleeping, she was unaware of the excitement she had caused.

Those were happy summer days, full of adventures and lessons in parenthood. On one occasion we were awakened by the strong scent of skunk. In our naïveté Don and I were sure we had seen it go in the house and that it was under our bed. When we awoke in the morning, we discovered what we had suspected was the skunk was my fluffy slippers!

Those were very happy summer months that we spent with a church full of loving people. They tried to talk us into staying and forgetting the trip east, but plans were made, and somehow, in our inexperience, we believed plans could not be altered. So we began packing and planning for a trip east. By that time we had acquired furniture and personal items that could fit only into a U-Haul trailer. So another chapter began for this little family of four—soon to be five.

CHAPTER 7

Daddy, I Want to Go Home

All adventures, especially into new territory, are scary.
—SALLY RIDE, FIRST AMERICAN WOMAN ASTRONAUT
TO FLY IN SPACE

On the Move Again

So it was that late in August of 1956, seven months heavy with child, I helped load a little U-Haul trailer with two cribs and all our worldly goods. We put the two crib mattresses in the backseat for Donnie and Terri's comfort and set off across the country for a new adventure. We did not know how long it would take the college to find a place for Don to serve while he was going to school. I had not yet seen a doctor, and I was anxious not knowing where our child would be born.

When we arrived in Indianapolis, we stayed with college friends while waiting for the placement office to put us into a church and house. Our three-and-one-half-year-old son best summed up our feelings in this classic statement: "Daddy, I want to go home!"

His daddy's reply was, "Son, we don't have a home." But after three weeks of homesickness, frustration, and concern for where this new little boy (we thought, surely) would be born, we were placed in a little church in a rural community called Rich Valley. It was a farming community on the outskirts of Kokomo, Indiana, north of Indianapolis. The little white church and beautiful colonial manse stood out in the middle of flat farmland, with a few farmhouses in distant view.

On October 20, 1956, only three weeks after we were settled in this cozy home, another girl (not the expected brother) made her appearance. We had another jewel, named Christine Louise, meaning "follower of Christ"—truly an accurate name. She was born in a hospital, not on the road in route to this new state of Indiana.

Children and Life's Delights

Two months later, with the newest jewel taking her equal position, we celebrated a joyous holiday season. We were very excited to celebrate this Christmas with our little family. We had carefully saved ten dollars for each child—a small fortune to us at the time. Back then ten dollars could provide several nice gifts under the tree. Our anticipation mounted as Christmas Eve arrived. We propped Christy, as she came to be known, in her buggy, and the five of us had a simple candlelight dinner, celebrating my twenty-third birthday. I remember it as a feast full of giggles and joy with our growing family!

Finally Don and I lovingly tucked little Donnie and Terri into their beds in the faraway upstairs. When all was quiet and we assumed sleep was near, Don disguised his voice, and—with a few "ho, ho, hos"—inquired into the children's behavior and then replied in his normal voice. Startled whispers passed between the two very excited children, and then all was quiet.

Very early the next morning, those two crept downstairs and into our bed to exclaim about what they had heard the night before and what they had just beheld lying under the tree near the foot of the stairs. Such was the joy of that Christmas in the snowy winter wonderland of Kokomo, Indiana!

We did not like having the children so far away in an upstairs bedroom, so during that Christmas holiday we moved Donnie and Terri into the study, next to our bedroom, along with baby Christy. But, more often than not, we had two little jewels in our bed, huddling together during a very cold winter full of electrical and ice storms.

During the day Don and I would only peer out the window at the glorious ice and electrical storms, often with two little heads tucked under our arms. Don and I had never experienced electrical storms where lightning hit the ground right before our eyes. Electrical storms gave way to snow and ice storms. What a wonder it was to behold when the sun glittered and glistened on this fairyland of snow and ice. The church was a short distance from the manse, so Don would carefully walk through ice and snow to his church study and sermon preparation.

To us, inside the house, huddling under a mountain of blankets in the subzero weather, with no electricity or water pump, it was a different kind of fairyland—one of love and togetherness. Even when the electricity was working, we had little money to feed this monstrous, fuel-consuming house, so we retreated to the kitchen to carry out our existence in this wintry climate. We turned the furnace way down, just high enough to keep the pipes from freezing, and turned up the electric stove in the kitchen (with the oven door open). We moved the TV, sewing machine, toys, and baby buggy to this retreat and continued to hole up for the winter. Only an occasional dash to the bathroom and bedtime would cause us to leave our snug kitchen.

Even the mice thought the kitchen was the best place to be. On one occasion I opened a drawer below the oven for a pan only to find a mama and baby mice in a huddle, trying to keep warm as well. They all scurried out as I was screaming, causing Christy to scream as well. I did not open that drawer again.

From then on it was not quite as cozy. But where did that poor mama mouse go to keep her babies warm? It was in the kitchen too that our love affair with Captain Kangaroo began. Our children learned so much from this kindly captain. For us it was a form of preschool.

Life's Never-Ending Lessons

It was in the middle of Indiana farmland that we learned to improvise. Winter did finally take its leave, and we enjoyed fragrant spring air, pigs snorting, and corn growing. How blessed we felt with these darling little jewels God had given us to polish. Life was good. We five were a happy family!

It was here too that we determined our children's religious training would not be left to others. We wanted our jewels to grow up knowing their Heavenly Father as one who intended goodness and mercy to fall upon His children. I developed my own home teaching. We wanted these children to know their Heavenly Father through love and not the fear that had crippled Don and me in so many areas of life. And it was here, in Indiana, that one of our favorite mottos became, "accentuate the positive, eliminate the negative, and don't mess with Mr. In Between."

As we observed our jewels, we watched the emergence of an abundant love and simple trust in their most adored Maker. My prayer became, "Oh God, please do not let us distort this trust and love these children have for you." We marveled at the infinite wisdom these two young children displayed. I believe all children are gifted with this innate knowledge of God, but we did think our children were exceptional.

Even the Children Learn Life's Lessons

Churches are not known for paying adequate salaries to young pastors, and Rich Valley was no exception, in spite of its name. It was indeed a very wealthy community, and this fact seemed to bother Terri the most. At the age of three, she noticed that the other children in the church had huge boxes of toys. Soon we found her pretending to be Janie or Nancy. So it was that she and her daddy began this ritual:

"No, you are not Janie."

"Well, then I am Nancy."

"No, you are not Nancy. You are Terri. It is Terri that we love."

The dialog continued throughout the year, as Terri compared others' material wealth and her lack. Her perception of her surroundings made an impact on her desires for her own life. She wanted to be the one with a whole barrel of toys.

My Goals and Dreams, Still in Place

It was a good year for Don and me—a year to reevaluate our goals and objectives in life. It was a year of commitment to one another and our precious little jewels. We did appreciate the grand state of Indiana, but we had a deep awareness that home was the Pacific Northwest. Though Don enjoyed his classes at Butler University, he wanted to continue with his graduate studies in familiar surroundings. With a son and two daughters gracing our home now, my first priorities remained to be a lover, perfect wife, and mother. I desired with all my heart to polish these jewels for the Kingdom of God. So it did not matter to me where Don completed his desired education. I would go anywhere with him.

It was in Indiana that I think obtained a clearer knowledge of what I wanted from life, marriage, and family. I did have a passion for learning and hoped to one day finish my education—though in that era it was more acceptable for a woman to be a good homemaker and supporter of her husband. A man's success was a wife's responsibility. I held all of my idealistic dreams and goals in my heart while I polished our three jewels.

Lingering Phobias and Fundamentalism

Don was often gone in the evenings doing his ministerial work, and I would read any material I could find in an attempt to expand my mind. We began purchasing books and carried on the habit throughout our marriage. On one particular night, when Don was out for the evening, and after the children were tucked into bed, I picked up the latest *Reader's Digest*. Most of my reading material was motivational and inspirational. But on this night, I read a story about a very young girl who had died of leukemia. The story terrified me. I wanted to stop reading, but I could not lay the magazine down. I was left shaking.

The article carefully described the little white dress the family had dressed their dead daughter in and how they had lovingly placed her in a small white casket. The article broke my heart. There was that word again...*leukemia*. It was the same illness that the couple in California said had taken their only child. After that night I often prayed, "Lord, if you want to teach me anything, please do it, but please do not touch these precious jewels that you have given us to polish."

The fear and phobias about death still lurked. My fear that I needed God to teach me something through death probably arose from a very fundamentalist movie I had watched as a teenager. It was at an evangelistic meeting, and the evangelist closed the meeting with a movie. The thrust of it was that a young couple did not want to go out as missionaries. They were described as rebellious to God's call. Then they lost their firstborn child. Heartbroken, they declared that they should have gone to the foreign mission field. They succumbed to the pressure from their church, and at the end of the movie we saw them singing, "I'll go where you want me to go, dear Lord," as they left for the mission field. The message, I suppose, was that God has ways of making you do what He wants you to do.

I did not like that theology one bit! Or perhaps it was then that I developed my own theology: that if you did what God wanted of you, nothing would happen to you or those you loved. Basically, if you did one, two, and three, then God would do four, five, and six. And surely God, in all His mercy, would never touch one of His jewels that I was polishing for Him! Surely!

Springtime in Indiana

Seasons pass quickly, and soon we rambled throughout the whole house in the spring of the year. How exciting it was for Donnie and Terri when they were allowed to stay up beyond bedtime to watch out of our dining-room window as the farmers did the night plowing, to throw the garbage over the back fence to the pigs that continually snorted at our back door, to roam the outdoors and smell the early tulips, or to eat pork chops given by the kindly farmers. How we loved those pork chops, ready to put in the frying pan. This was much better than when a kind farmer had offered us a chicken for our Thanksgiving dinner. We did not know what to do. He gave it to us live, and we were expected to kill, dress, and then eat it. Although I had seen my mother kill many a chicken on the chopping block back home, I had a weak stomach. Don was a city boy, and between the two of us, we could not bear to wring the poor chicken's neck.

More Adventure and Memories

We had many happy times in Indiana, and it made us nostalgic when it came time to head to the Pacific Northwest to bid the warm, loving people—these tillers of God's earth—good-bye. We would miss these Midwesterners who had watched over us and enjoyed our three little jewels. They loved watching Donnie and Terri hover over their little Hoosier sister, Christy, who was nine months old when Don decided to head back to the Northwest to finish his studies. We would miss the clippity-cloppety sounds made by the horses and buggies passing by our house. We loved seeing the beautiful, aloof Amish people—a real novelty for us from the Pacific Northwest. Donnie and Terri would wave at the people in the buggies as they passed by, but they would never wave back or look in our direction.

We loaded up our U-Haul once again and head back to Oregon. We decided on the southern route and encountered rainstorms, floods, tornadoes, and the bleak desolation of New Mexico. We stopped in California to see Donnie and Terri's birthplace, San Bernardino. While there we visited one of the elders from the little church where we had served. Mr. Bolster was not doing well. He had lost his wife and had moved into a retirement home. He seemed to have aged years since we lived in sunny California. We loved him even though he had some major prejudices. This was the same elder who had cringed when a black evangelist kissed our newborn baby boy. His wife had whispered, "Don't let that nigger kiss your baby." At that point in time, I had been too young to respond with an appropriate comment. Anyway, when this dear elder saw Don, he asked him to kneel so that he might give him a blessing. It seemed Don touched so many souls with his gentle compassion.

But the highlight of this trek west was our visit to Disneyland, which had just opened. Even little Christy, with her poopy diapers, loved our day there. (This was an era before disposable diapers, and we were not as prepared for emergencies as today's generation is.) Nevertheless, our visit began our children's love affair with this man, Disney, who seemed to mold much of our fairy-tale philosophy—the happily ever after theology! So many happy memories surfaced as we spent time once again in California—the place where Don and I had cemented our love. Happily we piled back into our car to travel the last miles of our journey home.

Please, Let's Put Down Roots

I was so ready to put down roots. Yes, we had to put down roots. I had lived in one town and one house and gone to one church for most of my life and was not used to such frequent moves. I was ready to settle in Eugene, Oregon, where our love had begun. Yes, the University of Oregon would be a good place for Don to continue his education.

I had totally accepted the belief that a wife was to do everything to push her husband ahead, minimizing her own need for education or advancement. In fact the philosophy of the day said that if a man was successful, it was because of the wife behind him. If he was not successful, it was the wife's fault. So no alternative was even discussed.

Don had taken courses at the University of Oregon while attending Northwest Christian University, and he felt he would do best in a known environment. It had been a fabulous trip west, but I was ready, ready, ready to unpack and settle down with our little family. This was before the feminist movement, and I was content to set my personal aspirations aside and to support Don in all he aspired to do.

CHAPTER 8

The Good Life...Our Own Fairy Tale

> Dreams are like letters from God.
> Isn't it time you answered your mail?
> —Marie Louis von Franz

Home Again

Once we were home in Eugene, we moved into a new little house with a built-in oven (which was new for that era), huge yards in the back and front, and three bedrooms...though still only one bathroom. Otherwise it was a truly modern, lovely home. We paid $12,900 for the house, and our payments were $99 a month.

It was such fun settling in to my dream home. We had a couple of months for Don to find supplemental jobs before he started back to school to gain more degrees. By this time, with our three darling jewels, I had gained much confidence in our family identity and I did not believe living close to Don's controlling relatives would impact our lives. They lived about one hundred miles away in Roseburg, Oregon. I was determined to take the high road and be the perfect daughter-in-law. However, his parents were still heavily involved in telling us how to live, what we could buy, and what we should do. They had put the down payment of five hundred dollars on this new little house, so they felt they had earned the right to gauge our every move.

Don worked at a grocery store, a service station (which embarrassed his mother), and weekends at a church, and he carried a full load at school. With Don's heavy work and school schedule, I was in charge of the children, the lawns, and all the homeowner chores, which made the neighborhood men envious of Don's good fortune in his workhorse wife. The man who had built our home lived on the same block of new houses. He would salute me as I was mowing the yard when he drove past. He would often stop to tell me his wife was not a happy camper when he asked her to do the same as the redhead down the street! I had worked hard growing up on a farm and thought mowing was a perfectly natural task for me to do. I saw nothing odd about my doing the yard work, but it seemed the other wives in the neighborhood would rather have coffee and gossip sessions and not be workhorses, as I appeared to be. But Don and I were so happy in our innocence and God's provision that we set what others thought aside. Perhaps the home-builder, who was also our neighbor, was jesting with me…only perhaps!

Dreams and Goals Once Again

The children loved our new home with the huge backyard and big oak tree to climb. It was a new, growing neighborhood with many young families, to the delight of our own children. They would have playmates besides each other for the first time.

Donnie and Terri quickly surveyed each new family. Donnie went to each door and made the introductions: "Terri, my sister, she's three and three-fourths, and I'm Donnie, four and one-half. Can you play?" And of course if our children played, we moms had to have a coffee klatch—close to a gossip session—each morning to discuss the neighborhood! We made dear lifetime friends in that neighborhood.

Terri had an insatiable drive to master anything she saw someone else doing. At four she was playing jacks with the older children with no problem while—try as we might—Don and I could not master the simple game! When she saw an older neighbor child play pick up sticks, Terri insisted we buy her the game, and she mastered it perfectly. What an incredible ability to learn new skills this child had.

Our days began at 6:00 a.m. and ended at 11:00 p.m. Don was carrying a full academic load in the mornings, came home briefly for lunch and hugs, and then worked an eight-hour shift. At his late-night shift at the service station, his two young helpers would delight in spending time with their daddy. They would take turns going with him, dressing in grubby clothes so they might wash down pumps, scrub windows, pick up papers, smile at customers, ride the hoist up and down, ride on the rear of the motorcycle, or simply watch TV in the office. Then two sleepy little workers would arrive home at 10:00 p.m. to drink mugs of hot chocolate. How they bragged about working for their daddy. This was an important time for us to schedule time for the children with their father; we made every minute count.

Happiness Abounds

Every weekend Don had a preaching point, which we loved. Our weekend drives to the little church where Don was assigned became an important and anticipated time together. Elkton, Oregon, is a little pit stop on the way to the Oregon Coast. We left very early on Sunday morning, so often the three little ones just slept. On these breathtaking drives, viewing mountainous terrain and driving through groves of trees and rolling Oregon farmland, our spirits were renewed. Since this was one of the few times throughout the week we could be together, we thoroughly enjoyed this time. Don always prayed for God's guidance before we left.

Aunt Vildy, my dear aunt, who often came to stay with us, went along on this weekend preaching point a few times. Aunt Vildy was my favorite aunt, and I believed I was her favorite niece. She had no children living, and most of her nieces and nephews felt they too were her favorites. She said Don prayed for heaven's help and then drove like hell. It was difficult to keep that Oldsmobile less than seventy miles per hour. Perhaps our angels did work overtime on those weekend drives!

The little township of Elkton, where Don preached, was overpopulated with churches—almost one for every family. But ours was usually packed each Sunday, for our congregation did love their young pastor with his lovely wife and darling children. At least those were the comments we overheard. Every Sunday we were invited to a different member's home, and during the course of our visits we listened intently to our hosts' needs. Donnie and Terri became very perceptive about people, and Terri seemed to catalog all the information in her incredible memory bank. This gave us an opportunity to instruct our children to never disclose any intimate conversations that had been entrusted to us.

It was not all listening, for these people were farmers and enjoyed the outdoors. The men loved Don because he was a gun enthusiast. They would get their guns out for target shooting—something I had learned to do with Don in sunny California by shooting baby-food jars. The men delighted in my ability to hit targets so well. While Don and I were busy with the adults, the children were occupied with kittens, puppies, chickens, pigs, sheep, goats, cows, lice, and other creatures. When it was a horse owner's turn to entertain us, Terri was in heaven. Waiting for that dinner engagement was almost intolerable for her. Donnie could not be coaxed, threatened, intimidated, or bribed to ride, but if a horse was tame enough for Teresa to sit on the saddle alone, she was in pure ecstasy. It was there in Southern Oregon, at a parishioner's barnyard, that Teresa's love of horses and the outdoors began. But leaving these lovely country folk each Sunday evening meant only the beginning of another exciting week back in Eugene, our urban setting.

Every Day an Adventure

Playmates were plentiful in this neighborhood, and Terri insisted on inviting them all into the living room, where Don and I had placed our old nineteen-inch TV, to watch four o'clock cartoons. I usually made oatmeal cookies, but I wanted them to last to each payday, which was every two weeks. This mattered not to Terri, who believed that in order to watch cartoons with the neighborhood children; one must serve cookies and bananas. I was sure the thin spot on the carpet was from the neighborhood children watching cartoons at our house each day. Teresa's simplistic solution was just buying a new rug! I loved having the children there, so how could I fault her insistence on feeding them all?

I learned many practical lessons while we lived in this house about what is really important in life. Our immediate neighbor had an immaculate yard and did not allow any of the children to play in it. He spent most of his time screaming at his stepchildren—a girl and a boy—and at our two older children. Conversely, the young mom across the street, a Catholic with five children, was far from perfect. She had a messy yard and a disfigured foot, but she was a delightful neighbor. Together we decided we would rather have human flowers than immaculate yards with untouched flowers. So we poured our money, time, and energy into human flowers. That family had five such flowers, we three, all beautiful and tenderly cared for.

Though the hours were few that Don and I could be together, there was always time for tokens of love. When no surplus money was available, we just got more creative. For special occasions I would write "I love you" on a pie crust. Don would leave little notes of tenderness in a pocket, or we would have a family bubble bath together. This ritual was to become one of the children's treasured memories. If they wanted to explain to friends that they had neat parents, they would tell them about our family bath. We tried to explain away our embarrassment by saying, "That is a Japanese custom."

Accidents

It was not uncommon to run to the nearby doctor for stitches for scalp wounds or split chins. But I was totally unprepared, after a long day with out-of-town relatives, when Teresa came running across the backyard with blood spurting from her ankle. The blood continued to spurt as she entered the house. It took one look, and my head spun before I regained composure. I knew this injury was very serious.

Someone grabbed a towel and wrapped it around the wound, and off to the doctor's we went. Fortunately Don was home for a dinner break and was able to drive us to the doctor, not too far away. After many sutures were sewn into place and the blood was soaked up, a very calm little girl explained what had happened. Workers were building a new house directly behind ours. Twenty feet to the left from our back door, a house frame and floor had been completed—a perfect place for adventuresome children to play after the carpenters went home for the day. But this day the carpenters had left a small hatchet behind for the curious to find. Of course Terri, the curious one, would be the one to find it. The cut was two and one-half inches long—a clean cut to the bone, but it had missed the main leg artery by a hair. The doctor marveled at his little patient's composure while he was closing this gaping wound.

I became well acquainted with the sight of blood. Only a few days later, Christy was standing on an old-fashioned chair, watching me can fruit, when the chair lunged forward, catching three of her little fingers under the chrome rung. Once again we rushed to the emergency room, towel wrapped around Christy's bloody fingers. I stood by her as the doctor deadened the hand, not fainting as I watched him sew up those precious little fingers.

To have thought these mishaps would limit Teresa's exploration was vastly in error, for with a bandaged leg she hopped throughout the neighborhood as usual. It was only a couple of weeks later when Teresa was carried home by a neighbor, oozing blood once again, that we suspected maybe this little flower was accident prone. She had been sliding down the neighbor's slide, and when she reached the bottom she ripped a beautiful *L* incision on the same leg that had only recently had another bandage removed. Right then we ruled out a modeling career. But at the tender age of five, Terri was undaunted by a few minor injuries and never seemed bothered by her many scars.

Birthday parties were yearly affairs for all the children, and a commonly heard threat was, "If you are not nice to me, you can't come to my party!" It was a neighborhood where children learned to fight, forgive, and tolerate. Enemies turned into friends, and friends turned into enemies. If the neighborhood squabbles became too much, they would be resolved with our Tuesday-night outings. At least it seemed the fun of an outing brought out the giggles, and any squabble was forgotten.

Because of Don's status as a student, we had access to the student-union movies. Through these movies we exposed our little family to some of the great minds of the past, such as Helen Keller, Albert Schweitzer, and Albert Einstein. Their little minds were challenged and stretched to overcome difficulties. It was amazing to me how much comprehension these little ones displayed. It was then that I suspected children's educations should start earlier than at five years old.

Spiritual and Music Education

Throughout our time at this small church of lovely people, the children participated in the church programs. Donnie could not tolerate the kindly laughter his appearance and recitation caused, but Terri reveled in the center stage and had to be instructed when it was time to sit down. She would rather stay on the stage, smiling and waving to those in the audience.

This little angel was not all saintly, though. A neighbor in Eugene shared with me that some of her prize bottles were missing. She said Terri had asked for them, and since her request was denied and now the bottles were missing, she was the prime suspect. Don and I simply said, "Terri, take Anne's bottles back." She went straight to her secret hiding place and returned the bottles with apologies. A lecture on the topic of how people need to trust in our honesty and character ensued. She never took anything without permission again.

At the end of our fairy-tale street ran a creek full of crawdads and an area of wide-open spaces. Under the watchful eye of an older brother to protect them from the perils of such a place, the girls played cowboys and Indians in a jungle of tall weeds. And who would have thought crawdads would be such a delicacy? Yes, we did eat them. With each season came more delights for these children to explore—that was until five-year-old Donnie headed off to kindergarten, leaving his playmates wishing they too could go to school.

We had begun to order the Seventh-day Adventist Bible storybooks, one a month. We desired for the Word of God to become a part of our children's very fiber. We wanted them to grow up believing that God is our loving Heavenly Father rather than a wrathful God who seeks vengeance. We believed if they developed in this incubator of love, they would not turn their backs on their Christian faith in their teen years.

We also wanted our children's lives to be well rounded in other areas. We thought music lessons would help them learn inner discipline. So when we heard about a studio piano advertised for the sum of $150, we bought it on a monthly payment plan. Education and music were very important to us. We believed the piano was a gold mine for that price, and indeed it did prove to be a gold mine for the children—and even to children to come. They would set the timer and devote many hours to developing their musical skills for many years.

Extended Family Joy

The time came for my young sister, a nursing student, to be married. The ceremony was to become a family affair. Don performed the ceremony, and each of us was to have a part. My sister and I had always agreed I would sing at her wedding, but we had not counted on me being an expectant mother at the time. I feared all the attention would be on my growing belly, but I was mistaken, for all attention was on the frills and flowers and smiling faces surrounding the happy couple. I sang "My Hero," which had been sung at our wedding.

Donnie was a ring bearer in his little white suit, and Terri and Christy, were darling little flower girls in their frilly pink-and-blue dresses. Terri became so enraptured by the event that she forgot to stand still, and during the most solemn prayer, she backed right off the platform where they were all standing. With crimson face she simply smiled at those who had peeked up from bowed heads and climbed back to her marked *X* on the stage.

The wedding continued uninterrupted. It was a lovely wedding, and it brought back happy memories of our own wedding, which had taken place in the same Christian church seven years before. It was just one more happy adventure for our little family.

Little Saint Teresa Evolves

It was the September after Terri had despaired over her big brother being able to go off to kindergarten. The time had finally arrived for her grown-up departure also. It was with hyper anxiety and a knotted stomach that she entered Mrs. Johnson's classroom. Mrs. Johnson had a reputation for being an outstanding kindergarten teacher. She was not beautiful by worldly standards, but she had an incredible and unique ability to understand children. Terri soon developed a love for her, and she became "Mrs. God" in our home.

Terri entered every activity with her whole being, and she was soon assisting the less-motivated children. I suspected bossy tendencies, but Mrs. Johnson diplomatically said Terri was so advanced that she used her as an assistant. How charmed we were at her first school performance. Terri had constructed her own Indian costume from brown paper bags and simply gyrated while singing "Itsy Bitsy Spider." When she spotted her family in the audience, it simply motivated her all the more, and we had a command performance. What a charmer!

Family Increases

In December 1959—completely ignoring Don's marriage-and-family professor, who declared that anyone who had more than two children was contributing to grave world problems—we anticipated the arrival of Todd Jeffery to even out our lopsided arrangement of children. I was quite embarrassed to be pregnant, for once again Don's parents did not think we could afford more children, and with Don's marriage-and-family instructor concurring, my guilt was compounded.

But when this beautiful jewel arrived, who cared about others' opinions? Todd Jeffery turned out to be Michele Kathleen—undoubtedly most feminine, with dimples and captivating charm. It was a simple afternoon birth while Don was in class. How could I not be happy with this blond, dimpled jewel? Michele means "angel or messenger of the Lord." Even though this little girl made the family even more lopsided with females, Donnie, Terri, and Christy were at home doing handstands and somersaults with glee at having a new sister to love.

Alan Beck was right when he wrote about little girls, "Little girls are the nicest things that happen to people. They are born with a little bit of angel-shine about them, and though it wears thin sometimes, there is always enough left to lasso your heart…"

Phobias Always Lurk

My heart was full, and my workload picked up speed with a new jewel in the home. In the spring of the year, Donnie began acting strange. He began just sitting in front of the TV when he came home from school. He looked pale and ate little—most unusual behavior. I did take him to the doctor, all four children in tow. Dr. Pugh was very solemn after he finished drawing blood for testing. He said it would be twenty-four hours before we would know if it was mononucleosis or leukemia...*Leukemia!* Oh Lord, what a hideous word. The story I had read in Indiana came flooding back. With anguished hearts we waited to hear that it was only mono, and rest and vitamins would soon have him in tip-top shape. What relief!

A siege of scarlet fever followed soon after Donnie had recovered from mono, with all three older children taking their turns in bed, very ill. We were giving them their antibiotics daily. We thought their symptoms were under control, but Terri's fever kept creeping up, and she suffered from persistent vomiting. Finally, in spite of the mounting medical expenses, we called Dr. Pugh to come to the house. He was a very stern doctor who said not to be penny wise and pound-foolish when it came to children's health. Since Don was a student and only a part-time employee, we did not have medical insurance, but the doctor was emphatic that the children needed complete bed rest and strong antibiotics until the scarlet fever had been sufficiently arrested. Young parents have much to learn about health issues.

More Adventures

Eventually everyone recovered, and normal life resumed. We rejoined Don on the weekly trips to his preaching point. On one of our Sunday home visits, we met with a family who raised pugs—beautiful little dogs with squashed faces, much like bulldogs' faces. I was smitten with a roly-poly little animal who defiantly insisted on jumping in my lap. It was instant love—but with a fifty-dollar price tag, no way! However, when, at six months old, Mr. Beans had not yet sold, he became ours as a love gift. At least five-sixths of the family thought it was a love gift. So it was that on a Sunday night, Mr. Beans rode home to Eugene, all cuddled in the backseat as though he had been waiting for six months for this very thing to happen.

Our glee was dampened by Don's rage, for Mr. Beans set out to destroy anything the children of the neighborhood had not yet destroyed—including our neighbor's immaculate yard! This little defiant animal found the neighbor chasing him off his property a most entertaining game. And if the neighbor stepped over the line into Mr. Bean's territory, a leap for the seat of the pants was in order. Even though we had no fence, the neighbor and Mr. Beans kept a property-line truce…most of the time!

We never were able to convince Jake, our next-door neighbor, or Don of this little animal's beguiling charm, but our four children believed he was a treasure sent directly from God. No dog, I am sure, has been so showered with kisses, and no children ever received the same number of kisses back. One of my cleanliness rules—not allowing animals to sleep in human beds—was broken, and Mr. Beans would choose a different bed each night, including ours…right in between his lover and his hater. I believe he was trying to win over that one-sixth of the family. When we went to visit friends—my sister's in-laws, who lived near us—Mr. Beans was most welcomed, so people said; however, he immediately went into their bedroom, lifted his leg, and marked his territory. Some people's words are more gracious than their feelings, I'm sure!

When school was out, we took time for short trips to lakes and clam digging at the coast; these were times for exploring the handiwork of our Creator. On one such outing to Multnomah Falls, we stopped on our way home to see friends of mine. Gert had been one of my mentors as I had grown up. She loved children and was always taking children who needed love into her home. I had been one of those children as well as one of her daughter's dear friends.

When the initial greetings were over, I could tell by Terri's quick glances around that I did not have time to usher her to head off an outburst. She blurted out, "Eee, what a messy house! But if you think this is bad, you should go to the bathroom!" Our friend, whose least priority was housecleaning, put me at ease (sort of) by responding to Terri's exclamation, and they became lasting friends. Besides, Gert had a horse, and in Terri's eyes the cleanliness of the house became inconsequential! On the way home, I gave Teresa a lengthy lecture to help her see that such candid honesty should be handled more discreetly, if at all.

In our lovely new home, our most happy family hosted many slumber parties that took place outside our bedroom window, under the stars. At that time in history, it was safe for children to sleep unattended outside, to leave keys in the car, and to leave the house unlocked, all without fear for our safety or that of our children. Often we tucked our children and neighborhood children into their sleeping bags only to later hear a tap, tap on the patio door, all of them wanting to come in and be closer to a mommy and daddy.

It seemed we always had a neighborhood full of children at our house. At night, when I tucked our own angelic children into bed and remembered screeching at all the children throughout the day, I was overcome with remorse. My goal was to be the perfect, calm, loving mommy. I felt like such a failure on these occasions, for try as I might, I still joined the neighborhood screamers. All of the neighborhood children said they liked to come to our house because I never screamed like their mommies. (I think it must have been the cookies!) Yet in spite of my failures, each morning was an exhilarating new day starting with "I love you, Mommy."

Overflowing Heart

Life was good in Eugene with our loving family. I suppose that is why I wasn't very excited when we were asked to be ministerial candidates in Colfax—a little community in Eastern Washington, in the rich wheat-growing county of Whitman. It was reported that at one time in the '50s, it had been the richest county in the nation.

It was July, the month of our eighth wedding anniversary. In view of that fact, we welcomed a trip to celebrate the occasion. Don had finished two degrees and was still working on another, so we had assumed we would stay in Eugene. But we wanted to be open to God's direction, so we piled our always-ready travelers into the car and headed east, trying to keep open minds.

The warmth we felt in that church on July 26, 1960, was indescribable. We were celebrating our eighth wedding anniversary and our most happy life, and as Don delivered his candidate sermon, I scanned the audience, and I wondered about the feeling rising within my heart. A potluck dinner was held following the service so we could get acquainted, and it seemed like we made instant friends. Don and I agreed on the way home that we could easily fit in with these beautiful young people (most in their twenties, as we were), but there would be so much at stake if we left the University of Oregon…so we thought!

We dismissed the lilt in our spirits and headed back to Eugene, having acknowledged what a wonderful weekend—and a perfect anniversary celebration—it had been. The chairman of the board, Larry Brownell, continued to call and write letters, asking us pointed questions about our beliefs and church philosophy. But soon it was time for school to begin.

Summer ended, and as September arrived Terri was entered first grade with great gusto. She would no longer be part of a protective carpool but would join her brother in the cruel world of the school bus. There was a neighborhood boy with a kidney problem, and the children at the bus stop made fun of the noticeable urine bag worn under his pant leg. Terri could hardly tolerate such injustice and was ready to take them all on single-handedly…even with bows in her hair, a scrubbed face, and a dainty dress! In her defense of the helpless neighborhood boy, she too became the victim of childhood bullying and, on many mornings, found more and more reasons to dawdle and find excuses to stay home. The children learned much give-and-take in this neighborhood, as did their young parents.

It seemed Terri's varied cultural experiences had put her ahead of her class in maturation. The gentle compassion she shared at home was also present at school. On the days Terri's teacher, Mrs. Whitlock, thought she could not make it through the day with thirty noisy first graders, she told me that Terri—perceiving the teacher's frustration—would come to her and say, "That's OK, Mrs. Whitlock. I love you." Mrs. Whitlock said all the frustration would drain away in the face of this little angel's love.

Teresa was her teacher's admirer, and we heard in detail about this beautiful lady with the blond hair and lavish wardrobe. Teresa's eye for good taste continued. Was this because from the beginning of polishing these jewels, I had kept them scrubbed, polished, and picture perfect? My older sister said I followed my children with a broom and washrag! From a later perspective, I may have been in error to have them always polished and perfect.

A Dream Fulfilled

The Colfax offer did not disappear. After negotiating with the awesome chairman of the board, Larry Brownell, and after much prayer, Don did accept the call to be the minister of the Colfax congregation…if he could finish his degree at Washington State and we could sell the house I loved. Continuing Don's education seemed to be the lesser problem, for the real estate agent was very dismal about the possibility of selling our house. It was December, and there were three other houses on the block that had not sold during their ninety-day listings. Our price was a little high, but we signed a thirty-day listing. We signed with the agent a day before Christmas, so when the realtor called the day after Christmas with a couple wanting to look at the house, we were surprised, to say the least. Christmas celebration was still evident throughout the house, but we took a ride, lest our six bodies compounded the clutter.

That evening the real estate agent called us to tell us our house had sold—the easiest sale he had ever made, he said. He had not even had time to put up a sign. We truly felt this was God's providence that we leave this chapter of our lives and move on to the next. So on February 1, 1961, waxing and polishing ourselves right out the front door into the rain, we left a glistening, empty house full of memories, watched a moving van pull out from the drive with all our belongings, and climbed into our loaded car, experiencing both tears and anticipation. We were on our way to a new adventure!

CHAPTER 9

Camelot

> Opportunity dances with those
> Who are already on the dance floor.
> —H. Jackson Brown, Jr.

Snowy Camelot

We arrived about the same time the moving van and crew arrived. Soon they were unloading our household of furniture into an old, recently remodeled three-story house. Crunch, crunch went the frozen snow under our feet as the children scrambled out of the car to explore their new mansion. And indeed the huge, old house looked like a mansion standing against a bluff, resting in its shade. I had left our youngest, fourteen-month-old Michele, with my mother in Clarkston until we were settled. Colfax was only about sixty miles from where I had grown up, so we could easily go pick her up when we were securely unpacked and moved in.

We had learned a lot about this community during the six months of negotiation. The community was wealthy, the wealth having been accumulated over the years from the agriculture industry. The wealth of wheat and livestock ranches, in most cases, had been handed down from generation to generation. At one time Whitman County's per capita income was the highest in the nation.

Pure Country Living

We entered to find a house full of women cleaning with gaiety and laughter—what a warm welcome on that crisp, sunny winter day. The kitchen counters were laden with foods and delicacies of the rarest kinds. The children scampered upstairs to select their bedrooms. All four bedrooms were upstairs, and it had been decided beforehand that Donnie and Terri—because of their ages—would each have a room, and Michele and Christy would share one bedroom. Donnie took the room at the end of the hall that faced the bluff—surely a seven-and-three-fourths-year-old's delight!

Terri took the room on the north, the one in the middle of the hall. There was barely enough room to turn around in, but it looked like a fairyland to Terri because there was a window facing a big oak tree. Outside Terri's window, she could also see a very old house surrounded by an iron fence covered with overgrown ivy. I found out later that the old and mysterious-looking estate belonged to Mrs. Perkins. Her family had been one of the first to settle in this community, and the street we lived on was named after them. Indeed we learned that our home too was one of the first handsomely built estates.

Mrs. Perkins's house looked like a scene right out of a horror movie to me, but the eerie view out Terri's window did not alarm her at all. She could only dimly see into what looked like a kitchen through a small window with a lace curtain, a single lightbulb dangling from the ceiling. The overgrown ivy made me think of a drama from Alfred Hitchcock. Remembering my own childhood phobias, I would have been terrified with the view. But Terri's love of Agatha Christie, even at this young age, was only enhanced in this little secure room.

Christy, just three, would share the large bedroom next to ours with fourteen-month-old Michele. They would be more secure next to Mommy and Daddy, although these little jewels were happy with anything and were always good-natured about their older brother and sisters' demands.

Can Life Get Any Better?

So it was that after a day never to be forgotten, including a tasty home-cooked dinner and pastries to melt in your mouth that our "good-nights" rang out through that upstairs sleeping dorm. As night fell we piled into newly made beds, all feeling tired but good...really good! Surely our Heavenly Father had led us into green pastures. We were all happy with our decision to leave our beloved Eugene and to take on this new season of life. We knew nothing but joy! But the friends we had made in Eugene would continue to be dear friends.

Unfortunately Donnie and Terri had to explore their new school the next day rather than the bluff behind their new home. It cannot be said that school was a pleasant surprise, for progressive teaching methods had not reached this small rural community. Donnie and Terri discovered that school here was a necessary evil. The school system had an entirely different philosophy from the one in Eugene, where, in first and second grades, children were already learning foreign languages. For these two young explorers, school would have to be endured, and then, along with Mr. Beans, the secret trails on the bluff could be explored with utter delight.

Don had been working monstrous hours and going to school full time, and I could see this new life was exactly what I had longed for. We would now share in ministry together. I liked that! The church and manse phones were connected, so I could buzz Don on an impulse and declare my love.

The community itself lent itself to our oneness, for I was always included. This community, which was overpopulated with churches, included the ministers in all civic functions—and there were many. We moved right into a full schedule with the church program, for our love relationship with the church had already been growing for six months.

However, we were to learn that not all newcomers to the community experienced the warmth and openness we had. Colfax held a reputation of being a closed community. We were eager to fit in to this unique church, and these dear people gave and gave to meet our every need. We had instant friends, as though we had grown up there. But it was a different story at school, and our children soon learned they were preacher's kids and outsiders! For both Donnie and Terri, this was a difficult adjustment. But Terri was determined to be accepted by her peer group, and soon she was inviting other seven-year-old girls to spend the weekend in her adventure land; in turn she was spending weekends with friends, especially the ones who owned horses.

I exchanged babysitting with other young mothers or hosted children in our home. So though we no longer had a neighborhood full of young friends, there were children in the community for our children to befriend, but adjustments came slowly. For Christy and baby Michele, playing Barbie dolls and getting to go with Daddy to the church office were enough. Don had many evening meetings, and I wanted to join him on these occasions, but what would we do for a babysitter? We had not been in the habit of hiring people to watch our children. And I did not feel comfortable asking the other young mothers to watch our children, especially when some of them would or should have been at the meetings.

Friends and New Life

With shyness and apprehension, Marcia soon came into our lives, forever to be loved. She was a junior in high school and one of the few teenagers in our church. We wanted a reliable babysitter, and she came highly recommended. The first night Marcia babysat, the children didn't say anything as we left, nor did Marcia. We were concerned, but it turned out we had no cause to be, for when we arrived home all four children were clinging to her, and she was dubbed our governess.

Winter turned into spring as we lived each day with a sense of adventure. Ruth Lowe, one of our delightful church members, invited us to visit her wheat ranch, located across an old railroad bridge. We had no idea what lay ahead of us. Ruth and her husband, Curt, defied description. Ruth was loud, wore her hair in old-fashioned braids, and wore clothes she had worn, mended, and re-mended for years. Her husband, who had lost an arm earlier in his life, wore overalls. Neither of them was in vogue with the rest of this wealthy community.

As Ruth told us, she did not desire diamonds but that rich Palouse land. True individualists, they defied any social pressure to be other than what they were. Curt, unpretentious as he was, won our hearts completely, though it was a rare occasion when we saw him in church. When he wasn't farming, he spent his hours in the back room of the local saloon, playing cards. Don and I earned Curt's acceptance, which he did not hand out easily. Don offered to clean his rifles, as it was a difficult task with one arm...and they formed a bond that lasted until Curt's death a few years later. Terri too observed his genuineness but admired him only from afar. He and Ruth did not have children of their own, and he never gave our children permission to approach him or step out of their prescribed role of being seen but not heard.

For our first visit with these new friends, Ruth had given directions, telling us we would have to park by an elevator warehouse some distance from the house. Then we were to cross a field and a small footbridge, and she would meet us by the railroad trestle. We were unprepared for what was in store. Not only did we behold the most gorgeous, rugged, uncivilized scenery we had ever seen in our lives, but we were expected to cross that railroad trestle by foot, fifty feet above the rushing Palouse River. We looked at Ruth aghast, and Mr. Beans— who went everywhere with us—placed one paw on the first tie and then noticed the rushing water below. He refused to budge! Ruth laughed at our city fear and, with her booming country voice, said she'd take us across in shifts. She grabbed young Michele from my arms and picked up Mr. Beans, tucking him under the other arm. Then she told Don to take Donnie's and Terri's hands and follow her. She returned to secure an arm around my waist and take Christy in the other arm, instructing us not to look down at the water but to keep our eyes straight ahead. We sighed freely once on the other side—only to remember we would have to cross again to reenter civilization.

What rustic living we enjoyed. There was an open-pit fire, with a huge iron kettle filled with frying potatoes—my favorite dish in the world. These warm, relaxing hours made us forget about the trip back across the trestle, especially when Ruth convinced us she would get us back across. She shared that she had crossed the bridge in the middle of winter in subzero weather and late at night, with no accidents.

Don spotted the groundhog hunting sites and observed this would be a hunter's paradise—and what a place for target practicing. The sound of the shots would ricochet down those canyons. The children's eyes danced with the grandeur they beheld. With Ruth escorting us, there would be many more such outings. Our feeling of accomplishment that night could not have been greater if we'd conquered Mt. Everest! We all agreed we had to take all of our out-of-town family and visitors to this earthly paradise. However, we never did gain the courage we hoped when we faced crossing the trestle—nor did Mr. Beans, for that matter. Even so, Curt and Ruth's place became our favorite getaway.

We enjoyed taking the children groundhog hunting, but when Don and Donnie shot a groundhog and then went the distance to check it, Donnie observed that it looked too much like Mr. Beans, and that was the end of his hunting. On those outings with the children, who were wearing either cowboy boots or tennis shoes, it was not uncommon to step over a rattlesnake unaware until you heard its rattler or to be snatched up by Ruth, who knew only too well what lurked on the trail. In retrospect I wonder at the risks we took.

The little footbridge we had to cross before we came to the trestle was thirty feet across eternity. Sometimes there was even a torrent of rushing water flowing under it. It seemed we all shared the same fear of heights, including Mr. Beans. On one particular occasion, he decided it would be better to swim the rushing torrent rather than walk across that shaky footbridge. Pugs have very short legs and are not known for their swimming ability, and soon Mr. Beans was drifting downstream with the current. Before Don could respond to our screams, Ruth was in the water waist deep—clothes and all—to rescue Mr. Beans and receive face-licking thank you. Thereafter, Mr. Beans insisted on arm taxi service from car to house! How much a part of the children's lives this lovable animal had become.

One Sunday after church, we came home to find Mr. Beans lying at the back door. Our perfect little world collapsed in one moment at the sight of him. Evidently he had been hit by a car and had made it that far before he died. True, Mr. Beans could infuriate us beyond words and then tilt his head and look into our fury with disarming defiance, seeming to say, "Catch me if you can!" (That was especially true when Mr. Beans had Christy's unnamed turtle in his mouth.) But now the tears flowed, and we wondered how we could possibly survive the loss of a human being when our grief was so great over a small animal. Don and I tried to kiss away the hurt from the tearstained faces, but nothing would suffice until we made a trip to Spokane to find a new pug puppy.

All the children loved Foo Doo, but it was Terri who scrubbed and brushed and passed on to him the same discipline she received from her daddy. Foo Doo continued the tradition of taking turns sleeping on the children's bed. Though we loved him, he never displayed the orneriness Mr. Beans had. He did not delight in our excursions to Ruth Lowe's wilderness. He preferred to remain in the comfort of his home, choosing a bed to sleep on and jump down from when he heard our car return (for sleeping on beds during daytime was not allowed). At night he most often chose Terri's bed to settle into after giving each child a slobbery goodnight kiss. However, we were never to find another pet quite as human (or as infuriating) as Mr. Beans.

The summers passed far too quickly with so many adventures at our beck and call. We enjoyed activities not only in Colfax but at my brother-in-law's place as well. He lived in Clarkston, where I had grown up. Often we made trips down the Lewiston grade, an unbelievably curvy and winding steep grade, which left the children wide eyed! Chuck owned several quarter horses was a horse trainer and he had a whole family of horse lovers. Terri listened to every word Chuck spoke and stored the horse wisdom away for later use. Any chance she got, she was feeding the horses oats and kissing their cold, runny noses. Her insatiable desire for her own horse kept her pleading with her daddy. Thinking she would outgrow this phase, he casually promised he'd buy her one when she turned thirteen. That was a mistake!

Any free night was family movie night. Colfax had one movie theater, but there were other theaters within driving distance. In the 1960s there were great family movies, and I am sure we saw every one. This exposure added another dimension to Terri's personality. She usually reenacted the various roles on the way home and kept us in an uproar with her precision. Little Meme, as we began calling Michelle, was old enough now to enter into the family fun, and so the laughter and happiness on the way home from these movies had an added dimension with her humorous giggle. After these happy family nights, we would crawl into bed knowing how good it was that we had come to Colfax. A round of goodnights would be heard from each of those love-filled rooms over and over until the last sleepy goodnight trailed off into dreamland.

Marcia was becoming more and more a part of our lives—not only when babysitting but just to have around. What a delight she was. She drove her dad's red and white pickup. With glee the children would usually con her into taking them in the back of the pickup for hamburger or somewhere…anywhere! Marcia had an openness about her that was refreshing. She treated the children like thinking adults, and they responded likewise. But one evening when she was babysitting, the children were acting out to the point where she went into a room, closed the door, and dissolved in tears. Four little people slipped "I'm sorry" notes under the door, and when she tucked them into bed—still silent—she heard them ask forgiveness for hurting their best friend's feelings.

Marcia accompanied us to conventions and family camps, always as our governess and friend. Marcia's own words can best describe the relationship, taken from a project she turned in for school credit.

My Small Friends

Two years ago our church gained a new minister and family. We learned that the family consisted of four young children. From the very beginning, we got along very well and my first babysitting experience with them was delightful and I became to know what winning characters they are.

All four are wonderful children, mainly because of their happy home and loving parents. Donnie and Terri get good grades in school. Christy is the charmer and a prospect for the title of "Miss America 1980." Michele is a natural clown and thrives on amusing others.

There is no jealousy among the four children, and they play together well. Oftentimes we have disagreements, but this is only to be expected. I find it very rewarding to take care of these children—for what is sweeter than Christy's smile, more puzzling than Terri's math problem, funnier than impish Michele, and what can warm the heart more than hearing Donny recite to perfection "The Lord's Prayer," the perfect end to our evening together? The end.

How we loved the ministry in Colfax: all the community involvement, the entertainment in our home, the gaiety of Christmas parties—the home fireside ministry, as we called it. But I knew if failed to polish the jewels entrusted to us, we would fail indeed. So we made sure we gathered these four jewels around us each day for family devotions: a time for Bible stories, a time to thank our Heavenly Father for His goodness to us, and a time of instruction God's precepts. Their young tender hearts were so receptive, and they had no hang-ups or rebellion to this family tradition. We did not teach them that they had "little black hearts" as was the custom of many conservatives in this community. They simply learned more about this magnificent Jesus whom they had always loved. When Terri heard some opinion contrary to her image of Jesus, she would take it straight to her daddy. How often she overheard her daddy releasing someone from the bondage of hellfire-and-damnation preaching, only to see that person blossom in a new understanding of God's love, not the God they were taught to fear and cringe before.

To say that we always lived in an atmosphere of love is not to say there was no discipline. For indeed Don still held a severe and strict upper hand that I tried to soften with tenderness. It was at this point in time that we began encouraging the children to share their feelings as long as they did it in a courteous manner. So an open dialogue began, with us correcting many errors in our ways. Still, did we have model children? Hardly! When she was corrected, Terri cross her arms, put down her foot firmly, and out her lower lip ready to give her defense. She looked like a mimic of Tinker Bell in the movie *Peter Pan*…and that trait stayed with her.

Blessings upon Blessings

Christmas became an extravaganza. Each year we tried to make it a time for family and celebration. It became a family tradition to attend the Christmas Eve candlelight service, with Don preaching and me singing a solo or singing in the choir. Then we would all go out for my birthday Chinese dinner. Finally, we would tuck four little sleepy heads into bed so I might wrap late purchases. We always made sure we had an equal number of presents for each child under the tree and that equal money was spent on each child. Early the next morning, we would light the advent candles and read the story from St. Luke. After the children were sent on a scavenger hunt to find their gifts and surprises, we would usually take off to attend the Ice follies in Spokane, Washington; stay in a motel; or take in the latest Walt Disney movie. If nothing was planned, we would walk through blizzardy snow downtown—a few blocks away from where we lived—for hot chili. During some Christmas holidays, we might even attend hog butchering parties to make German sausage. We packed the day and week full of pure celebration before the older children went back to school.

We were included in every community and family event, which gave us a broad experience of the culture of this blessed community. We would often spend Sunday afternoons with other families, boating, bird hunting, or just conversing. Our bonds were growing very strong with all the families. Though we missed some aspects of Eugene, we were very happy that we had made this move.

Later in the summer, we shared in the epidemics of ringworm and boils. The public swimming pool was swarming with heads that had purple-painted spots covering the circular bald spots. Teresa's long, fluffy ponytail covered her silver-dollar-sized bald spot. The boil epidemic was not as easily camouflaged. We had several bouts with strep infections. Terri was very seldom ill, but when she was, it seemed she felt worse than anyone else. We did worry at these times, remembering Dr. Pugh's comments about being penny wise and pound foolish concerning our children's health. On one such occasion when Terri was ill, she wrote us a love note:

Dear Mother and Father,

I'm going to give you the best Christmas gift you ever had. That is because I love you. I'm going to stop fighting with the family.

The thing I personally want to thank you for is your kindness to me. You let me stay overnight with people. When I'm sick, you're always near.

I love you.
Teresa

Terri romped, played ball, and climbed through the forts on the hill with Donnie and his friends. Her daddy, who had an aversion to bossy, domineering women like his mother, was fearful her tomboy traits would not allow her to develop into a soft, feminine beauty. He was never around when she played Barbie for hours with her little sisters. However, it was her father who would come home after work and say, "Terri, let's go groundhog hunting at Ruth's." She would run over and get the neighbor girl and be ready before he asked twice.

She loved to be in the company of her father, whom she emulated. She thought he was the greatest. What he did, she did. What he said, she said. What he read, she read—and that was a problem, for he was reading *Archy and Mehitabel,* and she would take it from his nightstand and read it also. You have to have a sense of humor to appreciate Don Marquis's writing without grammatical notations. But Terri's dad thought the book was far too mature reading for his daughter. Archy, a cockroach was once a reporter, and Mehitabel, a cat, was once Cleopatra; it was a satire to be sure. Mehitabel's lines "along comes another batch of these damned kittens/it is not archy/that I am shy on mother love/god knows I care for/the sweet little things/curse them" simply sent Teresa into hysterics. She was so quick to apply this to the reality of her acquaintances and was often to recall and observe this paradox. When she would listen to parents complain of their children's behavior, she would break into a knowing smile!

Colfax was a matriarchal community, and Donnie became very hostile to females always telling him what to do at home, school, church, Cub Scouts, and piano lessons. It was about this time that he decided he had too many sisters, and it was Terri—after seven years of inseparable companionship—who became his scapegoat. He no longer wanted her playing with his friends. She was too gangly, and he did not want to sit by her in the car, for her hairy legs bothered him. Don was the continual referee. Truces were declared only under their father's insistence or if a family outing necessitated their togetherness.

We didn't become alarmed with this new warfare in the household, for we noticed that when we vacationed in the Doty's' houseboat, they still swam together, fished, and laughed at the same practical jokes. It was a beautiful truce when they both requested that their father baptize them on Easter Sunday 1963. Donnie was ten, and Terri was nine months and three weeks behind him. They said resounding "I do's" when their father—with a lump in his throat—asked them, "Do you take Jesus to be the Lord and Savior of your life? And do you believe that Jesus is the Christ, the Son of the Living God?" As is the custom of the Disciple of Christ church, Don baptized them by immersion. They both wore white robes, and Don dipped them with a hankie over their noses into the baptismal. My heart danced for joy for these two precious jewels.

The truce lasted for one day! It seemed Terri could find something nice to say about the ugliest person, but she had trouble getting along with her brother. Her angst against her brother was just as strong as his against her. Also, when we had young friends around, she found it troublesome to include her two younger sisters. Is not the angelic and the devilish found in each of our personalities?

Soon Marcia, our beloved governess, was to graduate and go away to nurses' training. It was going to be difficult to let this beautiful young friend walk out of this chapter in our lives. It was a mutual time of tears, as a letter slipped into my hand indicates:

In a very few hours, I'll walk across the stage and receive my diploma from high school and close the door on so many things. Maybe it's just because I'm so sentimental, but there are a few things I'd like to say to you because you do mean so very much. The entire Gibbs family is one of the most wonderful families I've ever had the pleasure of knowing! Funny how six wonderful people just happen to all be related. I'm sure you're fully aware of it—but your children are four very special little guys to me. I simply love to stay with them and usually you are the only ones I ever babysit for anymore.

One thing for sure, I know I'll never forget you. When you first came, I knew that you were someone who would be a true friend. No words could ever tell how much I've enjoyed the times spent with your family. Every place you've taken me always resulted in a wonderful time. Ruth, last night you said you'd rather be alive and unnoticed than be dead and a hero. Don't you ever believe for one minute that you aren't important! You probably are thinking I'm just a mixed-up teenager who has a crush on someone—no, I'm over that. The tears I'm crying are very real, and my feelings are very deep…

There are so many things I'd like to do just one more time that I probably never will. There's the future to look forward to, but already I have many memories. No matter where I happen to be on a Sunday morning, my heart will be in Colfax at our church.

I know I'll never forget you. You can throw this letter away if you like, but at least I know you know now how I feel. I guess I could tell you just about anything. They say though that you don't talk about friendship—you feel it. What I feel for you is very special, and I want you to know I think I make a good choice in choosing my first "grown-up friend."

My love and respect always,
Marcia

This treasured letter found its way into our box of special memories. And it was not the end of our involvement with this lovely young girl!

Some Ripples

Not everyone was as kind as Marcia, though. One evening, when we were entertaining two couples, one woman said to the other in what she thought was out of my hearing, "Christy is the pretty one." It was true that Terri's two front teeth were only halfway down, she had a host of freckles bursting forth, and she was as gangly as many girls this age. However, I didn't pretend I hadn't heard what the woman said, and I answered back in fury! "All of our children are beautiful…we have no *special* ones!"

We had no tolerance for church members or relatives showing partiality to any of the children. We were determined to preserve the uniqueness of each child. We believed this needed to be done within the family as well as within the church family.

There were two distinct factions within this beloved church: the liberal conservatives and the conservative conservatives. We refused to take sides or show partiality to either group, as we loved them both. So when the members saw our intolerance of partiality being shown to our children, it put them at ease, knowing that each one of them would be accepted for his or her uniqueness. However, the factions took their toll on Don, who was always trying to get them to see eye to eye and blend together.

Teresa continued to develop in this incubator of love, though she was demanding and highly motivated to experience all aspects of life. We referred to her as our squeaky hinge as well as Tinker Bell, for she usually succeeded in what she wanted to do or have. Her father, as with all the children, remained her constant idol. Once, when he returned from an out-of-town meeting, she slipped him the following note:

Dear Daddy,

We missed you very much. We are glad you are back, because you are a good boy all the time. And also you are nice to us. So we would like for you to have a happy father's day.

Love,
Terri, Don, Christy, Michele

And another note was sent to Don when he was in the hospital for nine days:

Dear Daddy,

I hope you get better soon. I's lonesome without you.

Get well soon.

Love,
Terri

On another occasion, when Don and I were working in a youth camp for a whole week, my aunt Vildy came to stay with the children. Here is a letter we received:

Dear Mom and Dad:
    I miss you very much. But we are getting along fine. Michele doesn't cry anymore and doesn't wet the bed. Aunt Vildy made some doughnuts and cinnamon rolls. Christy and I polished Aunt Vildy's fingers and toenails. We went to Bible school yesterday. We are going again today. We hope you are having a happy time. Donnie is driving me crazy learning his memory verses. Aunt Vildy has my hair in four braids. It stays up pretty good. Foo-doo is fine too. His dog friends come over and play with him. Good-bye now with love from us all.

Your children,
Terri

Christy
Don
Michele

Pursuing Degrees

Don was still slowly working to finish his graduate degree at Washington State University in Pullman, only a few miles from Colfax. He was hoping to finish the degree with the classes he was taking but still receive the degree from the University of Oregon. I was his sole typist, editor, and critic, but the children participated in their own ways as well. They loved the nights they could attend class with their daddy. For instance they attended a class on abnormal psychology, studying the effects of children in epileptic fits. It had little adverse effect, for they thoroughly enjoyed the evening out with their dad, along with a Coke…which was much different from washing down gas pumps earlier in Eugene.

They also became subjects for some of his studies. The experimentation Don did for a probability-theory course left us in awe. Surely Terri must have had a photographic memory. Don used several subjects—church members, neighbors, and children—and tested each subject's recall. He arranged a stack of cards with a sequence of numbers. Then his subjects were to recall, in order, what they had viewed in different time spans—in other words, fifteen minutes, thirty minutes, eight hours, and then the next day. Terri was the only one out of a group of adults and children, male and female, who was able to tell what she had seen with absolute accuracy at every interval. It was incredible; the other guinea pigs of the experimentation thought so too.

Does This Camelot Have to End?

We became deeply and emotionally involved with a couple who moved into the community. Dick was a state patrolman. They came to our church with two little girls. When Shirlee, the wife, was diagnosed with cervical cancer, we helped care for their two darling girls, Sue and Pamie, who were seven and four—the same ages as our two youngest daughters—while she went through various treatments. To say the heaviness that interloped in our fairy-tale existence was not welcome would be to put it mildly. We had a firsthand view of Shirlee's fight and suffering. It was intense—something we had never experienced before. Still, we all remained optimistic about the outcome.

Shirlee's illness was followed in November of 1964 by the assassination of our youthful president, John F. Kennedy. He had not gotten our vote. (Many Christians thought it was heresy to elect a Catholic president.) However, we were unprepared for the reaction of our community. I was working part time for the county clerk at the courthouse when the tragedy struck. My boss's comment was, "They should have given the guy [Oswald] a medal." Negative emotions ran high throughout this conservative community. For us it was a time of personal heaviness over the injustice in the world we lived. We all grew a little serious that dreadful week. The festivities of the holidays seemed a little less carefree that year. Our hearts turned more to the spiritual than to our celebrations.

Shirlee was to enter a Spokane hospital in January for radical surgery. Believing that one should put so-called legs on one's prayers, I prepared for a fun-filled evening. We had one other couple, along with Shirlee and Dick, over for dinner. Later in the evening, other couples joined us to help us achieve what we hoped for—a light evening for Shirlee to remember while recovering in the hospital with her husband.

It was a joyous and laughter-filled evening. Most of the young husbands were full of unending jokes and fun. While the children romped upstairs, the adults played charades and other foolish games. We all put on the facade of gaiety—all except Shirlee. While playing charades she kept referring to death. It made my heart pound, and I wished she wouldn't do that—a Freudian slip, I suspected. Everyone was trying to maintain stiff upper lips for Shirlee. However, in spite of all our fears and Shirlee's references to death, she wrote on her calendar that evening "a memorable evening at the Gibbs'."

The next morning Shirlee's husband, Dick, took her to Spokane, Washington, about sixty miles from Colfax. The nature of the surgery meant she could not be in the small Colfax hospital. Her husband stayed with her. Don and I drove to Spokane and waited with Dick while she was in surgery. When she came out, we could not imagine the pain she was in. One could not brush against the bed frame without her shrieking in pain. The outcome looked grim, and after a few days—after enduring indescribable pain—she kissed her beloved husband good-bye. In spite of our prayers, it happened. We lost Shirlee. Our tears flowed copiously; the days were gray, and our faith was severely wavering.

Shirlee's mother, Vicki Vann, a stand-in for Carolyn Jones in Hollywood, came to stay with Dick and the girls. She was not equipped for family life, having already been through several husbands. She had placed Shirlee in parochial schools while growing up, as she pursued her career. As unique and different as she was, she was a celebrity in the community—and to Terri especially! Vicki gave Terri a gold bracelet and dubbed her St. Teresa; she knew a great deal about the Catholic Church, though she was now practicing yoga as a religion.

There was a mutual love between Vicki and us. She felt we were the angels sent to care for her daughter, for Shirlee and Dick had lived in Colfax for only a short time before she was stricken with the dreadful disease. Out of Vicki's broken heart, she gave us this poem:

She Was in Your Life for a Little While

And she knew how you loved her so.
There within the hearts of both of you
Cherished memories of her grow.
One thing we can't be forgetting now,
She also had memories too.
And if she were here to tell me
She would tell me "to give one to you"—

To remind you of all the salvation
She stored up within her dear heart,
Every time she would talk to you
With the love of God you'd impart!
This gift…is one of her treasures
And somehow I know she would say,
"The joys of life truly measured
Are in treasures you give away!"

Her loving hands have designed this
And each thread is so entwined,
If you look you will find her heart there
That she wove as she bided her time.
And now she is with her "maker"
And in secret she comes to our hearts
To reveal that God will take her
Where sorrow and joy are apart!

Out there…if we but knew His story
Of heaven and all of its worth,
There would linger on His earth!

—Grandma Vicki

We saw much evidence of God's concern for this beautiful family, though our hearts would never be quite as light again.

On the day of Shirlee's funeral, the church was full of patrol officers from all over the state. The front of the church was banked with flowers nearly covering the casket that lay in the corner, right by the choir, where I sat. The choir was to sing for the service. I was asked to sing a solo, but I knew I could not. Don was able to get through a sincere tribute to this beloved young woman with only tremors in his voice.

Small miracles occurred in the days that followed. I loved Shirlee's girls as my own and took them with us on excursions. It is odd how life often works. As Shirlee's husband, Dick, was struggling to deal with his grief, be a parent, and hold down a job, Mary—a very sensitive and loving person who had been the nurse who cared for Shirlee after the final surgery—walked into Dick's life to love him and his girls. We considered it a mini miracle; we grew to love Mary and supported this union even in our own grief over losing a dear, beautiful friend.

Our faith had received a devastating blow. However, in the Colfax community, death was seen as a common occurrence, and the community philosophy seemed to be "Live, drink, and be merry, for tomorrow we die." I wondered what was wrong with these people! This scripture came to mind over and over: "The righteous perish, and no one takes it to heart…" (Is 57:1, NIV).

We were still wrestling with the concept of God's protection and healing power when one clear evening we traveled to Palouse, thirty miles away, for a fellow pastor's farewell dinner. The pastor and his wife had become our good friends, and now they were leaving for more schooling in the East. We took all four of our children along and shared a happy evening.

On the return trip to Colfax, we hit a mudslide that had occurred while we were enjoying ourselves in Palouse. We were driving a red Buick hardtop. Three children were in the back, and Michele was on my lap up front…and there were no seat belts in the '60s! The car spun several times before sliding into a telephone pole—the only one in several hundred feet—that stopped us from rolling completely over. One small doorframe hitting that telephone pole was all that saved us.

We were stunned and terrified. As we climbed out of the smoking, totally demolished car, Terri said, "I'm sure glad you prayed before we left, Dad." I was glad too! Surely God was watching over us that night. We climbed back to the highway through ankle-deep mud and walked to the nearest farmhouse, which happened to be Marcia's family home. Marcia's mother, Martha, fixed us hot chocolate, and Paul Faires, Marcia's father, took us home.

We said many rounds of good nights that evening before any of us could go to sleep. The biggest irony of that night was that one of the state patrol officers had given Don a ticket for driving unsafely for road conditions, even though the officer had not been at the site, and Don had been totally unaware that a mudslide had happened. The officer had only heard about the accident. We had not met this particular patrolman, but that same officer showed up at church a few weeks later and deposited a bill in the offering plate. We wondered if our friend, Dick, also a patrolman, had talked to him. We never heard the truth, but that officer and his wife became our dearest friends over the years. They eventually shared in our lives and celebrations and became forever friends.

So Much Hurt

That summer brought many changes. During our four-year stay in this beloved community, not all was roses. Some farmers in the community were supporting an extreme right-wing individual who broadcast over the local radio station. His name was Carl McIntyre. His main thrust was anticommunism, but it was said by some that he was antieverything. Some people of the community complained he was very obnoxious and disturbing to listen to. Many of the ministers, but not all, felt he was doing more harm than good and wanted him removed from the air. Local congregations were being split within by the polarized opinions.

We had become close friends with both the Nazarene pastor and the Methodist pastor. The Methodist pastor had only recently arrived in the community. He and his wife were friends with whom we could let down our hair. We so enjoyed our times together playing cards—drawing the curtains to hide from the neighbors' views, as cards were considered by some religious groups in the community as sinful, and we did not want to offend anyone. After a full day of church activities, we would have a relaxing evening with these new friends, eating egg, pickle, and onion sandwiches or yummy pastries one of us wives made, or whatever we could conjure up on our limited salaries. Our children rode bikes together around the small town or just played on our hill while parents created their own entertainment. We never worried about the children, for they were reliable, and it was completely safe.

Our Methodist pastor friend was very proactive and vocal. The local radio station invited all pastors to present morning devotions each day of the week. When it was the Methodist pastor's turn, he did not give a devotional but began lambasting this defrocked Presbyterian minister, Carl McIntyre. Our Methodist pastor friend was immediately cut off the air. From that point on, the community was at war. The new Methodist pastor was called names: red, pink, a communist, a friend of Khrushchev. Such things were said to his children at school, and at times their lives seemed to be endangered. Donnie and Terri observed this whole affair with wonderment and fear. These children were their friends. The opinions of the elders soon became repeated on the school grounds. The whole community became embittered and out of control. The Methodist minister was run out of town!

Our church was not involved, but we felt some of the community fallout. Some of each pastor's congregation was involved with the John Birch Society, a radical organization that declared that each family needed things like a bomb shelter and firearms as well as approving of radical Carl McIntyre. It made every minister's job a little more difficult to keep peace and balance between these two opposing factions. It was intrinsically delicate. Our Methodist friends also put us in a delicate position, for our church did not think we should be friends with a rabble-rouser, the Methodist pastor!

Erroneous Offer

I suppose this explosive situation in the community was the reason that when Don was offered a teaching position on the coast, he did not evaluate the long-term ramifications of making a commitment to a school and community sight unseen! He signed a contract before ever visiting. His ultimate vocational desire was to teach in a Bible-related school, and this seemed to be the experience he needed.

The Grays Harbor College president was a good promotional man. He painted the position as a dream job and Aberdeen as a dream place to live. After signing that contract, we got up early one morning to drive to Aberdeen to check out this quaint little town, as it had been so lovingly described. Quaint?

Hardly! From our point of view, at least, the housing was lousy, and the weather was indescribable. We found the whole experience disappointing. On our return trip, the car was full of tears. When we arrived back in Colfax and to the safety of our home, the children ran for the protection of their rooms. We wished we had never heard of Aberdeen, Washington.

However, we believed at that time that a contract should not be broken. Later, we found breaking contracts was a common occurrence among educators. How could we leave our friendships behind? How could we leave our rambling house so full of happy memories? But the die was cast!

CHAPTER 10

Seduced by the Dark Side of the Force

> Dear friends, do not believe everyone who claims
> to speak by the Spirit. You must test them to
> see if the spirit they have comes from God, for
> there are many false prophets in the world.
> —1 JN 4:1, NLT

Brokenhearted

There were no ready-made friends to greet us in this strange salty-air, wet, windblown city…no nourishing delicacies gracing the kitchen counters…no small tokens of welcome and love. How accustomed to those tokens of love we had become. I left my heart in Colfax, among those dear wheat farmers who were our friends. What painful adjustments lay ahead!

It was quite a contrast living in Aberdeen—the wettest community in the Pacific Northwest—compared to living in one of the wealthiest communities in the nation. Our new community bore the sad statistics of having the highest rates of juvenile delinquency, suicide, divorce, and tooth decay in the state of Washington. It was a seaport town, but it had been off limits to the military during World War II—such was the seamy history of this place. Many people had been shanghaied on the riverfront during the war. And to this place we brought our innocent children!

However, the natives claimed they had the best educational system in the nation as well as the best living conditions anywhere. Don was delighted to be a part of this system, and we were happy to have our children exposed to this caliber of educational system…if it was true! It was stated that the indigenous children wanted to get their education elsewhere and then come back to the harbor to teach or work—hard to believe from my perspective.

There was no decent housing for rent, and housing was still more economical in 1964, so we purchased a newly built home in Central Park, just outside the city limits of Aberdeen. It was a lovely house, and we enclosed the rear of the single garage and made a fourth bedroom for Donnie. We also enclosed the over-cover between the house and attached garage to make it warmer and enclosed for when the children could not play outside. It made a perfect place for parties as well as a great play area.

It was now that Donnie wanted to be called Don, since he would be entering junior high school soon. So to distinguish between the two Dons, we called our son Don Ralph.

None of us—except maybe my husband, Don—was happy with the whole move. The contrast between Colfax and Aberdeen was glaring. Could we survive in this wet, muggy atmosphere? No one seemed overly friendly. No one was there to greet us.

We visited a Disciples of Christ church, since this was the denomination Don had been ordained in, and we felt a loyalty. But the congregation met in a musty, smelly building, and the domineering pastor declared we were there to help him. He had been in the military and assumed, given our association, that his church would be the church we attended. I wanted to run back to Colfax after that first Sunday.

The local Presbyterian pastor heard there was a new young college teacher and former pastor at the local junior college campus. The pastor called Don and asked us to visit his church, as they needed a youth pastor. This was our first introduction to the Presbyterian Church. It was a lovely, big church with an awesome choir, so Don accepted on the spot. When the other church's pastor heard of this, he wrote to the state secretary for the Disciples of Christ church in Seattle, to have Don unfrocked. We were shocked. However, Earl Van Doren, the state secretary, said that by all means he would *not* unfrock Don. Further, he gave Don his blessing for whatever Christian service he was in.

I did not want to go to that musty church where my beloved pastor husband would not be preaching and caring for a flock, nor would I be the first lady of the manse. The church gave me the jitters! But I cannot say I was happy about any church in Aberdeen. I did attempt to sing in the Presbyterian Church choir, for my life had been based in church and music. The pastor was extremely liberal, and at times I doubted I would fit in this congregation, which was much larger than what we were used to. But I really did try. We began groping our way in this unfamiliar setting. I taught Sunday school for intermediates, the same age as Don Ralph and Teresa. So began our bittersweet journey.

Trying to Make It Right

Paying no attention to the rain, Teresa—no longer Terri—was determined to make the most of this new environment. She found that Aleda, who lived next door, loved horses as much as she did, and although Aleda was younger, the two of them shared many hours playing with plastic Breyer horses under the eaves, sheltered from the rain. Teresa began dreaming of the day she could run a real horse in the open space behind our property. Indeed she was now eleven and was still asking her father for the horse he had so casually promised some years ago. A horse would have been nice in that open field amid all the wild blackberry bushes, but Don had taken a cut in salary to go into teaching. Against my better judgment, I knew I needed a job.

I went to a local employment agency to see if there was work for me. I did some testing and found I was 100 percent accurate with numbers. The employment office alerted the National Bank of Commerce, which was more than happy to hire me. Even with my income added, a horse had to wait, for we felt music lessons were more important to reach life goals than buying a horse. We did enroll Teresa in a riding academy with a German man called the Major. Teresa loved him and the opportunity to ride horses weekly. She looked forward each week to that one day she might mount a horse for one joyous hour.

Don Ralph decided piano was not for him. He would take up the saxophone in school. So we signed up Teresa and Christy for piano lessons with Myrtle Wood, a unique petite, gray-haired lady. Miss Wood had never married, and her house had Aberdeen's musty smell plus the aura of loneliness within its walls. Sometimes the girls were so fascinated and frightened by her almost otherworldly existence, I wondered if they were learning piano. The daily hours of disciplined practice surely had to be accomplishing more than a weekly trip into the haunting world of Miss Wood. We were quite proud parents when the girls played their first recital and first duet together.

However, this was not as happy an experience for the girls as I had anticipated. After each lesson the girls laughed at their quaint ethereal teacher, and sometimes they cried. For this reason we put them on a long waiting list with Marianna, who lived in our neighborhood. Gene Stensager, Marrianna's husband, led a community choir. Marianna accompanied her husband on the piano. She appeared to be so lighthearted; I thought she would be a more fun teacher for the girls. Her husband also taught music at the college. We became friends and associates.

Marianna had three sons, and we hired Mark—the eldest, sixteen—to be our babysitter. We were still missing Marcia's competence and were leery to leave our jewels with just any babysitter, but Mark proved to be an exception. Before we found him, we'd had a sitter for our four jewels that did absolutely nothing but sit in a chair while Don and Teresa prepared their own lunch and did the household chores without the babysitter even conversing with them. We had never had a male babysitter, but we thought we would try Marianna's son. After one evening with Mark, our children would hear of no other options. Later Marianna had an opening in her teaching schedule, and the girls were more than happy to be under her masterful tutoring. Her husband was the music teacher at Grays Harbor Junior College where Don was now the department chairman of the Sociology Department. I also began singing in Gene Stensager's community choir. It was my small salvation from feeling totally abandoned and like a fish out of water!

Losing My Identity

I was good at my job as bookkeeper at the bank. I went in every morning at six forty-five and finished my job anywhere from 2:00 p.m. to 5:00 p.m., depending on my accuracy. Most days I finished between 2:00 p.m. and 3:00 p.m. If there were errors, I had to stay until they were found and corrected.

Even though I had worked at the courthouse in Colfax a few hours a week, I had still been the beloved first lady of the Christian Church. Here in this Aberdeen bank, none of the management cared who I was, how many children I had, or anything about me except that I did a masterful job for them. My immediate supervisors were heartless and demanding. It was a painful time for me, as the job made it necessary to leave four-year-old Michele with a babysitter—another instructor's wife, named Beulah. It was not a day-care learning situation but a house full of screaming small children, with a screaming caregiver! I cried tears for both Michele and me each night knowing what was coming the next morning. I felt so cheated, and I felt I was not accomplishing my calling of polishing jewels for the Kingdom of God.

We dropped Michele off at the babysitter on our way to work. Since Don and I both had to be at work so early, the other three children had to wait for the bus alone, often in the rain. Fights easily broke out at the bus stop, and there was much bullying going on. My heart was heavy on those days. On the days my book did not balance at work, I had to stay and find the error and correct it. Therefore I was unable to be home when the children arrived, to listen to their stories about the excitement or cruelties of the day. I believed this time in a child's life was when bonding and encouragement from parents was necessary. Would Don and I ever be able to compensate for what I believed to be neglect?

We declared army-like responsibilities for the children. We insisted their beds be made before school. We outlined chores to be done and homework and piano practice to be completed all before we got home. We trusted them to carry out these responsibilities and believed it was good training. Yet I was missing out on very important time with my jewels. On those days when I worked late, Don would come home and get everyone busy preparing dinner. His military approach was lacking in tenderness. Once Christy said, "Dad, you don't make a very good mother!" However, we did make dinner itself a time of laughter and discussions, a time for questions to be answered, and a family devotion time. All the day's frustrations were vented at dinner, and as the mediators Don and I tried to help settle things and bring resolution.

Learning to Adapt

Weekends became times of retreat. In this soggy place, the only recreation we became adept at was clam digging, and how we all loved it! We prided ourselves on our success the first time we dug and ate clams, only to learn from more experienced natives that we had thrown away the tender parts of the clams and eaten the tough necks. We made a quick rescue trip to the garbage to retrieve what we should have eaten, which was fortunately enclosed in a baggie. The weather was always cold, so there was no damage done to the part we had so carelessly thrown away.

On those clamming trips, we came home with split fingernails and grazed arms from searching for the clams clear up to our armpits. But in those brief getaways, we found peace and togetherness—and we enjoyed many clam dinners, cooking and eating the right parts of the clams!

I had grown up in a very dry climate, and the rain, wind, and continually overcast weather in Aberdeen made me depressed. I longed for that dry climate, but I tried desperately to tolerate the wind, the rain, and the sand of the beach. When I was quite young, I had spent time at the beach in my aunt Vildy's cabin, but the high, dry climate of the mountains was more to my liking. Here my hair always went frizzy in the salt air. I had not known I could get badly sunburned even when it was overcast, and I remembered the horrid sunburns I'd suffered as a child. I do not remember Aberdeen ever being warm enough to be outside and get sunburn! Also, in this wet, muggy weather, I was developing a throat fungus, which interfered with my singing.

On the other hand, when Don was ten, his father had a nervous breakdown and had to be taken to the beach to recover. So the beach was not totally unfamiliar to Don. For the children it was one more exhilarating experience. Teresa loved the wind and rain blowing in her face and seemed to be in a fantasy world of her own. As she built sand castles, real castles and dreams were forming in her heart. She became very pensive and more and more creative.

As often as possible, we made trips to the Tacoma mall or to Portland to dry out. When we opened our suitcases on these weekend trips, we noted our clothes were damp, which we never noticed while in Aberdeen. But a movie, the motel swimming pool, eating out, and the family closeness of that breather made the Aberdeen experience tolerable. The best part of Aberdeen was getting out of town on those special occasions.

Teresa always invited a friend along to share in the family fun. She was a master at making new friends and embracing them, and she was soon part of a foursome that also included Debbie, Tracy, and Dona. Don Ralph was the studious one, and having these girls always around made him retreat. He and Teresa were still at war. Her friends were giddy and silly. Why, he wondered, did he have to have all these sisters with all these girlfriends? I sometimes worried about crippling him socially because of all the females in his life. I wanted him to grow up to be a masculine young man, just as his sisters were growing to be feminine young women.

St. Teresa Growing Up

At school Teresa was the new girl with the freckles and long blond ponytail. She enjoyed the attention. She came home with everyone either loving her or hating her, no in between. Her emotions became erratic. There were so many frustrations with becoming a young lady. She had insatiable dreams and plans. Teresa's dad did not always concur with them. In fact to her, it seemed he said no more than yes, and off she'd go to her room, slamming the door, only to be instructed to open it and close it properly. As a fifth grader, Teresa was beginning to become involved in a whirlwind of activities in school and after school. Don and I thought she was a bit too involved, but it seemed she wanted to taste everything life had to offer. She aspired to be at the top in all she did and took great pride if she achieved that goal. Once when I came home from work, I found this note:

> Dear Mom, look what I got. I got an A, Dona got a C. For once I beat her. I forgot to tell you, and I couldn't wait. Good-night. Happy dreams. Love ya. My papers are over on the cupboard. Teresa

We were acutely aware of how some parents push their children to achieve, hoping to realize their own dreams through their children. How different it was for Teresa. She was pushing her parents with her insatiable drive. Evidently she felt secure enough in her family's love that she would say to her friends things like "oh, my father will take us" or "my mom will cut your hair for you," always volunteering whatever service was needed. And in this way, her friends started thinking of us as the ideal parents. Her gratitude compensated us for our time a hundredfold, for we would find her little notes of thanks.

Teresa wholeheartedly embraced all her friends, so she could not understand when her devotion was not returned. She wondered if this was what growing up was all about. Letters from summer camp showed frustration:

> July 13
> Dear Mom,
>
> I love it up here. You forgot to give us some envelopes. Would you send me some money for envelopes? Roxy said there were envelopes at the canteen, and I haven't got enough money. My counselors are very nice. I'll give you our schedule:
>
> Rise 7:30
> Breakfast 8:00
> Watch 8:30
> Clean Cabins 8:45

Well I got to go now.

Love ya,
Teresa

July 15
Dear Mom,

I changed my mind. I know everybody, but nobody wants to play with me. So I'm not going to have any fun. I try to make them like me, but I guess they don't want to. The reason I had to say good-bye is because we had to get our cabins clean and then go on our Ex. groups. So I'll finish our schedule:

Ex groups 9:15
Free time 11:30
Lunch 12:00
Rest 12:45
Swim or Crafts 1:45–4:45
Games 4:15
Dinner 5:30
Free Time 6:15–7:30
Vespers 7:30–8:00
Campfire 8:30–9:00
Snack 9:00
In Cabins 9:05
Light Outs 9:30

But we don't get our light out till 11:00.

Love ya,
Teresa

That letter almost sent us after her, believing she was having a friendless week, when this letter, dated July 17, arrived.

Dear Mom,

I'm mad. You haven't written to me. Every day someone gets a letter. I wait and wait but you never write, and I'm not going to write another letter until I get at least one.

Now I play with Linda and Louise. We really have fun. Roxy said the other girls didn't like me. She also said she liked me no matter what. (Please excuse writing.) Mom, the weather is beautiful up here. The water is just like a bath. I love it up here, and I know you will too.

Bye.

Love ya,
Teresa

I knew puberty brought ups and downs with emotional upheaval, but when it is your children going through the experience, you become like a lioness with her cubs. Who of us cannot remember deep hurts inflicted on us in our own tenderness and impressionability of youth? Teresa needed to be loved by all and did not do well with rejection.

Don Ralph was small for his age and was often a target for the big bullies. It made the gap between him and Teresa greater, for any bullying she witnessed would be met with rage in her brother's defense. One particular young man named Paul Mathews was tall and obese and felt empowered by his size. He loved to see Teresa enraged even more than he loved bullying Don Ralph. This embarrassed Don Ralph, for he was the target only because Paul wanted to get his sister's attention. As with most preteen boys and girls, Teresa looked older and acted older. So it was that the same groups that accepted Teresa were always physically threatening Don Ralph. They knew she would fly into a rage and chase them…what delight for the boys! But for the young male ego in jeopardy, it was no delight.

However, Don Ralph was not bullied for too long, because he became the top academic student as well as muscular and fit. Don Ralph had excelled at the top of his class since second grade, and he soon was in accelerated classes, admired, and accepted. He and a girl named Meghan were the two top students throughout Don Ralph's time in Aberdeen. Eventually Don Ralph and Teresa's roles changed, for he hit a growth spurt while she remained petite.

Polishing Jewels

Don and I took part in all school activities, including chaperoning school dances, and we even allowed the children to have a dance in our covered garage room. Teresa asked me to speak at a student assembly on the subject of parent-teenager conflict. During my talk I made a comment—"I am in my teenager's court, and I trust my children"—that brought roaring applause and a standing ovation from the student body, and I became the ideal mom in their eyes! Teresa could not have been more elated (and I was a little pleased as well). This was truly how I felt. Children need to know that you are in their court and that they are trusted.

Slumber parties became the norm, and by then Teresa's brother had become part of the motivation. Teresa chided her brother for running around with other squares from the band rather than with the athletes. Don Ralph was becoming very good at the saxophone, and we thought his friends from the band were all high quality as well as studious. I suppose today they would be called the geeks! Don Ralph was exercising and exploring medical books in his spare time. While Teresa ran with the cheerleaders and the popular girls on rally squad, Don Ralph would get up daily, put on his cutoffs, and run or ride his bike in the mucky rain before school. Teresa's friends began noticing her brother for who he really was, and once again Teresa and Don Ralph became friends.

Fearful and Unhappy Experiences

As Teresa came into her teen years, she became a very beautiful young lady and the subject of the male gender's eyes. It seemed she was better able to adjust to each of our new environments than the rest of us; however, Christy and Michele were both struggling for acceptance in this closed community. We lived in the exclusive part of Aberdeen called Central Park, where new homes were being built, and the professionals were moving in. One neighbor had a party and told her daughter, Christy's classmate, that we would not be invited, as we probably would not drink or be comfortable. She said we were too religious. Of course our being religious would not have affected our interactions with neighbors, but she was rather snooty anyway, and we heard later that the party was a flop! This neighbor was also new to the area and was trying desperately to fit in with the professionals.

Of course this whole scenario affected how the classmate treated Christy. The irony is that we would have gone and probably enjoyed ourselves, but—true—we probably would not have drunk any hard liquor. We did not make an issue of others' drinking and were usually accepted in any social circles, so being excluded was a new experience for us.

Michele was struggling with anxiety more than anything. I felt it was because I had to leave her with a screaming babysitter. To say Aberdeen was a new golden experience for our children or for me would be stretching the truth. I cried too many tears, suffered from the constant rain, missed my friends, and was not singing solos or being in the ministerial role I believed I had been designed and gifted for. I had much guilt, and I never felt safe in the community or felt my children lived in safety, as we had in Colfax.

On one occasion when I had balanced at work without error, I was able to go home early. I had the car and would later pick up Don. This would give me a chance to fix dinner and make cookies for the children's arrival. As I entered the highway that would take me to our home in Central Park—a drive of five miles from work to home—an old, battered car pulled up beside me. As the driver drew level with me, he kept peering into my car. I could see how creepy and disheveled he was. I knew he was eyeing me and trying to get my attention.

His evil look permeated and consumed me, and I was terrified. The hair stood up on the back of my neck! I hardly knew what to do. Should I keep driving or turn around and head back into town? Should I keep going and turn into my driveway? I tried to keep my eyes on the road as he drove immediately beside me, giving me the most seductive and evil looks I had ever seen. If I sped up, he sped up. If I slowed down, he slowed down. I feared his intent was to rape me. We had no cell phones, so I couldn't contact anyone! I hoped surely he would continue on as I turned to go into Central Park.

However, he turned right behind me. I pulled into our driveway and ran quickly to the door, shaking all the way. I was almost unable to unlock my door. But I did get in before he could even get out of his car. I entered the safety of our home, shaking uncontrollably. There was a strip of gravel in front of the house where guests could park. He pulled onto that gravel area and revved his car for several minutes, gazing through our big front-room picture window. I stood by the now locked door, catching my breath before I could run to the kitchen phone to call Don.

After totally messing up the gravel on our parking strip, the man in the car finally left. I never quite recovered from the fear I experienced that day. I watched my children a little closer and prayed a little more for all of our safety. At about the same time, Don was telling me about a gay teacher who kept pursuing him. What on earth had we gotten ourselves into in this perverted town? All of our innocence faded into skepticism. But even in my newfound fear, our celebrations with our jewels—clam digging, outings to Portland, and other family times—softened my unhappiness somewhat...but the children were not seeing the fun-loving mom of Colfax.

Going through puberty was difficult for Teresa. She had an inability to control her temper that we had not seen before. Once she threw her clarinet down, broke it, and had to wash the Volkswagen bus for several months to pay for the repair. After her fit of temper, her dad gave her a whack on the behind. She laughed at him and said it didn't hurt because she had her girdle on. (That was the era when most females wore girdles.) Then Don slapped her on the face for laughing, which sent her into her room crying and left a dad feeling like a heel. He apologized copiously, but he never got over his uncharacteristic action—even though Teresa forgave him before the night was over.

Teresa always saw humor in human relationships. On several occasions in Colfax, when she and Don Ralph had been fighting, Don and I would make them sit face to face until they could get along. This always set Teresa into fits of laughter. One could never stay angry with her for long. She never held grudges and her dad very happy and grateful for that fact. In spite of adolescent emotions, she retained innocence and the same angelic spirit she had come into our lives.

Conflict

I worked at a job that I excelled in and was bringing home an income that very much helped our ailing finances. At this time our salaries were comparable, but later I was to bring home more than Don—not good for the male ego!

Don was so enjoying being on the college campus with young people who were eager to learn. Even with our financial pressure eased, I missed being the first lady of the manse, involved in ministry and sharing in all community activities. Don excelled in his teaching, and students loved him. I tolerated the church we attended, although I never felt a part of the congregation, and I was far too conservative for the pastor's comfort. The pastor's wife refused to attend church even though she had been one of the pianists for Dr. Fuller's church in Southern California (the *Old Fashioned Revival Hour*). She said she preferred to stay in the background. I could not understand this, as I longed to be back in my fishbowl. One of the elders, Tyson Jones, befriended Don, and we did become friends with him and his wife. However, he had become involved in the current charismatic movement and wanted Don to explore it more deeply with him.

The Full Gospel Business Men's Fellowship International was in town and hosting a dinner at a local restaurant. Tyson and his wife invited us to attend with them. We had Mark come over to babysit, and we went. I liked the Gospel preaching I heard, but all the talk of being baptized in the Holy Spirit both excited me and utterly terrified me. I knew our lives had been lacking since we'd left Colfax, but this was too much. Don, being a college teacher, was a prime target for the charismatics. This was in the early days of the charismatic movement spreading across the nation. They were always looking for recruits, and it so happened that Don became their target. However, we did come to love the Joneses and spent many weekends at their lake cabin, swimming and waterskiing. Don listened to what Tyson had to say and went to many home meetings with him. I joined him some, more than I wanted to at times, for there was such pressure to receive the gift of speaking in tongues. My mind was usually on being away from the children, as I was sacrificing the precious little time I had to be with them in the evenings.

Jim Galligan and his soloist traveled from Portland, Oregon, to teach about this new baptism in the Holy Spirit. I had such uneasy feelings when I was in his presence. He targeted Don, and I'm sure he sensed my disdain at his manipulation. I also felt he was far too familiar with his soloist, while his wife remained at home in Portland. It seemed the soloist's singing sent him into rapture, and he could not keep his hands off of her. She was quite seductive as well as attractive, even when singing gospel music.

We met Jim Galligan's wife later. She was a plain, unadorned, pious woman who was totally submissive to her husband. Here again this idea of a Christian woman being unadorned offended me, and I did not feel good about Galligan's ministry arrangement. I was totally committed to my husband and wanted to be his mistress and constant companion as well as his ministry partner. I could not understand her allowing another woman to minister with her man!

Unbending Authority

The demands of my job kept me focused on doing my work well. Though I was a faithful employee, I cannot say I enjoyed working at the bank, for many evenings found me crying over some event of the day. When Michele started kindergarten and became ill during one morning session, the school called me to come pick her up. My female supervisor said I could not go, stating, "Get someone else to care for your children. You are under our authority now." Hence Don had to leave his class and pick up his little blond daughter.

Another occasion that brought tears and intense anger was when one of the four bookkeepers was to say good-bye to her young husband, having just a day together before he was leaving for the military. She asked to have the day off. We other three bookkeepers had agreed to do her work at no extra pay to give our support. This same inhumane supervisor would not give her the day off. The young bride sat at her desk throughout the day with tears streaming down her face. What if her husband was killed and this was their last day together? We other three bookkeepers glared at the manager that day, not caring if we were fired or not. I suspected our immediate supervisor had only numbers where there should have been a heart! I do not believe I ever adjusted to this strange philosophy, and it is a wonder I was not fired. It was certainly before employee rights and sexual-harassment laws existed.

Weather Blues

Though I grieved every day and longed to return to my beloved Colfax, two years had already passed in this foreign country. On my drive into work, I kept count of seventy-three days of rain—not mist but downpours—and then gave up the count. Missing my former life intensely, I became very depressed. I believed I was light deprived to the point of depression.

I was semi-active in the women's ministry at the Presbyterian Church, and at one luncheon one of the leaders had just returned from two weeks in California. She said it had not been an enjoyable trip for her. She had become very depressed with being in the sun every day. She was so glad to get back to her rainy, cloudy beloved Aberdeen. I just sat in silent shock, for I believed the horrid Aberdeen weather was a reason for depression.

CHAPTER 11

Some Breaks in the Fog

A single sunbeam is enough to drive away any shadows.
--St. Francis of Assisi

Don continued to excel on campus, became the department chairman, and truly was an outstanding teacher. He led the Presbyterian youth group, which grew under his leadership. It was a fun group of youth but very different from our work with youth and children in Colfax. There was not the same level of bonding with the teens or the hilarity we had known before.

I continued to feel like a fish out of water. So when Don came home one evening and told me he had been accepted to attend a summer institute in Boulder, Colorado, I could hardly contain my excitement. I would have to give up my bank job, which had allowed us to live without financial pressure for the past two years, and there would be no guarantee of a job when we returned. Don had his summers free from teaching, so the timing would work out perfectly for him. He could attend through a government grant, and the subject was anthropology—a field in which Don had extreme interest. The excitement built daily. The children, especially Christy and Michele, missed Colfax and would gladly go anywhere to get away from this rain-infested coast! I believed even Foo Doo, the pug, wiggled his tail more—and, of course, we had not an idea in the world of leaving him behind.

Don received his summer institute acceptance early in the spring, so it seemed like we had forever to make preparations for the trip. We went to the mall in Tacoma to purchase camping gear, sleeping bags, and whatever we felt might be needed for roughing it for ten wonderful weeks away from this place. I did not even entertain the thought that I would have to return to Aberdeen.

The day finally arrived in June when we started our trip in our blue 1956 Cadillac. Again we had a U-Haul hooked on behind that held the things we would need for the ten-week assignment. We had rented an advertised basement \apartment, sight unseen before we'd left Aberdeen. Boulder, being the home of the University of Colorado, was well aware of the housing needed for summer school students and did much advertising. We were hopeful that we had made a wise choice.

We were hardly out of town when life took on a glow once again. I felt I had rejoined the living. We made the trip an educational journey, stopping at the gorgeous campus of the Mormon Tabernacle in Salt Lake City. We were fascinated by the history along the way. The Air Force Academy provided us with a most challenging sermon along with a chapel full of handsome young cadets. Of course a stop at Bob's Big Boy for hamburgers was a must. We also stopped at Boot Hill Graveyard, which was overgrown, rocky, and just as spooky to me as any ordinary cemetery. There was much laughter, fun, and quarrels in the car as we made the four-day trip.

Pure Joy

When we arrived we were pleased with our sight-unseen selection, for our apartment had three bedrooms: one for Don and me, one for the girls, and one for Don Ralph. Foo Doo slept with whomever he pleased. We had a gas stove, which was a new experience for me, and on one occasion I tried to light it and ended up singeing my hair and severely burning my hand. I vowed I would never have anything gas operated in any home. I later wished I had kept that vow!

Foo Doo wanted to go with us on all adventures and did not like being left at the apartment in the daytime, so he would get even with us by leaving little deposits by the children's beds—something he had never done before. Once he got out and wandered away. When he did not come home by nightfall, we had four very sad children. We put an ad on the local radio, and he was soon found. Foo Doo had wandered five miles from our apartment, looking for us. We watched him a little more closely from that time on and tried to include him in as many outings as was possible.

The sun shone every day, and the beauty of this state was unbelievable. Don started classes right away, and the children and I would drop him off and head for the Boulder Reservoir to swim the day away. We discovered, while at the reservoir, that another young woman with two little girls was also a professor's wife. Gay had taken leave of her job, as I had, to join her sociologist husband, who was attending the summer institute. We soon became friends, and Don Ralph became the tutor of five girls in daily card games.

Gay and the girls were our daily companions as well as other children who would enter Don Ralph's card games. We used a lot of baby oil as tanning oil to protect us from the intense Boulder sun. Every single day the sun shone. I was one happy camper who eventually went home with an awesome suntan—my first!

One of Don's new class friends was named Pete. He and his wife, Lois, became lifelong friends as well. We spent many hours with them on the weekends, exploring historic Colorado and the city of Boulder. Evidence of the gold rush days was everywhere. Pete and Lois loved children but had none of their own, so they took great enjoyment in sharing our four. A trip to the Denver museum included our first experience seeing the skeletons of mammoth dinosaurs. Our young children's world was ever being expanded. There were so many things to enjoy in this glorious Colorado sun, including open-air concerts and lectures at the commons!

We spent one weekend at a Colorado dude ranch. Teresa spent most of her time in the corral with the horses, which were all fairly lethargic. However, when we went on a trail ride, the turn of events proved they were not all lethargic—or friends. The six of us were all following the lead horse when the horse behind Christy's bit her horse on the behind. Off Christy's horse galloped, ahead of us all. The guide had to gallop ahead and stop the horse before we resumed our ride. From that time on, Christy did not trust horses or share her older sister's love of them. I'm sure if Teresa's horse had galloped, she would have said, "Let's go!"

We attended a fabulous Disciples of Christ church facing the grandeur of the Flatirons, as they are called. The majesty of these flat-rock mountains left us breathless. It was just a spiritual experience to look out the full-length, clear glass windows and gaze at the Flatirons. It was there that we first heard about situational ethics, which could, perhaps, be the philosophy where nothing is a sin; there are only choices. At night we would all go to the Missionary Covenant church and delight in the old-fashioned gospel music. It was the type of music I had sung in our church quartet as a youth.

We longed for gospel music in Aberdeen. It made my heart jump with joy, as I did want a heartfelt experience with Jesus. I wanted an experience that moved me beyond the mundane existence of Aberdeen. I wanted to live in transcendence, which I was not able to find in Aberdeen. Perhaps that was why Don was enamored with the charismatic movement. I had studied Paul, the skeptic in the Bible, and had noticed he did not throw out reason but combined reason with rational arguments. I wanted to do the same, but I wanted my faith to be heartfelt too. The dilemma of the charismatic movement was still bothering me in the back room of my mind!

Don Ralph took a paper route in our Boulder neighborhood and pulled around a little red wagon. Teresa was his able assistant. This was the beginning of Don Ralph and Teresa's work ethic, which followed them throughout life. (They both secured jobs before they were sixteen.) Don and I would get them up, provide a snack, and make sure all was well before they left with their little red wagon full of newspapers. Those early mornings, leaving at five o'clock, were always gorgeous and never cloudy. There were many benefits to that route: real bonding, learning a good work ethic and how to please customers, and realizing what a brother and sister can do together. Don and I would have breakfast ready when they returned. Our delightful days and joyful togetherness almost made me forget all about icky old Aberdeen.

On other weekends we would go to Left Hand Canyon and play in the streams and pools of water. Don would wear only his cowboy hat and jeans, and the rest of us would wear as little clothing as possible. Those days were like a return to the Garden of Eden, with us never wanting to leave this garden of the Lord!

It was in Boulder that Teresa began seriously painting. We took her gift for granted and just assumed we had very gifted children. But we did wonder how this child could take a piece of cardboard, or whatever was available, and make a beautiful painting in minutes. It was here that we began buying special paint sets for this young artist.

The savory history of the area kept us spellbound for the full ten weeks. Saloons had been plentiful during Colorado's gold rush, and our children were enraptured with "The Face on the Barroom Floor," which has become so famous. For one week of the ten, Don went on an archeological adventure down to Mesa Verde with his classmates. We wives and children who were left behind had no regrets, for we lived it up at the Boulder reservoir, eating out or taking picnics with us. As we lay in the sun, we all agreed that life did not get any better than this…but all the while, I knew I must return to Aberdeen, so I began preparing myself for that day.

The shops were awesome, and clothes were designed for the sunny weather, so before we left we took a shopping trip with Pete, Lois, and the children to get their next year's school clothes. When Teresa tried on the clothes, we all noticed what a lovely young lady she was becoming. All of a sudden, both she and Don Ralph looked like teenagers. They seemed a little more mature after this ten-week trek, but would they be ready for the rainy, musty return to Aberdeen? Yes, the children agreed it would be nice to be back in their own rooms and no longer living out of suitcases. However, we would miss Boulder and would talk about this experience for years.

Clothes never looked this inviting in Aberdeen. It seemed all the clothes there were dark and drab, so I wondered how these fashionable clothes would look in soggy Aberdeen. The two younger girls looked so adorable in their new school clothes, still looking very much like children. They too would have to re-adjust to the climate and attitude change, or could we keep this positive attitude when it began raining once again? No one knew.

Must This Joy End

When we returned to Aberdeen, the angst that had existed between Don Ralph and Teresa was but a mist of memory, for they became tight once again, sharing life as brother and sister protectors. I was so grateful to the Lord for these jewels, seemingly sent straight from the throne of God! We all seemed a little closer to each other and to our Lord. My heart danced with the overflowing love I had for Don and my children.

We returned to Beatlemania, and our teenagers joined in. We so enjoyed the world of teenagers. The rain was there, and the charismatic meetings were still trying to pull us in, but I did not return to the bank. I was grateful. Instead I applied for an opening for assistant director of an Office of Economic Opportunity (OEO) program. I was hired on the spot. The director was an absentminded ex-pastor who often came into work late—or did not show up at all. And it wasn't too long before the board of commissioners appointed me as director. It was unusual for a woman to hold that kind of position at that time in history, and it was also unusual that I made more money than Don did as a college instructor.

I was in charge of what were called grassroots workers, who were on welfare. They would go out and explore the poverty of the community, which they knew all too well. We started many programs for the less fortunate in the community, such as Head Start and educational classes. I much preferred this job to the bank job, as I was able to be what I felt was a more humane boss: listening to my subordinates, making them my friends, and in part making my coworkers my own little flock, in the same way we had in Colfax. However, I saw many improprieties going on when leaders of the organization would breeze into town, making massive per diems for acknowledging what we already knew to be the needs of the community. Even in this local program, it seemed, the government was not above corruption!

The Charismatics in Full Force

Now that we were back from Boulder, the issue of the charismatic movement loomed again, and we spent hours pondering the meaning of it for us. There was an Episcopal priest, Father Bennett, in Ballard—near Seattle—who claimed to be filled with the Holy Spirit. He had caused quite a stir throughout Christendom. Under duress I agreed to go with Don to Ballard to hear this oddity. It would give us all time together away from icky old Aberdeen, as little Michele had described it when we first moved there.

The service lasted for three hours as Father Bennett shared his experience. I was confused but very interested in anything that would bring back the fairy-tale existence we had experienced before we'd moved to Aberdeen. In my heart I wanted all of God's blessings for our family and was sure we had walked away from our anointing when we left Colfax, so I listened intently.

During the singing and worship time, I looked over at my children, who seemed to be enraptured. Christy and Michele had sat in this meeting for several hours without complaint. At home they could hardly sit for one hour! With her innocence and lack of inhibitions, Teresa simply lifted her hands and worshipped Jesus. The glow on her face was like that of an angel. There was no mistaking that she appeared to be in the presence of the Lord…no inhibitions!

So I was more confused than ever, for it did not seem natural to me that in order to be filled with the Holy Spirit, you had to babble in an unknown tongue. However, in Teresa's innocence, she wanted whatever the Lord had for her. So it was that Teresa enjoyed the experience of what was called baptism in the Holy Spirit.

Searching or Deluded?

Back home Don continued to follow the small meetings conducted by Jim Galligan. I was skeptical, having heard Jim tell stories that I believed verged on the occult. I nearly choked when he described how he was leading a retreat and mice got into the food supply. He said he prayed the Lord would bind their mouths, thus protecting their food supply. On another occasion he described how he and other leaders were so anointed and blessed that oil literally ran out of their shoes. The stories continued, but the one that annoyed me the most was when he said he cast out evil spirits from attendees at one of his conferences and drove them into the pillows in the room. In my opinion we were hearing more and more stories of mere white magic. I had often felt the presence of the Lord in my life, but I felt what I was hearing was heresy. But still of the mind that woman is to be subservient to man and follow his leadership unquestioningly, I followed along, letting Don decide!

The Joneses wanted us to fellowship with these people when they came to town for home meetings. I believed their main motive was to get a dynamic college instructor to be a leader in the movement, so he might attract all his students. Indeed Don was a popular advisor at the college, and many students felt they could share anything with him—even their sexual encounters. The free love movement was just beginning to sweep the land with popularity! This too was the era of the Ouija board, and students were dabbling in sessions late at night with this new game. One student told Don the Ouija board pointer chased him. Now, it may have been the weed he was smoking that had him believing this— these game sessions often included smoking marijuana and/or using LSD—but I felt both Christians and non-Christians were dabbling in the spirit world, and strange things were happening.

Don did guide students to stay away from such things and to seek the power of God in their lives. I respected him for this, but I was still leery of the movement he was exploring. We had bought an Ouija board for our children. In fact at the eighth-grade dance we held in our covered garage room, some of the children played this spooky game in a bedroom with no lights on, touching knees and enjoying the time apart with Teresa. After Don's students came to him with stories like being chased by the pointer, we threw our Ouija board in a burning barrel and watched it explode. Good riddance! We wanted no part of the occult in our lives or our children's.

This whole movement—and the people involved—gave me a sick feeling in the pit of my stomach. However, it was my belief that all of mankind was and is searching for transcendence. I observed it in others. I observed it in myself. There is a longing in our hearts. We want to overcome our human frailty and touch the face of God. We want to transcend our human limits or experience. I believe that in the deepest, innermost part of each human being is the desire to discover God's vastness, to slip from our finiteness and explore the mysteries of the Infinite. And living our gloomy, rainy experience in this coastal town, we were indeed ready for transcendence.

So, knowing this desire in my own heart, I had to be more forgiving of those I believed to be misled champions of God. I wondered if they had made baptism in the Holy Spirit an idol to worship rather than God Himself. To me it had become a form of controlling their destinies and controlling others' behavior. These people were seeking thrilling experiences—for example, speaking in tongues, being slain in the spirit, and white magic. It seemed to me that these things had become substitutes for real worship and the transcendence of God.

But Don and I were gracious. We had them into our home, but I did not allow them to pressure me to submit or to embrace a strange language. "Just open your mouth and start babbling, and the baptism will come," they said. I just listened, trying to hold my tongue! I always had a sick feeling in my stomach after they left. Maybe it reminded me of when my father tried to force me to wash my hands in his dirty water.

Don and I had been united in most of our beliefs, but this movement put a split in our spiritual relationship. Don admitted after the fact that he had become a charismatic addict—the very thing he warned his students about, teaching from the book *True Believer*. The younger children were very confused by this movement and began to feel they were less favored by God. It put fear in their hearts as well. It was not a good time.

The old problem of outside expectations and pressure lurked for Don, as so many of these wannabes tried to manipulate him into doing their bidding. It was the same old story he had sought to be free of in the past. It seemed to me that these self-proclaimed leaders had unconstrained free spirits as well as searching for power. Some of the charismatic leaders said if they were asked to speak, they would just open their mouths and let the Holy Spirit fill them. That seemed pretty lame to me. I believed you should study, work, and then ask the Holy Spirit for guidance and wisdom. However, I continued to be conflicted.

The Joneses had pursued our friendship when we'd attended the Presbyterian Church, and we certainly needed friends after coming from Colfax, where we had been so intimately joined with the whole community. Then there was the fact that the Joneses had two of the most handsome sons around; Teresa and her girlfriends made sure we kept that friendship alive.

Reality or White Magic

In no way do I want to minimize the value of a deeper relationship with the Holy Spirit, but for me it seemed there were many fraudulent leaders in the charismatic movement practicing occultism activity to gain followings. "Power tends to corrupt and absolute power corrupts absolutely" wrote Lord Acton, English politician and writer. Too much total authority or power can lead to one's destruction and hurt countless people in the wake.

The charismatic movement created a schism in the Christian community. It became a test of who was more spiritual, whether you raised your hands and spoke in tongues or not. In David's prayer in the Psalms, he prayed, "Lord, take not thy Holy Spirit from me." I too had prayed that on many occasions. I believed that these men who wanted to be leaders distorted the reality of the Holy Spirit in one's life. I cannot measure their accuracy, but I sincerely believed it to be white magic.

Only honesty gains grace, so I was conflicted as Don pursued this movement at the insistence of his friend, Tyson Jones. I had no desire to either embrace the movement or to follow these leaders. History and the testimony of many indicate that this new movement did bring power and a renewed closeness to God. However, sometimes the crossover from holiness to white magic is so slight as to go unnoticed by many. These cults do not take on graven images but raise up individuals to god status. They make claims of controlling the elements, healing the sick, raising the dead and uttering words of prophecy and ultimate wisdom. They do hold an attractive lure for those of us who are seeking transcendence. We are tempted to make these psychics little gods and entrust our lives and futures to them.

I was too much of a skeptic and still noncompliant enough that I did not allow them to take control of my life. I believed that none of us has the whole truth and nothing but the truth! Then again, it appears Satan distorts anything good and makes areas of it corrupt. One needed a spirit of discernment to know the difference between the white magic and the true touch of the Holy Spirit. Oh, how I prayed for discernment! What God intended for our good was being distorted, to my way of thinking.

In the Midst of Confusion...Blessing

One of the would-be leaders was a man named Bishop Stanley, who was part of the Greek Orthodox Church. He had attended the one Full Gospel Business Men's Fellowship Don and I had attended. Bishop Stanley had made a missionary trip to India, and while he was there he met a fellow Full Gospel pastor who had a seventeen-year-old son who wanted to come to the United States to study. Bishop Stanley told him, "You come to the United States, and we will get twenty people to donate money to support you and pay for your schooling."

The young man, Abraham Philip, did come to the United States. By now he had turned eighteen. He excitedly looked forward to meeting his supporters in the land where money grew on trees, but there were no supporters waiting, nor had Bishop Stanley sought any. When Abraham—or his name of affection, Raju, as we called him—arrived in Seattle, he called Bishop Stanley, still holding the business card with Stanley's name and address. Bishop Stanley had forgotten all about his offer, so he brought Raju to see us. When this beautiful Indian youth walked through our door, I immediately thought of Bell Kari, the young girl who had given me the gold bangle bracelet so many years ago, and my dream that had followed that meeting. Bishop Stanley thought maybe Don, as a college teacher, could do something for this young man. All we could do—and did do—was open our arms, hearts, and home to him. Don signed for loans for Raju to start school, and so I began realizing a longtime dream of mine: some involvement with India. Remember, I had fallen in love with Bell Kari, the young girl the missionaries from India had brought to my home church.

Raju enrolled in Pacific Lutheran University in Tacoma, Washington, where he lived in church basements and ate very little to survive. He spent many weekends with us and became part of the family. He had believed money grew on trees in the United States, and it was a huge adjustment to realize that was not so. We usually added Raju to our weekend excursions, wherever they might be to, or just had him come to our home. We could see how homesick and hungry he was, so I decided that for his comfort and for our delight, we would ask him to fix one of his homeland dishes: curried chicken. I provided a large roaster pan, purchased needed ingredients from the nearby market, and let him go to work. Raju was so homesick and hungry for his mom's cooking that he probably could have consumed the whole pan, but there was enough for all, and it surely was a delicacy.

Raju fit in as one of our kids: going waterskiing with us at the Joneses' lake, taking off in the boat without permission, standing on his head on the dock, and just being a warm addition to our family. Occasionally Don received requests to speak at Presbyterian churches close by, so he would have Raju fill the pulpit. Raju's father was a Pentecostal pastor back in India. Having grown up in this environment, Raju was equally Pentecostal and bombastic. He would take off in a high-pitched voice and not land until the sermon was over. I am sure no one understood what this young man from India had preached, but people fell in love with his spirit.

Over the years Raju developed powerful preaching skills, though. In addition he was eventually able to graduate from Pacific Lutheran University and the University of Minnesota and even earned a PhD. He became a successful microbiologist for DuPont, and he did it all without the help of those promised twenty supporters.

Diversion

This year was somewhat easier for me to tolerate because I had a different, better job. We became involved in the Driftwood Players, so our children could experience acting in the theater. I had always loved the theater. In my small hometown of Clarkston, the community concert series had brought many concerts and plays to town. I was at every one of them. Don had taken part in play productions in high school and college, so he was an agreeable participant.

All three girls took part in a Helen Keller production, but it was eight-year-old Michele who got a major role, as Greta in *The Sound of Music*. She stole the show. Don and I took small parts as a nun and a Nazi, since we needed to be at each rehearsal and performance as Michele's coach. On one occasion, on our way to the production, we already had our costumes on. Don had his arm out the window, with the swastika armband on his costume plainly visible. A gentleman was so stunned at seeing that swastika that he walked right into a light pole!

When some friends came over from Colfax to see us, we took them to the play. Before we left for the theater, their five-year-old son, Jonathon, picked up a small bat and clobbered Michele over the head, sending her into fits of screaming. We looked at Michele's tearstained face and told her that the show must go on! And indeed that was one of her best performances.

That was a fun evening with our friends from our Camelot, Colfax. However, it seemed to me that those charismatics were always lurking in the background to disrupt our family. Bishop Stanley showed up one evening at the production, and after the show he told me I had spoiled Michele for life by letting her take part in theater. Of course I did not feel it would impede Michele's personality or life. In fact her personality already showed signs of the theatrical, and I had met Stanley's wife, who was a plain Jane, wore no makeup and drab clothes, and never spoke unless her husband gave her permission. I did not want Michele to bear that description!

Positives

Life was good on many levels. As a sociologist Don was often asked to speak at Rotary Club and many other public events. Once he was asked to go to McNeil Island and speak to the prisoners at the federal penitentiary. On this occasion he opted to take Don Ralph with him. It was a fun trip for father-son bonding. It was interesting to cross over the river and onto the island to gain entrance, and Don Ralph was enraptured with both his dad and the prisoners.

When Don Ralph returned home, he commented to me, "Those guys have more manners than the kids I go to school with." The educational system, as stated, was one of the best our two older children had yet experienced from an academic standpoint, but what they were exposed to—bullying, gangs, and corrupt living—was an eye-opener to our innocent children and to my innocence as well!

Our children were flourishing in many areas of their lives. We spent many weekends at the Joneses' lake cabin graciously listening to their charismatic stories and watching our children develop their waterskiing skills. We were also watching all of Teresa's girlfriends fall madly in love with the Jones boys. This was our introduction to the teen years.

Era of Cults

The charismatic movement was not our only introduction to occult behavior. One of the board members of the community action program was a pastor in a local church. He was involved in sensitivity groups—a philosophy started by

Carl Rodgers—and he invited Don and me to attend a weekend group held at the coast in a small house. He gave me a glowing report of how beneficial it was as well as how much he thought I would enjoy attending. I had a babysitter stay with the children, and we attended—a ghastly mistake.

The theory behind Carl Rodgers and his movement was to break down the personality and then rebuild it. As we arrived and got settled with introductions, we were instructed to take a seat in the circle of chairs. Another gentleman, a pastor as well and the self-appointed leader, began with one of his church members whom he had invited. He told her she bored him to death, that she never said anything worth listening to, and was a miserable failure. I, who longed to be back in ministry and had loved our people very much, was astounded at this crass young pastor who dared to devalue one of his flock. She helplessly tried to defend herself. When she was weeping uncontrollably, he moved on to me, saying, "Who do you think you are, sitting there all superior and silent?" I was devastated.

Don jumped in to defend me and gave some sociological jargon, and the young pastor launched an attack on him. I was embarrassed by the pastor's behavior, embarrassed by Don's arrogant response, and totally crushed from being attacked. Who did this guy think he was, inviting people to his retreats only to attack them?

When the session was over, we were supposed to gather for a meal. There was no way to escape, as we had ridden with another couple, the husband a pastor from the local Presbyterian Church, who happened to be one of my OEO board members. How can you eat with your heart in your throat and an experience like none other looming over your head? It was worse than the charismatics! Neither Don nor I saw any value to this kind of amateur therapy Carl Rodgers had started. It was an attempt to exert the same type of control many cult groups did. Was this an era of cult control?

One of the attendees was the Associate pastor at the Presbyterian Church we attended. He had little to say about the meeting. Maybe he was holding his tongue, as he was a friend of the supposed leader that day. But as we shared our experience with the senior pastor and some of Don's fellow teachers, we began hearing how devastating this movement had been at YMCA camps, churches, and social groups. We heard about many divorces happening after such supposedly honest comments were made to spouses. The philosophy hit the churches as well, and many church members, friends, and family members were severely mentally wounded. Some of our very dear friends found themselves wounded by such groups, which seemed to be sweeping the country.

Our friends reported that some of the groups even turned into sexual orgies. A college friend who we knew well as an upstanding pastor made the statement, after he became involved in one such sensitivity group, "I didn't know Christians could have so much fun." We were not surprised when he and his wife—my friend—divorced. I do not know if he ever came to his senses. But it seemed evident that Satan knows where to dance!

After I recovered from the fallout, I felt an inner compulsion to be a defender of individual rights and to preserve the individual psyche more than ever. I could not imagine how tearing one's character down could bring about any good or redemption. I was reminded of the scripture to test the spirits or the very elect will be deceived. It seemed like someone was always trying to manipulate us into his or her plan for our lives, and all I wanted was to be free and walk in harmony with my Maker, celebrating life with my beloved and my jewels. Surely Christ came to set us free.

Another Interlude

That year brought both pain and enjoyment. I loved my job. I loved the precious children God had given to us to polish. It was not as painful as the four years prior. I did feel I had been given the highest calling possible—to polish jewels for the Kingdom of God, and now Raju was added to the equation. He fit in so perfectly! And then the joyous word came of another opportunity for a summer institute in Columbia, Missouri. How blessed we were, and how excited the children were for another adventure.

By that time we had purchased a Volkswagen bus, and we began planning what to take. In Columbia there were only high-rise apartments to rent. We still had Foo Doo, and now we also had Christy's cat, Fang. Of course we had to take them. We would not need to pull a U-Haul this year with our new Volkswagen.

Don's cousin was to be married at the end of the summer and wanted us to take part in his wedding, which was to be in Chicago, on our way home. Again the excitement grew. We learned our friends from the summer before, the Petersons, had also been chosen to attend the institute, and by then they had a baby son (due, we believed, to how in love they were with our children). It was May, and we began to make plans.

We had lived in this forsaken, barren land for four years. The force of the charismatic movement weighed heavily on my heart, so I was anxious to escape the pressure for another summer. I would focus on my husband and children, and once again we would just love, play, and study, and I would set aside my concerns over this white-magic movement for the summer.

We had received a request from our beloved former nanny, Marcia Faires, to share in her upcoming marriage to Jay, a redheaded mechanical teacher. We would arrange to attend their wedding on our way east. Young Christy and Michele were to be her junior bridesmaids. I was to sing, and Don was to share in the marriage ceremony along with Jay's minister brother. It was pure heaven to be back in Colfax with these dear friends. It was a glorious Saturday night, but I could not keep from crying over being where I felt was home.

When Christy and Michele wanted their daddy to baptize them the next day, Sunday, as their older brother and sister had been baptized, it was the same joyous occasion to hear these little jewels say resounding "I do's" to their father's question: "do you take Jesus Christ to be your personal Lord and Savior?" Oh, how I missed my beloved in the pulpit! After we left these dear friends—with dog and cat and four excited children in a crowded Volkswagen bus—we continued on our way to another exciting summer of family togetherness.

This summer Don was studying statistics, which was not as enjoyable as anthropology, and the weather was hot and humid, unlike in Colorado. We spent many hours inside our fourth-floor apartment to escape the heat. However, we had two teenage neighbors—a girl and a boy—who were Don Ralph and Teresa's ages. They became friends and spent many hours exploring as well as playing cards. We were happy for our children to meet these two, equally awesome teenagers and to share the experience of puppy love.

We again took every opportunity to visit historical sites and to attend lectures. Our weekends were full with the educational history of this territory. What fun we had, in spite of the humidity!

I had a new peace. The area was so rich in history: Hannibal, Missouri, is where the character Tom Sawyer grew up. We saw the caves Samuel Clemens (Mark Twain) had explored as a boy—and experienced claustrophobia ourselves. On another trip through Independence, we drove past Harry S. Truman's house. It was closed for the day, so we failed to see the interior. It still was a thrill. We took a trip to a wonderful, old historical restaurant on the

Missouri River, had catfish, and laughed and giggled the afternoon away. We were giving our children many cultural experiences.

My Search

I spent time sewing outfits for the upcoming wedding and reading scripture to see if I could put my questions about the charismatic movement to sleep! This issue had been bombarding our lives. One night I dreamed I was on a ladder reaching to heaven. I was trying to climb higher, pleading with an angel to bless me, as Jacob had pled so many years ago. The angel said to me, "I have already blessed you." Then he poured oil on my side. I awoke the next morning with an odd pain in my side that stayed with me all day. Actually it was not a pain but a catch.

As I pondered this dream and the unusual catch in my side, I could not help believing it was my answer to my position in Christ. I had been His since I raised my little two-year-old hand so many years earlier. I truly believed the Holy Spirit was active in my life without my babbling in tongues. At the same time, I read Sam Shoemaker's book, *I Stand by the Door*. His poem so touched my heart that it became, from that time on, my philosophy of what my calling was to be. It became my divine appointment in that fourth-floor apartment in Missouri. The poem is as follows:

I Stand by the Door

I stand by the door
I neither go too far in nor stay too far out.
The door is the most important door in the world—
It is the door through which men walk when they find God.
There's no use my going way inside and staying there
When so many are still outside and they, as much as I,
Crave to know where the door is.
And all that so many ever find
Is only the wall where a door ought to be.
They creep along the wall like blind men,
With outstretched, groping hands.
Feeling for a door, knowing there must be a door,
Yet they never find it.
So I stand by the door.

The most tremendous thing in the world
is for men to find that door—the door to God.
The most important any man can do
Is to take hold of one of those blind, groping hands
And put it on the latch—the latch that only clicks
and opens to the man's own touch.

Men die outside that door, as starving beggars die
On cold nights in cruel cities in the dead of winter—
Die for want of what is within their grasp.
They live on the other side of it—live because they have not found it.

Nothing else matters compared to helping them find it,
And open it, and walk in, and find Him.
So I stand by the door.

Go in, great saints; go all the way in—
Go way down into the cavernous cellars,
And way up into the spacious attics.
It is a vast, roomy house, this house where God is.
Go into the deepest of hidden casements,
Of withdrawal, of silence, of sainthood.
Some must inhabit those inner rooms
And know the depths and heights of God,
And call outside to the rest of us how wonderful it is.
Sometimes I take a deeper look in.
Sometimes venture in a little farther,
But my place seems closer to the opening.
So I stand by the door.

There is another reason why I stand there.
Some people get part way in and become afraid
Lest God and the zeal of His house devour them;
For God is so very great and asks all of us.
And these people feel a cosmic claustrophobia,
And want to get out. "Let me out!" they cry.
And the people way inside only terrify them more.

Somebody must be by the door to tell them that they are spoiled
For the old life, they have seen too much:
One taste of God and nothing but God will do anymore.
Somebody must be watching for the frightened
Who seek to sneak out just where they came in,
To tell them how much better it is inside.
The people too far in do not see how near these are
To leaving—preoccupied with the wonder of it all.
Somebody must watch for those who have entered the door
But would like to run away. So for them, too,
I stand by the door.

I admire the people who go way in.
But I wish they would not forget how it was
Before they got in. Then they would be able to help
The people who have not yet even found the door.
Or the people who want to run away again from God.
You can go in too deeply and stay in too long
And forget the people outside the door.
As for me, I shall take my old accustomed place,
Near enough to God to hear Him and know He is there,
But not so far from men as not to hear them,
And remember they are there, too.

Where? Outside the door—
Thousands of them. Millions of them.
But—more important for me—
One of them, two of them, ten of them,
Whose hands I am intended to put on the latch.
So I shall stand by the door and wait
For those who seek it.

"I had rather be a doorkeeper..."
So I stand by the door.

I finally found peace and was secure in my position with Christ...so I thought!

Always Hurdles to Overcome

A child of two years of age had fallen out of another fourth-floor apartment, and the sadness of this death, coupled with the humidity and lack of Colorado's beauty, made us all ready to return to Aberdeen—in spite of my dislike for the community and the happenings there. Further, in the apartment hallway, a young black girl accosted Michele and tried to take her ring off her finger. Michele had never experienced an incident like this, and she ran crying to our apartment. The children feared to leave the apartment without us.

We had never lived where there was a racist attitude—except for that elder's nasty comment in California. In fact there had been only one black family in Colfax, and they had loved Don and given us butchered chickens. We had considered them our friends. Also there was a young black missionary pastor who had kissed our newborn son and was our friend for many years. But in Columbia our family was often subtly made aware that we were not in our territory when we entered the elevator. Hate was directed toward us, and we knew it. From some of these terrifying experiences, we took a different view of the black-white issue. It was not all one-sided.

The ten weeks had come to an end, and with excitement and dread we started for home via Chicago. Our bus was filled with new clothes for the wedding, laughter, and an eagerness to see the sites in Chicago and watch our two teenagers be candle lighters. I had a new peace of mind since my dream of receiving a blessing, and Don returned with more knowledge of statistics, to be applied in writing his graduate thesis.

Don's cousin, the one to be married, had had his mom, Don's aunt, with him in Chicago for some time before the wedding. She would return home to Oregon after the wedding, so I invited her to ride home with us—still wanting to be the good niece-in-law! I so wanted happy in-law relationships with all of Don's relatives. However, Don was not overly thrilled. This was the aunt who had also tried to control his life. As it turned out, Don was probably right, as his aunt talked nonstop about their superior heritage and how lucky I was to have him. Well, I knew that, but not because of his superior heritage. It was because he was a child of the ultimate King of heaven and earth, and I loved him! He was my soul mate! And furthermore my ancestors had been involved in preparing the Underground Railroad for slaves to escape to Canada. Though I was proud of this, I did not believe it gave me a superior status to brag about.

However, we were determined to make this an adventurous trip for our children, so we stopped at Mt. Rushmore and slept out under the stars—until a rainstorm doused us and our sleeping bags, forcing us to run for cover in the Volkswagen bus for the rest of the night. The morning hours found us drying soppy sleeping bags before we could continue on our trip. We drove on to where Buffalo Bill was buried. Then we traveled through the Badlands and marveled every mile of the way at God's creative beauty.

What Next?

Back in Aberdeen life took on a different expectation, for Don needed only a few credits to complete his master's degree. I went back to the Office of Economic Opportunity, but it was not the same to reenter a job I had been away from for ten weeks. An understudy had taken my place while I was gone, and he was not very happy to give up his role and allow me back in leadership. The organization had lost some of its appeal under this gentleman's guidance. His style of leadership was not as warm, and contacts with the city fathers had become strained, so my reentry was not without some ripples.

The community was not quite as excited about the possibilities for alleviating poverty and had grown weary of the grassroots workers going door to door. We had some sexual-misconduct issues between the high muckety-mucks who came to town and the single grassroots workers. Some of the grassroots workers were lonely women who were extremely vulnerable to any male attention, and these government workers took advantage of that vulnerability.

My job was still putting money in the household account, but it was not as satisfying as it had been. More and more we talked about the possibility of taking a sabbatical, so Don could finish his degree. I was now taking classes at the junior college. Since I had completed only one year of college, I was anxious to eventually finish my own degree. This was my ultimate goal, although I did enjoy being Don's editor and number-one typist for his work. He needed to complete those credits for his master's, and a seed of creative solutions was planted and germinating. We began planning how he could earn those credits while still considering jobs, house responsibilities, and needed income.

Another Hurdle

It was to be a weekend of fun. Don Ralph had an intense stomachache after we had gone to a movie and had popcorn Friday night, but we still planned to travel to the Tacoma mall the next day. We assumed Don Ralph had an attack of the flu, but when the pain would not let up, we called our pediatrician. He came to our house—as they still did in that era—poked Don Ralph in the stomach, and said it was probably just a bellyache from popcorn.

The doctor had only recently stopped by the house when Teresa had sat too close to the fireplace and had caught on fire. When her sisters said she was on fire, she started running through the house with them and me in pursuit. I yanked her nightclothes off of her and was immediately able to put out the fire. Her quick-acting sisters had seen the fire spark soon enough to prevent a very serious mishap. While I ripped her clothes off, the other girls had a blanket ready to wrap around her. And now, only a few days later, the doctor was back again, telling us Don Ralph probably just had a bellyache from too much popcorn.

We continued with our plans to go to the Tacoma mall the same day, since the doctor was sure it was only a popcorn reaction. However, when we arrived, Don Ralph left the contents of his stomach all over the store floors. We hurried home and took him to the emergency room, where they found that his white blood-cell count was soaring. All tests indicated a ruptured appendix, with gangrene setting in. A very somber doctor immediately took him to surgery.

Don Ralph, now in the eighth grade, spent several days in the hospital fighting a life-threatening infection. The surgeon, an Adventist doctor, assured us how lucky we were to have him as the doctor on duty. We did not care that he was so arrogant; we were just grateful for our son's life. He lost a lot of weight and missed a lot of school, but he did recover.

Teresa and Christy continued to excel in their music lessons with Marianne Stensager. When Teresa and Christy gave a recital, playing a sister-act duet, Don Ralph said they were the best in the program. The sibling rivalry was ancient history…and we were glad. Michele was interested in dance, so we enrolled her in the local dance studio, but her eyes wandered. She was too interested in everything that was going on to concentrate on dance. So as quickly as her dancing began, it was over. It seemed like she was more interested in acting and people watching.

As Don continued to explore the possibility of finishing up the few credits he needed for his master's at Portland State University, excitement grew among the whole family. Don had been at Grays Harbor College for five years and was eligible for a sabbatical, so with joy in my heart at the possibility to get out of this rainy, scary town, I began rolling around possibilities in my head.

The Beginning

CHAPTER 12

House of Shekinah

> Even the wilderness will rejoice in those days; the desert
> will blossom with flowers. Yes, there will be an abundance
> of flowers and singing and joy! The deserts will become
> as green as the Lebanon Mountains, as lovely as Mount
> Carmel's pastures and Sharon's meadows; for the Lord
> will display his glory there, the Excellency of our God.
> —Is 35:1–2, TLB

Changes in the Wind

Don worked out a deal with Grays Harbor College that would permit him to study at Portland State for one year, allowing him to finish his master's degree. In the fall he would spend several days a week at Grays Harbor College to fill his contract requirements. At the end of the year, and with the completion of the degree, he would return to Aberdeen. So our plans and dreams began. He continued teaching with the same vigor while his family fantasized about living in Portland. We had survived five years in this barren land.

When summer finally arrived and school was concluded, we drove down to Portland to pursue what would be needed to finish up the master's Don had begun several years before. After he enrolled in the classes he needed at Portland State University, he went to Portland Community College, thinking that perhaps he could teach some night classes to provide extra income. He met Irvin Hummel, a fellow sociology instructor, who told him an instructor had just quit, and they were looking for a replacement ASAP. While the children and I drove around checking out different sections of this metro area, Don immediately started to teach sociology to the nursing students at Good Samaritan Hospital.

He observed that the students in the program were a high-caliber group compared to some of his former students. So began his summer of being exposed to Portland Community College and Portland State University.

In the fall Don was to drive back to Aberdeen two days a week to fulfill his responsibility to his contract. Then we would move back to Aberdeen, in theory, even though I was praying for a miracle so we wouldn't have to return. But for now I allowed myself to think only of the charming prospect of a whole year away from Aberdeen's rainy, godless community. I could dry out, be with my children, and join the living!

It was June by the time Don had taken care of some prep work for our new adventure. We drove to Portland and stayed at the same motel on Capitol Highway where we always stayed: the Rose. It was cheap and creepy, but we had memories of many adventures there from the holidays we had taken in the past five years. We noticed how damp the clothes in our suitcases were. But who cared about that now? We would soon be moving to Portland.

While Don taught those lovely nursing students, the children and I went about the city looking for housing. We checked with a Mr. Green, who owned a rental service that I located in the newspaper. We checked several places that had low rents of $165 to $210. They were all dirty and depressing or far out of town. Living in some of the houses would mean Don Ralph and Teresa would have to ride a city bus to school. Living in another house would mean that Christy and Michele would go to school by a mausoleum.

If the houses were anywhere near decent, they were already taken. When we could not find anything adequate in rentals, the rental agent suggested buying a house with a buyback clause. But when we checked out that option with Mrs. Hadley, a local realtor, she did not think it would be possible. So we went back to Aberdeen without results, but we still held to the belief that there had to be a house somewhere in Portland to suit our needs. Back in Aberdeen on a Monday morning, Don called our mortgage lender to see if we could get a loan on our equity. He said yes—the best-sounding response yet!

Miracles Galore

The following Saturday, July 6, we went to Portland and started looking through the paper for ads. We spotted one ad for a five-bedroom home with a low interest rate that was located in Beaverton, near schools, shopping, and churches. It sounded too perfect to be true, so we felt we needed to continue exploring all our options with Bill Snyder Realty, whom we had contacted—even though it appeared to us that he was trying to unload some humdingers on us. We almost put a one-hundred-dollar deposit on one house, but we decided to go out to lunch and discuss it first. We did not have an air of excitement about any of the houses, so while eating lunch we decided to check with our mortgage company again to be sure we could pull out equity. Also, before going home we decided that we would explore that one ad in the paper for the five-bedroom house.

We called Mrs. Hadley again, even though she had not thought it possible to use the buyback clause. She called the owner and asked if we could go through the house. He said he and his wife would take a drive, and of course she could show the house. When we were driving up to the house, the children's eyes lit up. Everything about the house was absolutely perfect, but we did not see how we could buy it, knowing we had only one year guaranteed to be in the Portland area. It was a good price and had been on the best-buy list for several months, and the realtor could not understand why it had not sold. The house would be perfect for us. It would be close to schools for all the children. It seemed to have a flashing neon light out front with our name on it! The children were euphoric with excitement…This was the first house we had seen that they showed any interest in, for we did live in a beautiful new house in Aberdeen.

We consulted our prophetess, Marie Stara. Marie had been married to a local judge, now deceased. She had become a dear friend in Aberdeen. She was not known for her beauty of outward appearance; she simply possessed a beautiful, discerning spirit and was above reproach. We knew she was a Presbyterian in good standing. She had dignity and intelligence and was not easily swayed by whims and diverse opinion. She was one of the few people associated with the charismatic movement whom I would trust. We had met her at some of those home meetings I had such unrest about, but she seemed so rooted and of sound mind that I trusted her judgment. She simply seemed to be in tune with God. There was no question in my mind that she was a grounded saint. I had little faith in most everyone in this godless community, according to my values.

We had become fast friends, even though she was probably thirty years older than I was. I often talked with her and shared my quest for quiet holiness, without all the hoopla. Now I spoke with her about our dilemma in looking for housing. She prayed with me and then later called to tell me the Lord had given her a scripture pertaining to our future:

Even the wilderness will rejoice in those days; the desert will blossom with flowers. Yes, there will be an abundance of flowers and singing and joy! The deserts will become as green as the Lebanon mountains, as lovely as Mount Carmel's pastures and Sharon's meadows; for the Lord will display his glory, the excellency of our God (Is 35:1–2, TLB).

We pondered her words. However, so much was up in the air about where to live, finishing the degree, and returning to Aberdeen that we wanted to make sure of any action.

We still had loose ends to tie up in Aberdeen. I was still working on plans to resign from my job after our plans were secure for the next year. Our thoughts were in Portland and the step we were about to take.

On Thursday we headed to Portland once again with great hope in our hearts that we were doing the right thing. It was on Saturday night that we signed a note for $3,000 and went home trembling, anticipating good news when meeting with our mortgage broker. We finalized our offer from Aberdeen on Monday morning. Thirty-six hours after we had made the proposal and paid the $3,000 note, the sale was confirmed. The house was ours! We would have a house payment of $164—fourteen dollars over our Aberdeen house payment, which our new renter covered. The whole deal went through like greased lightning! We were told no deal had ever gone through that quickly. However, the children had been confident this was our house when we first had looked at it.

The house had the typical multi-olive-green carpeting and the beautiful hardwood floors that were so characteristic of that era. The previous Saturday afternoon, in this five-bedroom, tri-level house, each child had picked out his or her bedroom, oblivious to all else—including the front entrance to the house, which displayed the most beautiful roses in brilliant reds. Other colorful flowers grew over the terrace, and there were many roving flowers gracing the whole property. We knew this was the house Marie Stara had described to us. The scripture she had given us stated "the desert will blossom with flowers. Yes, there will be an abundance of flowers…" What a gardener the former owner must have been!

Done Deal

Our heads were still reeling, but we did not feel secure in our ownership. We would still need to undergo a credit check. We had good credit but were still uneasy. I wanted the deed in my hand. We knew we were stepping way beyond reality in a faith move to be sure! Was it wise to buy a house to live it for only one year? Our jewels believed in the goodness of God, and they had no problem at all accepting such a miracle. They were ready to take occupancy immediately, so as soon as we could move our belongings, we would move in, without waiting the typical month.

Teresa immediately claimed the downstairs bathroom and shower. She labeled the shower with "Bod Cleanser." That was her new hip word for "body cleanser or shower." Then she made plans to paint the words "The Sound of Music" in bold black letters in the downstairs family room, where we planned to place the piano. She and Don Ralph took the downstairs bedrooms right next to each other, and right away Teresa also planned what color to paint hers. She wanted daisies on the walls and planned a green, yellow, and blue color scheme…It sounded like an odd color combination to me, but when it was eventually completed it was colorful and turned out beautifully. Christy and Michele planned to take the upstairs bedrooms next to the second bathroom and our chosen bedroom, which overlooked the huge backyard.

We went back to Aberdeen to collect our belongings with unspeakable joy in our hearts. We were amazed by how our prayers could be answered so rapidly and without the slightest ripple. We had decided to rent our home in Aberdeen, and we were pleased with our renter, at least at first. Two teenage boys were a little hard on ceilings when they played basketball in the house…but that rain! Our renter needed immediate occupancy as well, and it seemed every detail of the move was in place before we even prayed about it: "I will answer them before they even call to me. While they are still talking to me about their needs, I will go ahead and answer their prayers!" (Is 65:24 TLB).

With nothing but faith in our hearts, we loaded up a U-Haul to pull behind our Volkswagen bus. I drove the bus, and the three girls rode with me along with a not-so-happy cat and dog. Don secured a rental truck to be loaded with our furniture. My heart could hardly hold the joy. We were so thankful for God's grace and mercy in granting us this opportunity. We would surely walk by faith and believe we were in the midst of a miracle.

The Awesome Teen Years

Don continued to teach nursing students at Good Samaritan Hospital while I was home, unpacking and moving in. How good it was not going to work outside the home. Summer was for playing with my children. I thought they needed the experience of picking strawberries, so I made arrangements to ride the bus that came around our neighborhood to pick up strawberry pickers. That first day I bent down or crawled on my knees all day. I had a reputation of being fast at whatever I did, and I was confident we would make a bundle of money between the five of us. However, at the end of the day, my earnings were a mere $3.42! What? Someone must have made a mistake. I was used to clearing at least $150 a day—a very good income for a woman in that era.

On the bus ride home, a cocky boy threw strawberries and hit Teresa in the head. His language matched what our children had listened to in Aberdeen. Teresa jumped up and told the young admirer, in no uncertain terms, to lay off and mind his own business. He seemed stunned she was not happy with his advances.

At the end of the day, we all agreed that another form of income would be better. Berry picking had not been cost effective! So, instead of working, I signed the girls up for baton twirling and watched them perform at local parades. We just continued our joyful living, barely able to wait for the next day to see what wonder would await us. On the weekends we would go camping at Lost Lake near Mt. Hood, pick huckleberries, and in general just celebrate this newfound paradise.

Don Ralph continued to love playing the saxophone, and I wanted the girls enrolled in the best musical program available. I explored the possibility of getting them into the music program at Lewis & Clark College, a local school with an excellent music program. I took the two very resistant girls to the campus and enrolled them. The girls thought music lessons should not interfere with summer fun, but I did not know how long we would be there, and I did not want them to lose any skills they had obtained with Marianna.

Mr. Enman was an excellent teacher, but the girls said when he stooped down with his arms over their shoulders to watch their finger control, his breath was intolerable. They could not concentrate on piano with him breathing down their necks. So on the way to each lesson, I found myself praying that Mr. Enman would do something about his breath, so the girls would have better attitudes. Teresa and Christy both seemed to take to the lessons—in spite of their complaints—and moved ahead with speed and creativity. Though Christy did well on the piano, her desire was to be a dancer. Michele showed no interest in piano, so we would let her choose an instrument later, which turned out to be the flute.

We also bought Teresa a guitar, and she began giving us nightly concerts from her sunny bedroom with the daisies dancing on the walls.

Togetherness and Exploration

Teresa had wasted no time in creating her unique bedroom. It became our private prayer closet, where we said nightly prayers and listened to her dreams for the future. Her questions would always be, "Mom, who will I marry? What will my future hold?" She always wanted to peek into her future. I also pondered her questions in my heart. She seemed to live such a charmed life, with so many life questions! It was our custom to say each child's prayers with them nightly. This also was a time to share their heartbreaks and triumphs. I treasure those moments still.

We lived close to a Disciple of Christ church. It was just half a block away, so we first visited the denominational church of Don's ordination and childhood. The pastor's wife suffered from bipolar disorder, and she was most unfriendly and disturbed. The pastor himself seemed a bit unstable, and we knew we did not need that involvement. He probably suffered some from living with a manic-depressive wife. I wanted a stable setting in our lives here in this newfound paradise!

We tried another Christian church in downtown Beaverton. We heard a powerful sermon, and I was overcome with tears that Sunday. I don't know why. Maybe I was just happy to be out of Aberdeen. We continued our search for the perfect fit in a church for us and our children. I believed we needed a church with a solid, grounded, unemotional setting. I had had enough of the charismatic movement and what I perceived to be emotionally unstable people. I wanted to return to the solid faith of my childhood. What I really wanted was to be back in Colfax as the first lady of the manse. But I felt we did have a new mission here in Beaverton, and I would set the desires of my heart aside.

One Thursday evening on my way to the girls' music lessons, I took a new route to Lewis & Clark. This route passed Valley Presbyterian Church. It had a warm, inviting exterior, and I told Don later that night that I would like to visit that church on Sunday. We agreed to try another Presbyterian church, hoping it would not be as liberal as the one in Aberdeen. The sermon, preached by Bob Davis that Sunday, was powerful, and we felt an immediate bond. In fact I was sure he had prepared his sermon just for me—something about a proper fit.

We jumped into this new church without hesitation. I joined the choir and met the unforgettable conductor, Suzanne New. She can best be described as a lovable tiger! She was demanding and put out some of the best musical arrangements I had sung. I had sung in high school, college, and community choirs, and I was thrilled for this new opportunity. I later sang, under Suzanne's leadership, in a group called Bell Canto. That was a very special time.

We joined a Mariners group, and those dear members became our support group. Mariner groups were smaller support groups, since it was easy to become lost in such a large church. The church at that time ministered to about 1,200 members—a much larger congregation than our previous experience in church, so we were extremely happy for this small group of friends in the Mariners group. All the while we did not know what our future held. We just decided to celebrate our good fortune during this holy summer and wait for God to move.

Raju spent much time with us that summer. If we could work it in, we would go to the Joneses' cabin on the lake. We usually took a carload of young friends for a waterskiing weekend. But on one occasion, early in the summer, Raju wanted Dad—as he called Don—to find him speaking engagements. He had spoken in Aberdeen, so why not here? He had a strong desire at this point in his life to be an evangelist proclaiming the gospel of Christ. Raju seemed more comfortable in Pentecostal settings, so Don called the Assembly of God pastor in Portland to inquire. Pastor Swanson indicated they were having a youth meeting the next night and that he would be happy for Raju to share his testimony. Of course Raju did not want to go by himself, so he enlisted Don Ralph and Teresa to join him.

But Don Ralph and Teresa wanted no part of this setup! We told them it was only right that they should accompany their brother. They were still resistant, and their anger was directed at Don and me as they left; however, they were all smiles upon their return. It seemed there were very desirable-looking young men and women present who made the trip worthwhile, and Raju evidently did a fine job and was invited back whenever possible. The evening definitely ended better than it started out.

That evening also began a love affair for Teresa and much toleration for Don Ralph. He was at odds with the fundamentalist and Pentecostal control theology, but Teresa was not fazed by it as of yet. Perhaps Don Ralph had a little bit of his mom's noncompliant spirit. There was much control in all such more conservative churches. It was the good looking girls who attracted Don Ralph to any church!

It was the end of the summer, and we thought that since we had not lasted at strawberry picking, we would try going out to the bean fields in the nearby rural area of Hillsboro. The sun beat down on us as we began our day's work. Teresa attacked the job with vigor, like she did everything else, and when the younger girls screamed because she had grabbed their fingers rather than the beans, laughter resounded over the bean field, and other pickers wondered what was going on with this family of six. We all agreed we would use our earnings to make a last trip to Eastern Washington before school began.

We always had such a good time sitting in that dry Eastern Washington air, spending much time on my sister's deck, looking over the river and property that my grandfather had once owned. (He had bought forty acres dirt cheap—or was it sand cheap? For in the beginning that is what it was: fertile but very sandy.) Then there was my dear sister and her husband, Chuck. Chuck had horses. We all loved going to Clarkston, but Teresa was the one who wanted to go there to see the horses.

So Much Goodness in This Land of Milk and Honey

Soon Michele was to enter the third grade, Christy the sixth, and Teresa her freshman year, and Don Ralph was to enter Sunset High School as a sophomore. Where had the years gone since these precious jewels had been born into our home, bringing such joy? All of the children happily anticipated starting at their new schools, and all the pain and dislike of Aberdeen seemed to fade somewhere in the recesses of our minds. Life was good. Very good!

As we prepared for the fall schedule, still not knowing how this arrangement would work out, Irvin Hummel—the department chairman for Portland Community College—approached Don again and said Portland Community College would like to offer him a contract for the following year. Don's delight was uncontainable when he called to tell me the good news. He would have to continue to teach classes in Aberdeen two days a week, teach the other three days in Portland, and work on credits for his master's degree. Don continued talking and told me that was not even the best news: they would pay the contract back to the beginning of the summer, so he would be paid for the past three months. Miracle of miracles!

The miracles continued to flow without our doing anything other than praying without ceasing. Our hearts swelled at God's goodness to us. Surely we must have been doing the one, two, and three correctly to receive God's four, five, and six provisions! I prided myself on the fact that I was spending time in my prayer closet as a prayer warrior for the needs of our family. How good of God to be so faithful!

My entry prayer before God's throne was, "Lord, behold the handmaiden of the Lord." When the angel of the Lord came to Mary, telling her she was to bear the Messiah, this was her response: "My soul doth magnify the Lord, and my spirit hath rejoiced in God my Savior. For he hath regarded the low estate of his handmaiden…" (Lk 1:46–48). To serve God was the desire of my heart, and so it seemed our lives were under His protection.

Much to Learn

School began, and we were surprised by Christy and Michele's teachers. They simply were not the same caliber as the teachers they'd had in Aberdeen. I offered to be room mother for Michele's class. What an eye-opener! Mrs. Sitser had absolutely no class control. The children were wild and uncontrollable, throwing erasers and pencils. When I attended a parent-teacher conference session for Michele, I asked Mrs. Sitser about the classroom conduct. Her comment was that she wanted the children to like her, so she never raised her voice. It was her first teaching assignment and her last!

On one occasion Michele raised her hand to be excused to go to the bathroom, but her teacher refused, thinking it was just a ploy to get out of class. The resulting puddle on the floor was devastating to Michele.

It seemed unthinkable that we would miss anything about Aberdeen. But Don Ralph said in later years that he never learned anything new after leaving the Aberdeen school system. Not totally true, as he later added much learning to his education in academia and the military, but to date that may have been true.

Christy's teacher was intimidating in his demeanor, and on occasion he would throw things across the room in anger. He reminded me of a teacher I'd had in fifth grade who would hit students with a ruler for not complying with her outlandish instructions and then retreat to the attached room, screaming hysterically. I wondered if everyone has educational experiences that have emotionally crippled them.

I wondered whether I should go to work again, do some foster care work, or just enjoy being a homemaker once again. I had gotten used to coming home from work and then attacking household responsibilities, and I was still in the mode of starting my domestic work late in the day. I had enjoyed being the director of community action at my last job, but I still wrestled with the idea of shortchanging my roles of domestic engineer and polisher of jewels. I did enjoy working and desperately wanted to contribute to the financial needs of the family, but I decided for the time being to spend my time in prayer while the children and Don were at school. I knew it was not fair to take a job for one year, knowing we would be returning to Aberdeen.

The Joneses were proving to be caring friends apart from their charismatic involvement and offered Don a place in their home when he had to return for the two days a week of teaching. I desperately missed Don when he was away. We had rarely been separated overnight for any length of time. He would write little love letters to his children even though he was gone for only three days, encouraging them to cease any fighting and to be helpful to their mom in doing chores. We greeted him with hugs and kisses upon his return.

Still after Us

Of course the Joneses wanted Don to continue going to charismatic meetings, so they found all of the Portland area meetings and made sure Don knew the places, times, and dates of all of them. Were we still to be harassed by this movement? Though I must say, in Portland we heard some dynamic speakers who did not appear as kooky as those who went to Aberdeen to promote their wares! One speaker we heard in Portland was a pastor named Judson Cornwall. His preaching took us both to lofty heights and strengthened our aspirations to walk humbly before our God. When I sat in his services, I felt goose bumps rippling on my skin. His theology was so sound that his reasoning removed much of that white-magic theology from my memory.

Jewels

As usual Teresa had no trouble making friends, and our home became a gathering place for teenagers. I loved it. It took me back to my own involvement with youth, parties, and ministry. Don Ralph soon became top student, as he had been from second grade on, and was asked to join the jazz band, playing bass saxophone. Teresa was painting, and she was writing her own music and serenading us each night with her melodies. It seemed her life was one big miracle.

All the children were succeeding academically as honor students. I could not help but think we still had a corner on child-rearing with these naturally gifted jewels. God was so good to our family. In fact it seemed to me that our family was just one big celebration of happiness. People at Valley Presbyterian were commenting on our success, and some couples in our Mariners group stated they would like to hook their wagon to our star. That was a bad omen!

A New Commission

Well, if we had the recipe for raising perfect children, why not do some foster care? After Don and I went for the interview, the social worker was indeed eager to place a baby in our care. His name was Shawn, and he was four months old and catatonic. He had had no stimulation or the love of a family. He came with bedsores on his little bottom from neglect. We had him for four short months, when he began giggling, gaining weight, and was one happy little boy. Our four were constantly loving and hugging him and teaching him new little tricks.

I mentioned to the caseworker, a young girl just out of college, that if he came up for adoption, we were interested. That was one big mistake, for the social worker said we were getting too attached, and they would be moving him the next day. I wondered at such a philosophy. Who would this hurt more, the child to be moved from a loving home or a secure family who would have to make adjustments upon his removal? But my case was not to be heard, and the baby was ripped, screaming from my loving arms. Thank goodness that philosophy of placement of foster children has changed over the years. Michele was especially wounded when this little bundle was taken from us, and she continually said she wanted a baby brother.

Remember earlier when, as a young girl, I read the Bobbsey Twins book about a baby being left on the doorstep of the Bobbsey Twins' home, and I wished that would happen to me? That desire still lay deep in my heart. I had often told Don we needed another son to balance out our family. When he finally, out of the blue, conceded and said to me, "Maybe it is time to adopt," I wondered how this could be possible, since we had to return to Aberdeen after this miracle year…maybe! Also, where would the extra money come from to pay for an adoption? Medical coverage with Kaiser Permanente was basically free other than a one-dollar copay with each visit, emergency, or birth. I knew any child we adopted would be covered by our medical insurance after he was in our home. But many other questions swirled in my head.

However, since we were living totally by faith in this new paradise, we decided to go to exploration classes at the Boys & Girls Aid Society adoption agency. We went through the classes—a series of four—and afterward we were approved. Anyone could meet our jewels, whom we had birthed, and see that we were apparently successful parents. But I decided to set the whole idea of adoption aside. I believed life would go on, and if adoption was to be, it would all work out. In fact I decided to take a job in the office at Montgomery Ward. I had worked full time and had contributed an income to the family for the past five years, so subconsciously I felt I still needed to contribute to our growing financial needs. We needed to invest in art tools, purchase instruments, pay for piano lessons and voice lessons, and, most of all purchase the boat we desired. That had become our top priority: to own our own boat. As for adoption I was sure it would take a year or so, and by that time we would probably have to return to Aberdeen.

Miracles Do Happen

It was the month of November—hunting season, so Don and Don Ralph decided to go deer hunting in Yoncalla with some of Don's relatives. In fact, as I remember it, it was November 28, 1969. While they were gone, the girls and I did some baking and just hung out. Later Michele was in her room. In our tri-level home, the stairs to her bedroom were not too far from the kitchen. Michele literally bolted down the stairs and said the Lord had just spoken to her, telling her she would have a baby brother for her birthday.

Not wanting to shatter my little girl's faith, I said, "Meme, let's wait and see what your dad thinks." When Don and Don Ralph returned the next day, a Sunday, she hardly let Don in the door before she blurted what she believed with all her heart to be a word from the Lord.

Don listened patiently, and I feared our ten-year-old's simple, trusting faith might be shattered. His response surprised me: "I believe it was a word from the Lord!"

All I could say, holding my skepticism within, was, "We'll just have to wait and see!" Could I believe, and was I really ready to take on a baby?

I had been enjoying my Montgomery Ward job for two weeks. It was Monday, and as I sat at work I pondered the innocent faith of a ten-year-old. I decided I would call the Boys & Girls Aid Society the next morning. So Tuesday morning I gave the social worker a call to just see how the adoption process was going.

She said, "This is very odd that you should call me today, as we do have a baby boy we are considering placing in your home." She asked a few questions and then said she would call me the next day. We already had a baby crib set up in Michele's room from the foster baby we had cared for.

The social worker called the next day, which was December 4, and asked if we were ready to pick up our son. The overwhelming excitement in telling the children that evening cannot be described other than to say they were *ecstatic*! While the children were in school the next day, Don and I went to the Boys & Girls Aid Society with anxiety and fear to pick up a little bundle all wrapped in a beautiful blue crocheted blanket and hat. I knew I did not want to work and leave a new little jewel with a sitter, so after three weeks of work I gave my resignation to a not very happy boss.

This new little son had to be awakened to be fed. He was only five pounds in weight and needed a lot of stimulation. He was possibly a fetal alcohol syndrome baby, according to the social worker. Michele's miracle word from the Lord had come to be, and we took her to Farrell's Ice Cream Parlor to celebrate her tenth birthday on December 9—with her baby brother in tow! Cean Michael had been born on November 28, the day Michele had said the Lord spoke to her. Such a faith builder left us aghast at God's continual provision and daily miracles.

The whole adoption process had taken four months. On the way home from our birthday celebration, I made the statement that perhaps we needed to remember this miracle surrounding Cean Michael's birth in later years. How prophetic that thought became. He gave us a run for our money!

Celebrations Galore

Though it was difficult for Don to be in Aberdeen part of each week, life still remained one big celebration on weekends. Since our children had learned to ski at the Joneses' lake, we wanted our own boat and ski equipment, so our search began. We had promised Teresa a horse, but we had the whole family's desires to consider and not just one child's. Teresa too loved waterskiing, so it was not a difficult decision to put the boat ahead of the horse.

There were many boat shops in Portland, and we had great fun on Saturdays looking for the perfect boat for our family. Boating and skiing were to become our primary family sport. We purchased a blue tri-hull sixteen-foot boat. There were many rivers and small lakes—and most of all the big Columbia River— to explore. Boating became our weekend sport, and we often included some of Don's associates, who were masters at the sport and always included extra children.

While living in our Camelot, Colfax, we had often gone to church retreats on Liberty Lake near Spokane, and there was always recreational time for children to learn to waterski. Don Ralph and Teresa had been the first to learn. I had tried for five years to get up with no luck. I swallowed much of the lake, refusing to let go of the ski rope. But one Sunday afternoon I did get up... momentarily, and the aftermath of that brief success left black-and-blue bruises from my ankles to my chest. The skis had come off and slapped my body in the fall. From that point on, I decided I would be the ski coach rather than risking another collision with water and skis.

The younger children and Don learned to ski with our powerful new boat. This family sport brought many hours of weekend pleasure and summer activity. It became another love of my life, and we stayed from early morning, through the heat of the day, and into the cool of the evening. Often we would park the boat at a restaurant's ramp, and we would walk up the stairs to a fun-filled dinner. Time seemed to stand still, and it didn't seem that life could get any better! But life did continue to get better and better.

CHAPTER 13

So Many Good Decisions

> Life is a great canvas, and you should
> throw all the paint on it you can.
> --Danny Kaye

Since Portland Community College offered Don a tenured contract after his one year there, he had a serious decision to make. He had agreed to return after his year of working toward his master's, which he now had. He talked with the college president, Dr. Adams. It was decided if he would pay that year's salary back, they would let him out of his contract.

The children and I were euphoric. I think even Don had joy in his heart after his awesome experience in working on his advanced degree and teaching such motivated nursing students, as well as seeing how happy his family was. He had enjoyed his time teaching and his associates at Grays Harbor College. But could he refuse the offer from Portland Community College? *No!*

We were all so happy in Beaverton. Don Ralph and Teresa continued to be involved with the Assembly of God youth group as well as active with the youth of Valley Presbyterian, where we were all attending church. Teresa became active in most school activities, including choir, acting, and Sun Flares—a twirling team. She was also a class officer…leaving not one spare moment. She often had parties at our home for the church youth and for school friends. Teresa had a certain charisma that attracted both girlfriends and the boys who wanted to win her attention.

I too was doing a lot of entertaining of our new friends. Many friends were still coming to visit us from Colfax, and relatives also found our place in the metro area to be a drawing card. We were asked to take our boat to youth retreats, and this became a ministry to youth. (We also observed many romances starting in the boat—as well as breakups.) We loved having the teenagers around.

A Promise Is a Promise

Teresa, our young beauty who seemed to have it all, had not forgotten her father's promise of a horse. She had passed the thirteenth year of her life, and although she still had a horse-shaped brain, she had no horse! She began looking at ads in the paper and talking to school friends. She told her dad that now was the time, since we did not have to return to Aberdeen. Her joy was uncontainable when we found a young horse not too far from where we lived. The price was within our means, and when we went to look at the horse, Teresa went right up to it and fearlessly jumped on its back from the rear! The horse seemed not to mind, though the owner said no one had ever done that before, and he was aghast.

As was usually the case, Teresa had a girlfriend with her, and they were vying to decide who had less fear around horses. We talked with the owner and said we would have to find a place to keep this new money loser, but we would be back. Teresa told the owner, "Please don't sell it before we get back," and the gentleman, with a glint in his eye, said he would hold him if she made a small deposit. (I think it was ten dollars, which Teresa had with her.) So it was that this beautiful young horse had a new owner.

How little we had calculated the cost from that point on. Teresa had a friend at school who also loved horses and knew of a pastor, Rev. Hornshuh, who had space in his barn for another horse. The costs would mount as we calculated what it would take to rent the space and for hay, grain, shots, tack, and on and on. But still, a promise is a promise…right?

Teresa went home that evening and searched the Bible for the perfect name for her newly acquired miracle. She decided that Kishan would be his name. The young horse was very gentle and was a perfect match for Teresa's innate horse knowledge plus all the horse knowledge her uncle Chuck had shared. She learned to apply fairness, discipline, and unwavering love when she worked with Kishan. She said her father and Uncle Chuck had taught her how to handle children and horses.

It seemed these two were soul mates, for Teresa could communicate with Kishan on a superhuman level. The horse had not been officially broke, as horse people called it. But with Teresa, Kishan did exactly what she required, as though he knew she was fearless. They became one when she mounted her new beloved gift from God. The horse-riding lessons Teresa had received in Aberdeen paid off, for she was a natural, sitting like a pro on that beautiful specimen of God's design. A friend (the one who Teresa had declared had a dirty house) had given her a saddle, and in addition to that we added tack, hay, oats, and other items that her uncle Chuck suggested. She joked with her dad that a sports car would be a good follow-up for graduation.

And so it was that Teresa's romance with horses continued. She made friends with all the horse people in the vicinity. At that time we had only one car, so I would have to take Don to class, keep the car, and make sure Teresa arrived safely to where we kept Kishan. She rode him every day after school and invited her school friends to join her. The wide-open fields that had not yet been developed were a horse-and-rider paradise. Our gas bill mounted as well!

An Angel in Our Midst

We wondered how Teresa had time to maintain a 4.0 grade-point average, take part in Assembly of God activities, practice the piano, play her guitar, paint, write music, give her horse quality care, and always take time for Bible reading. Truly she was becoming a polished jewel! It seemed there were never enough hours in the day for this unique child of God. We felt so blessed. She always took time to declare her love and appreciation for her parents. Here is one poem she wrote:

> To a mom and dad who always care,
> To a mom and dad who are always there,
> From one little voice crying out aloud,
> From one little voice that is so, so proud,
>
> To share her life with parents like you,
> And make you happy and never feel blue,
> To show her love by feelings untold,
> To show her love by actions so bold.

She stands out of her crowd to show to you,
The love you've embedded in her too,
The tenderness that was put right there,
By the few words, "We always care."

By concern for me when I needed it so,
The strength when I had to face my foe.
You taught the thing that you thought was right,
You tried your hardest to bring us in God's sight.

You gave us hearts full of love,
You gave us God, who came from above,
But most of all you gave to me, the meaning of love
And how to be free.
And now we know as we look back
It's been a wonderful, wonderful past.
And it will be a wonderful future
Just as we all love God.

I just wrote to say to you,
We will always be more than true.
And that no other parents two,
Could have raised us as well as you!

Teresa sang with high school and college-age singers at the Assembly as well as with madrigals in high school. She always looked like an angel to us—always singing with such drama and upstaging all the other singers with her smiling face and almost transcendent appearance.

Don Ralph had opted to get involved with the Assembly youth along with Teresa, although conservative control was utmost and bothered him greatly. He admitted the girls were why he was involved there. He said that only the unattractive, forward girls at the Presbyterian Church showed interest in him. He also thought the Presbyterian Church was too dark and under lit.

Teresa was delighted to have Don Ralph involved along with her. We divided our attention between their involvement in the Assembly church and our interest in being involved in the Presbyterian Church. We attended Sunday evening services with the children at the Assembly as well as the special meetings they often held. I was happy with Valley Presbyterian, although my heart still remained as first lady of the Colfax manse. I needed to change that broken record!

A Child Shall Lead Them

Young Cean Michael was loved by all, and he delighted in our every activity and adventure. He was a precocious child and was difficult to control with four teenagers laughing at his every antic. At evening services, when he saw other people raising their hands in praise, he would lift his little hands and say loudly, "Halua!" One time when we were shopping at the Meier & Frank department store, he slipped away in an instant and went down the escalator before we could grab him. In our panic we rushed down the escalator, hoping to catch him before he became totally lost. We found him walking through the store without the least bit of fear or knowledge that he had done anything dangerous or wrong. He was definitely fearless. Try as we might, we could not convince him there were dangers.

On another occasion, when we went back to see Ruth Lowe, young Cean had no fear crossing the trestle, as his older siblings had experienced. He simply said, "Do it again!" When he put his little hand on Ruth's hot wood-burning stove, just to see what it felt like—which sent us to the emergency room—he was oblivious about what he had done. Even though he uttered howling screams, he seemed undaunted. We remembered this incident later when Cean, maybe ten or eleven, tried to hang himself just to see what it felt like. (This was after a young teenager we knew had hung himself and died!)

It was a new experience both to parent young children and to interact with teenagers, all the while trying to keep our equilibrium.

Not a Good Idea

We had befriended two couples who were a few years younger than Don and I, whom we had met at the Christian church near us. One couple had one young daughter, and the other couple had four children. The couples were exploring the charismatic movement in Portland, and when they heard we had some connections because of Raju, they wanted to hear more. They too said they wanted to hook their wagon to our star.

When the younger of the two couples tried to buy a home and were refused a loan even though the husband was a banker, we loaned them the $2,000 down payment. That did not go well. We had withdrawn the money from a life-insurance policy and were certain we would be able to pay it back and keep our policy. But the insurance policy was never repaid, and the friendship did not go well from that point on. We ended up letting the policy go, but we could have used it later in life. Our compassion got us into trouble on many occasions. But that was a lesson well learned!

A Family of Achievers

Don continued to teach nursing students throughout the year and was asked to be the speaker at the graduation. It seemed he was on a roll, for all his students loved him, whether he was teaching the nursing students at Good Samaritan Hospital, Portland State night school, or Portland Community College. He would walk into the classroom and have the students spellbound for fifty minutes, and he was also sought after for counseling. It was when he was teaching the Good Samaritan nursing students that Don met Father Truehella, the hospital chaplain. After Father Truehella heard Don give his graduation speech, he could not wait to make his acquaintance. He highly commended him for such a fine delivery to those graduates, and they became good friends and confidants.

As Don Ralph and Teresa approached their sixteenth birthdays, they opted to secure jobs. Teresa first took a job at a day care that was close to our house. We helped her learn the necessity of a good work ethic, for when her supervisor was not the most compassionate and Teresa wanted to bail out immediately, we helped her to see the necessity of sticking to a job. I too had learned this while working at the bank. I had hung in at that horrible job, even though it had provoked many tears from working with mean-spirited supervisors.

Teresa had taken this job during the summer, wanting to pay for some of her needed tack and desired wardrobe. It was to conclude when school began. She stuck it out, although she was much relieved when school began. I hated to see her work on top of all of her activities, but she had so many desires and now was a horse owner. When school started Teresa secured a job at the Boutique. It was a shop in the mall, also a short distance from where we lived. There, both staff and clients adored her and her style. She not only was an excellent salesperson, but she did the shop's window displays and the graphic design for newspaper ads.

Don Ralph wanted a car, so jobs were a necessity. At fifteen and one-half, he started working at the Arctic Circle, for they commonly hired workers younger than sixteen. That, too, was an exercise in learning how to deal with mean-spirited managers. When he turned sixteen, Don Ralph started at McDonald's and stayed there for many years, eventually paying much of his own way. He was so fast in his work that the company sent him to San Francisco to take part in a contest for best hamburger flipper. He was flown to San Francisco in Ray Croc's own jet, and besides that he took the prize for Best Hamburger Flipper in the Pacific Northwest.

Don Ralph definitely needed a car to attend all of his school and church functions, and of course he needed the wheels for his sister and her friends. At age fifteen and one-half, he spent time looking at car ads, and since he had money always in his pocket, he talked his dad into allowing him to purchase a '56 Mercury, even though it looked like it belonged in a junk pile. Don Ralph would rev it up and pretend, but he never drove it. He had only a driver's permit at the time.

When he turned sixteen, he drove the Mercury for a short time until he found a green 1950 Ford in excellent condition. He sold that pile of junk and bought the Ford. He parked in front of our house, which was surrounded by apartments. He had delighted only briefly in the ownership of this automobile, when one evening, very late, one of the residents, in a drunken stupor, drove into it. The Ford was demolished, and the insurance totaled it out.

With that money Don Ralph and his dad went to Hardtop Motors and found a Pontiac GTO that did not run. His dad took it to the automotive department at Portland Community College, where they rebuilt it. Earlier, when Don Ralph was first learning to drive, he had accidently driven into the frame of the garage, causing some damage—but more laughter than anything. Don, a car buff, was also enjoying the teenage car adventures as much as the teenagers.

Both our older children were heavily involved in so many things, and we wondered at their unnatural energy and drive to maintain all activities. It truly was a joy to be involved with these children. We wanted them to know we were always in their court, and we were enjoying every detail of this season of life.

Memories

It was not uncommon for Teresa to come home late from a date or work, flip on all the lights, land in the middle of our bed, and share the delights or drudgeries of her evening. She would say, "Dad, are you listening?" Between times of dropping off to sleep, he would mumble "I heard you." We both knew how much we would cherish these memories.

Don Ralph would not jump in the middle of the bed, but he would come in and sit on the floor, leaning against the wall. We would not have thought of closing the door to such open relationships. We always made the rounds of saying prayers with the children each night, except on the nights they came home too late. Often Teresa would pull me down on her bed and say, "Talk to me!" She always had burning questions to explore.

Still Lurking

At the Assembly it was characteristic to give testimonies. Our children wondered if you had to have great sin in your life before you could give a testimony to God's grace and love. In fact we wondered at the wisdom of sharing such gutter material, but it gave us an opportunity to share our theology of love and grace and the need to walk circumspectly all one's life.

The Assembly often had deathbed stories or movies that suggested if you did not make a commitment before leaving the building and then met death, you would be forever banished from your Maker. These deathbed stories disturbed me, just as they had in my past. They also greatly disturbed our children. This was especially true for Christy and Michele. After those evenings we would drive over to Farrell's, and over ice cream sundaes we would discuss how we felt about such stories. I wondered why we subjected our children to this extremely conservative and controlling organization, but it was, after all, their idea to be involved.

One evening the church had a guest speaker from Don's former Disciple of Christ Christian denomination. He was elderly and claimed he was now baptized with the Holy Spirit. He said he would like Don to come to his motel room, so he could share how he had come into this new experience. Since the children were riding in Don Ralph's car, Don and I visited the man. When I walked into his room, I noticed about ten prescription bottles on his nightstand, and he started to take pills from each bottle. Odd, I thought, after his speech about all the miracles in his life. He noted my resistance; for once again I found someone I didn't know trying to manipulate me to accept his every word. I did not think what he said had a ring of truth, and here again I felt a charismatic trying to pull me into his control.

I was angry and devastated once again. It seemed I was continually caught in this vice between the charismatic pull and my desire for soundness...and yet there was fire and enthusiasm here that our teenagers missed in other mainline churches. The irony (or blessing) was that the involvement was a good way to keep the teenagers off the streets.

Don't Let the Hurt Overrule the Joy

We were continually concerned about the charismatic influence at the Assembly of God church—especially speaking in tongues. This aspect bothered me greatly, but since Teresa was so involved and was enjoying her participation in all the activities, I had to set my inner feelings aside. She made so many friends through that church—both male and female! She took part in two plays: *A Man Called Peter* and *Quo Vadis*. She took the best actor awards for both plays, she was so convincing in her acting. In *A Man Called Peter*, she played a maid with such emotion that the whole audience was in tears and gave her a standing ovation. Her acting was not limited to the Assembly; she took part in theater at Sunset High School, while her brother played his bass sax in the small orchestra.

It did seem Don and I were spread very thin in our attempt to be all things to each of our children. Sometimes my mind was spinning with what I wanted to do and could find the time to do. Christy was beginning to take a real interest in dance and was very proficient. Michele seemed to have a flare for acting. However, Don Ralph's and Teresa's activities seemed to overshadow all other family involvement. Family activities and our two older children's school activities consumed the younger children's time, and it seemed we were all riding on Teresa's star for the moment. It was Teresa who filled our home with her friends, and I often said, "The squeaky hinge gets the oil!"

Valleys and Peaks

Don was usually teaching night school. It seemed he was much in demand to teach extra classes. Sometimes I felt like a married single. Of course we needed the extra income to support all our desires and activities, so it was a sacrifice I was willing to make. I was very proud of his academic achievements. No matter where we went in the area—shopping, to the movies, or eating out—some former student would stop Don to tell him how he had changed his or her life. He became a community icon! But still I wished he had more family time to join our nighttime school activities.

I was taking voice lessons from Eileen Manning for my own enjoyment, and Teresa decided she wanted to take voice as well. Both of us grew to love Eileen, who put on musical plays for the community. Teresa was cast along with me in *Amahl and the Night Visitors*. This is a very moving Christmas musical, and although Teresa had a small part, she upstaged every actor—including her mother. It seemed like from infancy on, she stood out with a certain angelic appearance in all she did.

We often had Kishan, Teresa's horse, in our backyard along with the many girlfriends Teresa invited over. Thank goodness we had understanding neighbors who kept silent even if they disapproved. We actually had awesome neighbors, and we spent much time talking over the fence or watching our children play in each other's yards. I did wonder, though, if they were glad on the weekends when we were gone with the boat…no horse in the backyard!

All the children became very competitive and competent in waterskiing. The boat was our family's most enjoyable sport and my favorite time with the family. The minute the weather was halfway decent, we were on the water. So much bonding took place on the rippling, warm water, in the sunshine I had so missed in Aberdeen. We were truly living the American dream.

Don Ralph's senior year had whizzed by, and now he was to graduate. He had enjoyed a great year playing football and his sax, working at McDonald's and driving his GTO. Teresa was about to enter her senior year, still extremely active and busy with her life. Amid our activities I planned a grand graduation party for Don Ralph, our first to graduate, and what a gala affair it was. So many dear friends came to celebrate with Don Ralph before he entered Lewis & Clark College. I was not quite ready for any of our children to leave home, so I was glad Don Ralph would still be living at home. It was so delightful to be involved with our teenagers, and it was both exhilarating and distressing to think of our children launching their careers.

Don and I squeezed in time for the children's clothes shopping at Lloyd's Center, our favorite shopping place, before school. We shared caramel apples at the mall and hit the summer sales. By the time we were finished, we were all dressed in Nordstrom's summer and fall fashions and looked like we had stepped out of the pages of *Vogue* magazine. We went from one celebration to another before school commenced again. These were joyous experiences in this glorious promised land of Beaverton. Could life get any better? Would this joy ever end? We were about to find out!

CHAPTER 14

Room 101

> How long must I struggle with anguish in my
> soul, with sorrow in my heart every day?
> —Ps 13:2, NLT

Turn in the Bend

The excitement of Don Ralph's graduation celebration was over. It was still fairly early in the summer, and I began having unbearable pain. After a few days, I decided I had to see a doctor. We had appreciated the insurance coverage with Kaiser through Portland Community College. The only problem was that we did not feel like we had a family doctor who knew our health history. When I went in, the doctor, whom I had not met before, was not sure what was wrong, but he opted to do a D and C—or exploratory surgery, as he called it—to find the source of the intense pain. I agreed, for the pain would not let up.

As it turned out, they did a therapeutic abortion. I was in such pain that I did not care what they did…that is until I came to and realized the whole scenario that had taken place. I had signed a release for them to do whatever was necessary. Evidently things were not quite normal, and it was for the best—so they said, but that did not help the despair that took over my whole being.

I wept! What had I done? The whole body, physical and spiritual, prepares for a child—even at the immediate point of conception—and when the body does not complete the process from conception until birth, there is great remorse, physically and emotionally. I would boldly state that every woman who has opted for this solution, either by intent or by innocence, disturbs her psyche, and some never recover. I did recover but not without great pain and remorse.

My heart was heavy, but we were still involved in summer swimming programs, outdoor sports, and preparation for the new school year. Teresa had trained her beloved horse, Kishan, to the point of perfection, and she was riding all over the vacant lots near our home. Our house was always full of teenagers, parties, laughter, animals barking, or a horse neighing in the backyard. How does one keep an attractive lawn groomed with a horse tromping down the grass? There was little time for heaviness!

Foreboding Hangs On

Now it was time to put the boat away and prepare for the next school year. We were glad Don Ralph would be going to Lewis & Clark; at least he would not be leaving home yet! Yet in spite of the excitement of a new school year, I still carried a certain foreboding in my heart. What was it? I did not need to be concerned about Don Ralph. He had graduated at the top of his class and was going to a local university in the fall to study the field of medicine. All our children had lofty ideas for their futures, and they all did well in school—including being members of the National Honor Society. Don and I were proud parents.

So why did I have such foreboding in my heart? I knew that our children were emerging as finely polished jewels and would soon be launching off to pursue their own dreams. Though that made me nostalgic, and I did not want this season of life to end, that was not what the foreboding was. I tried to put the uneasy feelings in the deep recesses of my heart into a locked room!

Everything was going along great in the early months of the school year. Before we knew it, it was already time for the holidays. We had a great Thanksgiving dinner with Don's parents, and a lavish, laden table showed our prosperity in this Promised Land. His parents even seemed to let up on us as they viewed our success. Christmas came with a tree surrounded by joyously wrapped and love-filled gift packages. During the Christmas break, we watched Teresa closely because she kept saying she felt like she had the flu. She even turned down some dates with friends. When she came into our bedroom in the wee hours of the morning on the day after Christmas, we knew something was very wrong. And so we took her to the emergency room.

Her white blood-cell count was way up, and the doctor thought it was probably her appendix. He opted to remove it ASAP. I still had the horrible foreboding in my heart as we anxiously waited for her to come out of surgery. I had to pace in the waiting lounge, as I just could not sit still because of my concern. During the surgery they removed a cyst on an ovary but found normal cells in the appendix. Her urine was normal, and the doctor said the blood counts were normal as well. She seemed all right afterward and was surprised by my concern.

Teresa seemed to recover quickly, and life continued on as before except for what I was feeling in my heart. What was this foreboding in my spirit? I just could not shake it. I had a foreboding when we were being pursued by all the charismatic people, but this feeling in my heart was different…Maybe it was just my remorse over the abortion still lurking. I tried to shove it deep within and out of my thoughts.

No Time for Regrets

After the holidays school resumed, and all the children were extremely active in school and church activities. Cean Michael was a bundle of energy. Chasing after him was not an easy assignment, and it seemed to take all of us to keep him corralled!

We had dear friends from college who had moved back to Portland. Also a friend from Colfax moved to Portland with her doctor husband. We decided to get together once a week, renewing friendships and solving religious and political issues. Cean Michael was always my little companion. He was an observant toddler, and at eighteen months of age he was able to give me directions to get to my friend Jane's house; she had recently moved to Portland. He so looked forward to these outings that he would stand beside me in the car, with my arm around him—no seat belts required yet.

On one occasion when we gals were enjoying each other's company, Cean was very quiet but seemingly entertaining himself. Later that night Don and I got a call from our friends, stating that their toilet was plugged. Don immediately went over to see what the problem was, knowing our son was the culprit. He had to take the whole unit apart and found several monkeys clogged in the lip, unable to come up or go down. This was a childhood game Jane had put out to entertain Cean. Don removed the monkeys, and the friendship was intact! It seemed this little guy was always experimenting to see what the outcome would be. Talks or lectures seemed to do no good.

A Dual Track

I was pulled in so many directions with the pressing needs of the family, but I was also trying desperately to put Teresa's scare behind me. This was difficult when she kept having flare-ups of unidentified fever and pain throughout her body. At these times we would rush her to the doctor, only to find the blood work showing nothing. The doctor said she was just recovering from the appendectomy compounded by her busy schedule and usually diagnosed it as pleurisy. Almost three months had transpired since that surgery, so it seemed odd to me that she would still be recovering. Does a routine appendectomy cause that many lingering symptoms and for that duration? My concern did not help the heavy cloud hanging over my head and heart.

We were facing other challenges as well, and it seemed to me that some of our joy was dissipating. The charismatic associations were seemingly taking a toll on my relationship with Don. He had been so dazzled by the charismatic leaders who had told him about all the power he could have. It seemed to me that he was more involved in this supposedly charismatic movement, his students, and being an icon on campus than he was in his marriage.

As I observed the movement, I noticed that the proclaimed new spirituality was linked closely to sexuality. The new sexual freedom was not only hitting the young people in high schools and colleges, but it was also influencing churches, sensitivity groups, and the charismatic movement. Though it did not affect us directly, the fallout was never far away. I wondered if the attention was going to Don's head, for he was being sought out at every turn. He was in demand for speaking engagements and more and more classes, such was his teaching skill. I continually wondered if I was a married single. What had happened to our team ministry? It seemed we had gotten off track and that our original dreams were losing ground. We were living on a dual track at best.

But in reality I did not know if my concern was for Teresa, about the charismatics, or about my needing a renewal in my marriage. Was the pressure just cascading in on us?

During that time, as was often the custom, some friends had come to see us from our beloved Colfax (Helen and Dale Culbertson). She had been our organist at the church where we served, and I had sung many solos with her accompanying me. She was also Don Ralph and Teresa's first piano teacher. Every Wednesday night when we lived in Colfax, Don Ralph and Teresa would ride the school bus out to the Culbertson's' wheat ranch some twenty miles from town.

Helen and Dale would then bring them home on their way to lead the choir practice. Such dear friends they were, and now they brought their daughter, Susan, who had grown into a young beauty. When Don Ralph saw her it made his heart skip several beats.

When the Culbertson's' visited Portland, we met them at the Plush Pippin, a pie house. Elsie, my friend from the old weekly coffee clutch, was Helen's sister, so she and her husband joined us for an evening of joyous celebration with these nearly grown young people. Susan's brother was also in the party, and Don Ralph excused himself and invited Susan and Craig to cruise downtown Portland in his GTO. So it was that at the pie house, Don Ralph was smitten with this newly grown-up beauty—a nursing student in Spokane.

Don Ralph was doing well at Lewis & Clark College, still working at McDonald's, and being a solid part of the family. Now he began making weekly trips to Spokane in his GTO, and soon Don Ralph and Susan became engaged. Don Ralph's draft number had come up at fifty-five, so—rather than be drafted—he made plans to join the ROTC. He enlisted in the Washington Air National Guard in Spokane—obviously to spend the weekends near Susan. For the next few months, their engagement gave us all great joy, knowing we would be forever connected to our dear friends from Colfax. My foreboding still remained at a subliminal level, but watching these two young people in love made our hearts bubble over with joy.

CHAPTER 15

Unthinkable

> What I feared has come upon me…
> —Jʙ 3:25, NIV

It Can't Be

I t was on a Friday in March when Father Truehella—or Father T, as we called him—caught me in the hallway at Good Samaritan Hospital and said Don had called, and I needed to go home immediately. I had been so impressed with Father T after Don had given the graduation speech that I had signed up to do volunteer work at Good Samaritan, thinking this would appease some of my foreboding.

I knew since it was the Friday before spring break, Don would be finalizing his grades, turning them in, and planning for a week of fun with the family. I learned later that as he finished up, he received a call on the intercom to call home. He immediately dialed home, and Teresa told him she could not stand up for pain. He left school immediately to find his beloved daughter crying and in pure agony. I drove home with a huge lump in my throat and adrenaline pumping through my body. When I arrived Teresa was writhing in pain. I took her to the emergency room quickly, and Don stayed home and waited for the other children to arrive from school.

When you go to the emergency room, you do not know who your doctor will be. We knew there was the possibility that a doctor we didn't know would be on duty that afternoon and that after we were checked in and paid our one dollar; we would be ushered into a room to wait for whomever. Indeed, an unfamiliar doctor finally came in. He was not friendly at all and abruptly told Teresa to get on the scale. She could hardly stand and began crying, and in response he said, "Stop being a temperamental teenager, and do what I tell you."

I was almost too stunned to speak, but I pointed out the little red markings on her skin and her pallor and said she was unusually tired since having her appendix removed in December. He ignored this information. I tried to control my crying and told him she was immobile from the pain in her legs. He did some initial tests and said nothing more.

Another doctor came in and gave her a Demerol shot, which seemed to ease the pain. He suggested it was probably a muscle spasm or pleurisy—as had been suggested before—and left the room. The nurse came in with a prescription for Valium and said the doctor would like to see her in a week. Both Teresa and I were crying on the way home and spoke very little. We were both angry and upset. Couldn't they gauge the intense pain my daughter was in?

When we got home and told Don what had transpired, he and I were both livid. We had another college friend we had connected with since moving to Beaverton whose husband was a doctor. We had run into her and her husband, Dr. Don Ramsthal, at a charismatic meeting. However, at this moment I did not care about their associations; we placed a call to Dr. Ramsthal and told him about our experience at Kaiser Permanente. He said to bring Teresa to his house, and he would look at her, but he said it would have to be later that evening.

We half carried Teresa into to his home about ten o'clock that night, on March 17. He gave her a morphine shot for the pain, and then he made a phone call to a local pharmacy for Empirin 4. Our doctor friend—who was in private practice, unassociated with Kaiser—was livid too, and he said he would make a call to Kaiser in the morning. When we told him Teresa's symptoms, he had his suspicions, but he kept them from us.

That was a very long night, with Teresa crying throughout from the intense pain, though she said it was somewhat relieved by the shots. Don and I tried to comfort her with hot pads and by rubbing her legs, all the while praying with bleeding hearts. We had gone through childhood diseases, like Don Ralph's mono, but this had a different feel about it. That horrid foreboding lunged out of my subliminal mind and hung over my head.

The next morning our friend demanded an appointment with a specialist for Teresa, as promised. Before leaving for the hospital, Don was in prayer and read the scripture Proverbs 3:5–8 (AMPC). Verse eight reads, "It shall be health to your nerves and sinews and marrow and moistening to your bones." I quoted that verse over and over in hope it would remove the terror in my heart.

Don and I left Christy and Michele at home to care for Cean Michael and drove to the hospital. We went to the main Kaiser hospital near Swan Island — clear across town from our home in Beaverton, our home of promise! I dreaded going to the main Kaiser hospital, as that was where I had spent time in room 101! The ride was painful for Teresa, and it seemed we would never arrive.

When we finally got there, the atmosphere was far friendlier than it had been in the Beaverton clinic the afternoon before. We again paid our one-dollar copay, and they did not waste any time admitting Teresa and placing her in a room. It was a Dr. Gurwith, an oncologist, who came in to see her. He said it was obvious she was a very sick girl. They took bone marrow from her breastbone for testing. We were asked to wait outside the room, but I could hear her screams.

As I paced, I watched all the doctors putting on protective gear before they entered Teresa's room. After some time—hours, it seemed to Don and I—a very somber doctor came out to talk with us. He said the marrow was so packed; they could not get a sample to test, which was an indicator of leukemia. In a callous tone, he said she was old enough that she should be told, and her dad said he would handle it.

When the doctor said *leukemia*, my body went limp, my legs buckled, and the hallway swirled about me. When Don helped me up, the doctor said we could go in now and talk with our daughter, but I was weeping. I felt like all the blood had drained from my head, and I was unable to move my legs, so Don went in and shared the news with Teresa. She asked where I was and told her dad she wanted to see me.

As Don came out of her room to tell me Teresa wanted to talk to me, he found me weeping uncontrollably, too stunned to move. I tried to compose my-self enough to walk, but my devastation at such news was complete. Maybe they had made a mistake, just like they had with Don Ralph when they thought his mono was leukemia. With that thought I walked into the room, a new sanctuary of prayer for all of us.

Teresa said, "Mom, you know God will heal me! This will give us an oppor-tunity to write a book about miracles that still happen." She seemed free from pain for the moment and was happy that they had found out she was not being a temperamental teenager! In her innocence she did not see the gravity of the situation. I looked at the blood spots still on her arms, indicating a low platelet count.

We were asked to go to another Kaiser clinic to speak with a Dr. Glass, who would be treating Teresa. He was a pediatrician as well as an oncologist. In a state of shock, Don and I kissed and hugged Teresa good-bye and said we would be back as soon as we met with Dr. Glass. When we arrived at the clinic, I was so distraught I could not go in but paced back and forth in the parking lot. In contrast Don seemed confident. He assured me Teresa would be OK, and he went into the clinic without me.

When he finished with Dr. Glass, Don told me what the doctor had said, although I was too hysterical of mind to comprehend it. He said Teresa had a 40 percent chance of beating this horrific disease, which had been diagnosed as acute myeloblastic leukemia. The doctors had told us they did not do a marrow test from the hip because of the risk of bleeding. If bleeding occurred, she would need platelets, and the blood bank was closed until Monday. They would start chemotherapy on Monday. The doctor made this diagnosis before he was able to get a bone-marrow sample, so sure he was of the symptoms. *Myeloblastic* meant the worst form of leukemia.

I was overcome. "What to do…what to do?" was all I could say.

Don called Dr. Ramsthal, our friend, to tell him of the findings. Dr. Ramsthal said he had suspected lupus or leukemia, either one an undesirable diagnosis. Don immediately called some of our friends requesting prayer. Indeed, news travels fast, and from that point on we began getting calls from our past and present acquaintances all across the United States.

When we went back to the hospital, it was already late afternoon, and in that room twenty of Teresa's and Don Ralph's friends were gathered around Teresa, joking and telling her to hurry up, get well, and get back to them. It was no fun without her, they said. She was so loved by all. There was positive energy flowing, and Teresa seemed to be at peace and her usual joyful self. I was still a basket case, but I tried to embrace her friends, who were giving nothing but hugs to Don and me. We thanked them for coming.

The Gorilla Who Walked the Halls

When Dr. Glass came to Teresa's room, he seemed very gentle and loving. He was a young Jewish doctor with young children of his own. At that moment my spirit was lifted, and I believed we could lick this and be a testimony of God's healing power. However, when I stated I would stay all night with Teresa, the supervisor nurse—a big, burly head nurse who had the appearance of a gorilla in a military uniform—was sent in to talk to me. Ms. Blackstone motioned me out to the hallway and informed me, "*No*, you cannot stay the night; you will need to be here at the end, not now!" I could not believe my ears. She did not even appear human, much less compassionate, as one who dealt with pain and suffering daily.

I said, "What end?"

An Angel of the Lord

When I told Don about the conversation, he immediately called his new friend, Father Truehella. There had been no chaplain on duty when we'd checked in—or at least one did not come to Teresa's room. When Don told Father T of the conversation with the military gorilla, all he could say was, "We do not practice medicine that way." He said he would come over that evening. And that he did. Teresa loved him instantly, for he took her hand and gently made the sign of the cross on her forehead, prayed for her, and said he would be on this journey with her. Such gentleness he showed her. It was such a contrast from that evil woman who had made our journey a nightmare. She would always be lurking around the many guests who came to see Teresa daily.

Father Truehella prayed with us, rebuked Satan, and declared he had no part in this child. I begged Father T to tell me he believed in healing. He stated that God loved Teresa far more than we did…and that was all he would say.

The gorilla lady came in and told us it was time to leave. Father Truehella simply prayed for her as well and took his sweet time in leaving the room. Seven pastors came and prayed for Teresa in the first nine days. But it was Father T and her own father whom she wanted near.

Visible to All

We were a visible family involved in church, school, and community activities, and we became the target of every religious and nonreligious group who had answers, solutions, or remedies. Teresa had already been noted for her tremendous influence through her music and testimony. As the word of her illness got out, we were surrounded by love and by many who really believed and expected a miracle. This strengthened my heart, or maybe I just made little compartments in my heart for fear and hope. After all, I reasoned, no way would a loving God take or harm this jewel. I did not believe God picked off the wings of butterflies just for pleasure!

I had prayed so often that if I was to learn anything in the way of living more righteously, God would teach me in any way other than through touching my children. Fundamentalist teaching really had imprinted on my heart that righteous living brought protection from the evil in the world. If you did not follow God's will to the letter, He would inflict something on you to make you change your ways and do His bidding. This was the inner battle raging in my heart.

One morning Christy read a scripture about the blind man, where Jesus stated this was not a sickness unto death. Christy became a rock who kept the home front from collapsing completely.

On Our Knees

Don told Teresa that after all she had gone through—referring to all of the earlier accidents in her short life—Jesus would not forsake her now. People in the charismatic movement began bringing us books on healing and miracles. I did not care about my feelings brought on from our experiences in Aberdeen with the wannabes. I was ready to turn over every stone to have my daughter healed and restored to health. When we got home, Don gave me a sedative, for I could not calm down. I needed to be at the hospital with my daughter. Suddenly it all fell into place: so this was why I'd had such a foreboding in past months!

Early the next day—Sunday morning—we went to the hospital. Because the chemotherapy could not be started until Monday, I spent the time rubbing Teresa's legs, trying to relieve the intense pain. Some dear friends came to be with us in addition to young and old friends coming to see Teresa throughout the day. Teresa set her pain aside and graciously received these friends. The room was always filled with laughter and love, but this was a totally new scenario for a family with a Disney theology!

Monday morning came, they did the bone marrow test in the hip, and it confirmed what they had suspected. I was hysterical with fear. Many friends continued to come to be with us. Don told Teresa the prognosis and treatment while I waited in the lobby, for I could not bear to be present. But when I did go in and began to cry again, Teresa once again said, "Don't cry, Mom. I think it is an honor. Now I can be on Kathryn Kuhlman" (referring to the healing evangelist's show, *I Believe in Miracles*). Again we were asked to go to the other clinic and confer with Dr. Glass. Once there I still could not go in. I wanted to run, run, run…anywhere, but I did not want to be in this scenario!

Dr. Glass outlined the treatment for Don, saying that 50 to 70 percent of those with Teresa's diagnosis were not able to go into remission, but Teresa's age was an advantage. He said they would start the chemo late that night. The intent of the chemo was to poison the replication of leukemia cells. The doctor said Teresa would have nine days of intravenous chemotherapy injections and then fifteen days of rest. During the chemo treatment, there would be intolerable vomiting in the great white porcelain. The doctor also said the bone marrow test had shown that the bones were 95 percent packed with leukemia cells, which was typical for myeloblastic leukemia.

Since we could not stay in the hospital, at least not yet, we went to a Full Gospel meeting that evening. I was so vulnerable and open for any word from the Lord that I agreed to go without hesitation. Don asked for prayer and stated the reason. A tall man who towered over me appeared to me to look like what an angel of the Lord must resemble. When he took me in his arms and hugged me, I nearly collapsed to the floor. It truly felt like God himself had touched me. I knew not who he was, but he was very gentle and affirming. He said nothing but was quietly speaking in what I thought was a foreign language. Was he speaking in tongues? I never saw that man again that evening. That night I was able to sit in the meeting without being offended, but I didn't comprehend a word that was said throughout the evening. I was too distraught!

We numbly got through that first nine days of chemo, which used a drug called cytosine. At the end of the first series of chemo, tests showed that the bones were still 95 percent packed. During that nine-day series, Teresa developed sores in her mouth, had a septic infection in her bloodstream, and was given amoxicillin (an antibiotic), among various other drugs, to control what was going on. They continually drew her blood to check on the count and to do cultures. She was given several packs of platelets as well as blood transfusions, and tubes were continually hooked up to many parts of her body. Who knew what was going on but the doctors?

Pastors from every denomination came to call on and pray for this young jewel, both in the hospital and when she came home. Her door had a sign that said no visitors were allowed, but they ignored it and barged in to see their young friend. The gorilla was still stalking the halls, peering in at the crowd every opportunity she had. Not once did she encourage us or give us support. Rules were her rule! But we did perceive that high powers in the hospital had silenced her!

Friends Galore

Teresa had dated Ron Miller for some time. He was a handsome, delightful young man from the Assembly. He and his sisters, who also loved Teresa, brought in stuffed animals and treats and loaded her bed with loving trinkets. Her room smelled like a floral shop, so crowded it was with flowers and plants. It was good this was spring break week. Usually spring break was a time to get the boat out on the water, for eating out, and for sundaes at Farrell's, but not this spring. Christy and Michele had to be left at home and in charge of caring for Cean Michael, preparing their own food and not really comprehending what was happening to their idealistic family!

Our dear friends, Durwood and Priscilla, were constantly by our sides, encouraging us. Durwood was a private detective at that time and always carried his gun. On one particular night, he bounced into Teresa's room, laid his revolver beside her, and said, "Teresa, you tell them either get the needle in the first time or…" which sent Teresa into hysterical laughter. To spend any time with Durwood was to spend time in helpless laughter, for he had jokes memorized for every occasion. He and Priscilla had two lovely daughters as well who became babysitters for Cean Michael. We were truly blessed with a plethora of friends who were constantly by our sides encouraging us.

Trying to Act and to Be Normal

On March 30 Teresa was finally able to go home. She had been in the hospital for twelve days and now would go home to have daily injections from a PICC line placed in her wrist. Our dear neighbor, Delores Mahn, who was a nurse, offered to come over and give those injections, making sure only medication was injected into Teresa's bloodstream. (It would be dangerous if air was allowed through the needle.) But Teresa was able to be home only until April 3, when she was in dire need of platelets and more whole blood. So back to the hospital we drove, with heavy hearts.

It was hard to keep the sessions in perspective, as Teresa was in and out of the hospital. She would be critically ill, and then in a few days she would be home and living life as though nothing had happened. This became our new normal. The sepsis, internal bleeding, and mouth sores were constant companions. She would go from hemorrhaging from every part of her body, ingesting the chemo, and sitting over the great white porcelain to being up on water skis in her pink polka-dot bikini. Even though it was her senior year, she did most of her school-work at home. She did go to school when she was able, and she kept her 4.0 grade-point average.

Teresa continued painting, writing music, and singing in those wonderful pain-free intervals. She almost had to make a weekly schedule to keep up with those wanting her to sing at Christian coffee shops and churches and even in the hospital. She really was gaining a reputation of being St. Teresa. In my heart I was wishing I had named her Jane!

In the midst of this whole saga, Teresa was able to go to her senior prom with a delightful young man named Michael Baugh. He gave her a wrist corsage that covered up the PICC that was still visible on her wrist. Prom occurred during one of her good periods, and everything seemed so normal, so natural, and she seemed so like the same Teresa, with boys in pursuit. She would accept no sympathy and was determined to stay in the same active role she had adopted from birth on. In fact she was finding great satisfaction in her ministry of music throughout the metro area. Her friends did not run from her but seemed to want to be with her constantly.

Because we were so visible in the community, we became the talk of churches, Don's college associates, and the children's school. Didn't friends always say they wanted to hook their wagon to our star? We were invited to a Wednesday night healing service at the First Baptist Church in downtown Portland. Everyone was proclaiming Teresa was to be healed for the glory of God. Even with all my angst against the charismatic, I could not risk leaving any stone unturned. As I sat there not knowing anyone, I felt an arm go around my shoulder. I looked to my side and behind me to see who it was who had touched me…All hands were in laps. I was puzzled.

This was the same season when Don Ralph had fallen in love with Susan and become engaged, and he was now making weekly trips to Spokane for his National Guard assignment, just so he could be near her. We tried to keep everything in perspective, delighting in this new love but unable to completely enter into their happiness.

During one of Teresa's reprieves, our beloved Colfax church was in transition and needed a pastor, so Don was asked to drive over on weekends and be their interim pastor until they found a full-time pastor. Though Teresa was scheduled for a bone marrow test on the Thursday we were to leave, Dr. Glass said, "Go ahead; we will schedule it a week later." We took Teresa and one of her current boyfriends, the one who had taken her to the prom. It was like an escape from our present reality and was so refreshing. Don once again preached a dynamic sermon, and it was so good to be back in our Camelot, if only briefly!

Back at home Teresa was in the midst of a good reprieve. We had brought all the flowers and gifts home, and her room looked like a flower shop. And more flowers continued to be delivered daily. Dr. Glass did not apprise us of the prognosis weekly. Well, if he did, I perceived only the positive. We saw only the effects of the chemotherapy, the platelets given, the blood transfusions, and then the reprieves. Teresa had such gratitude in her heart for all the people who sent cards and flowers and continually came to see her that she wrote the following song and sent it with a thank you note.

Sometimes

Sometimes, I just want to open up myself to your Spirit and let you take me away so gently. When I imagine myself as a stallion, tossing my head and kicking my heels, I feel strength surging through and through me with energy and life. Then I feel like a bird, hand in hand with you, soaring gracefully, quietly over your peaceful blue skies. This is how I would describe your refreshing touch. It gives me life boiling in every vein. I feel I could move a mountain with the power of life that flows through my veins. Then I am brought into the presence of my Father God. And love in its purest form permeates my being. I feel so at peace and so quiet in my spirit, and yet at the same time I feel such power and strength. I love, my whole being loves my God, and I want to please him with all of my heart, more than I have ever wanted anything. I want to give back all that he gives me, to make his day worthwhile. I want Him to proudly and lovingly smile upon me. I want Him to be pleased at what He has made and is making of me. At times when I am still enough to take what is offered and relax in His divine loving Spirit, I come back all afresh, whole of mind, spirit, and soul, with strength overabounding, ready to conquer the world again. I sure do delight in God. In Him I have real life!

At that time I was reading about St. Teresa, and the similarities between these two young women named Teresa were alarming! The words shared were so similar to our daughter's spirit and heartbeat. The words made me uneasy, even though I knew how tender our Teresa's heart was to her Heavenly Father. St. Teresa continually proclaimed her love of Jesus. When I got to the part of the book when St. Teresa died at the age of twenty-four, I had to put it aside.

Turning Over Every Stone

During one of our earlier weeks at home, Teresa was developing the painful sores in her mouth again, but other than that she was bored, unable to be with her horse because of the low blood count and at risk for massive infections. My choir director, the gentle tiger, shyly came to the house. She wondered if it would be all right to bring us something. I said of course it was all right, and she went to her car and brought in a fifty-pound bag of carrots and a lot of garlic. She also had a juicer but saw that I had one too. She was one of those health nuts, and I welcomed her and the carrots instantly.

Don and I had both begun to fast, for that was recommended by the charismatics, claiming it would help God to hear our prayers. I was like a dutiful child, doing everything I was told. We did not laugh at Suzanne for her home remedy, for we were willing to try anything. Besides that we loved Suzanne. When Teresa began running high temperatures and suffering from severe headaches along with the mouth sores, we would put carrots and garlic through the juicer. Ruth Lowe, the lady who lived across the trestle in Colfax, had sent a juicer earlier. She too believed in home remedies.

When we had a quart processed, Teresa would drink it without complaint, although she said the garlic really burned all the way down. We did note the yellow tint to her skin as well as the continual smell of garlic. However, a temperature of 102 degrees would come down to normal within twenty minutes. This drink became a daily ritual. When I asked Dr. Glass about the carrot juice, he said, "Sure, if you don't care if she turns yellow!"

Teresa would try to go back to school only to return home after first period. The sores in her mouth were unbearable as well as the headaches and the leg pains. This told us that all the cancer cells were not yet destroyed. We were in a continual fog of disbelief but numbly kept up the fight. The good news was that Dr. Glass had decreed we could spend day and night with our daughter, against Ms. Gorilla's decree! And from that moment on, we never left her side except for brief moments when it was necessary to take care of pressing matters at home.

What Is Normal?

In May Teresa's former boyfriend's family, the Millers, invited our whole family to join them for a ski trip to Cove Palisades, a favorite lake for waterskiing in Central Oregon. They had children who were our children's ages as well as the son who dated Teresa. They were devastated by the news of Teresa's illness, as they loved her even as their own. Teresa seemed much better, so we agreed to the trip. It had been some time since the last series of chemo, so we felt her blood levels were high enough not to endanger her further.

The Millers had gone earlier to set up camp, but Don could not cut classes to leave until later. We arrived about ten o'clock at night, after having to drive up a very dark and winding road to the campsite. The campsite was dimly lit by only lanterns, and the stars were brilliant in that Central Oregon beauty, but it was no place for our daughter who was battling leukemia. By the time we got there, Teresa's mouth had begun bleeding, and nothing would stop it. So Sharon, Ron's mother, and I decided to take one of the cars and go back to a motel in Madras, about fifteen miles away. We would stay there until we could either go back the next day or take Teresa home.

At ten o'clock at night, it was extremely cold in that mountainous lake air, so it was a good move to go to a nice warm motel room. Once we had checked in at a motel, in two rooms, Teresa was able to take a bath, read her Bible, and comfortably climb into bed.

This was so different from our usual family recreational times. Was this the new normal? I was trying to hold it together for my daughter, but Sharon said she really needed to talk to me about her marriage issues. Sharon and I shared the room next to Teresa's, so she was able to hear our conversation from the adjoining room and asked me later, in private, if there was no one who loved her husband as I did mine. She had not yet witnessed the chasm that was growing between Don and me. Was it a chasm, or was it just this unbelievable situation we had found ourselves to be the central characters?

I pondered our situation, and I knew my love for Don was deep. Perhaps this new drama in our lives was causing him to retreat, like he had as a child. He felt responsible for making everything OK for his young family, and he had learned to hide his fears as a young child. I wondered how he was able to continue to teach with this sword of Damocles swinging heavily over our heads.

Miracle of miracles, the next day we did go back up to the lake, as the bleeding had subsided. Teresa had a fabulous time. Daytime brought very hot weather with nothing but sunshine, and she spent much time up on skis. It was just like old times, and it was easy to completely forget what had transpired the night before. Several young guys vying for her affection made the day seem perfectly normal. And I watched, as always, for the smallest sign of healing.

Help or Harm

When we got home that Sunday night, another charismatic acquaintance came to the house and stated the Lord had spoken to her, saying, "I have called her, but I will not take her home. I have a work for her to do." In fact she called several times with new prophecies, all claiming healing. We really became a target for the charismatics once again. However, now I was looking only for signs of answered prayer instead of for the white magic I had observed previously. I was too distraught to even register whether it had the ring of truth.

I felt more comfortable, though, with a call from a friend from our Valley Presbyterian Church—Venita Frye, whom I considered a saint. She said she had called together a prayer meeting, asking only those who believed in miracles to come. Another Presbyterian church in Portland called to tell Don their whole church was in prayer on Teresa's behalf. We received calls from people we had never met. One such gentleman called to say he had a prophecy for Teresa. He said God would heal her and shine through her to others, which in turn would bring glory and honor to His Holy Name. Again I prayed, "Oh, dear Lord, please do not let this be white magic." And then it happened!

Monsters Descending

Teresa's medical routine was still chemo, in the hospital, out of the hospital, rest, periods of normalcy, and packets of platelets, transfusions, and fighting blood infections. It was like a roller coaster of despair and hope…up, down, up, down. Our hearts sped around.

It was a Tuesday evening, and Don had a night class. Teresa was lying on the couch in much pain and distress. During this time she was staying at home and making periodic trips to the hospital for outpatient injections of the chemo. The other girls were doing their homework. It was a lovely spring night. A lady we had never met, called and said the Lord had told her to come to pray for Teresa, and of course, not wanting to leave any stone unturned, I said that would be fine.

When I hung up, Christy said she had a bad feeling and said she wished I had not agreed to let the woman come. Soon there was a knock on the front door, and when I went to open it, there was a woman in a wheelchair and four scruffy-looking young people of indeterminate age. They were extremely dirty and shabby young men. They did not wait for an invitation to enter but barged in; pushing Mrs. Petersen in her wheelchair and saying they were there to see Teresa. We had heard about the Petersens, who were involved with Father Bennett in Ballard, but had never met them. Teresa was lying on the couch, visible at their entrance.

Before any of us could say anything, they pulled out their bottles of oil and started mauling Teresa with their oily hands. They started praying in loud, almost screaming voices, all babbling, while claiming healing. They described her as a dirty old man with sores covering his body. They said they perceived great sin in her life. Then they told her she needed to confess her sins before the Lord would heal her.

By that time Teresa was frightened, saying nothing but looking to me to rescue her. When both Christy and Michele started to cry and Cean ran for cover in my arms, the unwelcome group abruptly left, believing they had accomplished their mission, never saying a word to anyone but Teresa. They left, dancing all the way to their dumpy-looking car. One of the scruffy-looking guys was shouting "hallelujah" all the way down the inclining lawn to their car. They had left havoc within the walls of our home.

Christy said, "I want my dad. Please get my dad." I knew I could not reach Don, for he would be in class, so I called Dr. Ramsthal, and he came to be with us until Don got home from class. While Dr. Ramsthal was there, a lady who was charismatic called from Aberdeen to tell me I had to praise to defeat the enemy, which only made me cry harder. Following that call, Susan's aunt called. She said she just wanted to quote Hebrews 10:35 for me: "Do not throw away this confident trust in the Lord…"

Our phone rang without stop: calls from people we knew, had met only briefly, or did not even know. I felt like ripping the phone off the wall…but I did answer each call. I guess I was waiting for that one miracle call!

Could It Get Worse

We were all distraught over the invasion of our privacy, and we knew not how to assess those people. Teresa became sicker as the night wore on. She was bleeding from the mouth and running a high fever. Early the next morning, we rushed her once again to the clinic, where they would do more blood cultures. Dr. Glass said she had to be admitted to the hospital. We had to set the horror of the supposed ministers of the Lord aside and start this new battle. (We never saw nor heard from Mrs. Petersen or her cohorts again.)

Throughout the day Teresa would doze off briefly only to awaken and ask, "Is the throne room still present?" We had shared with Teresa the story of the Shekinah Glory following the children of Israel as they roamed in the Sinai desert for many years. And yes, it truly felt like the Shekinah Glory was surrounding us, or surely we would not have made it. We were shattered from those thoughtless charismatic people invading our home.

Teresa's mouth was hemorrhaging; it seemed the whole mouth was sloughing away, giving her a new mouth. The crisis of that night passed, but we realized the battle was not over. She continued to cough up blood and phlegm and was unable to lie down. They kept giving her drugs to help alleviate the pain in her head. X-rays were taken that showed a growth in the back of her neck to be the cause of much of the pain. She was taken off the antibiotics, though she remained on heavy doses of pain medication.

The next morning Dr. Glass told me our daughter had nearly expired during the night. I knew, for both Teresa and I had felt the presence of God in her room. Don was at home with the children and preparing for early morning classes the next day. I had spent most of the night on my knees in prayer. Dr. Glass told us they were trying to kill the leukemia cells but were not 100 percent successful. Teresa would need another series of the injections of cytosine, and she would also need to have radiation treatment for the breakout on her neck. That would start immediately. She was not released from the hospital that day.

Teresa continued to battle and fight for her life in the hospital. This hospital stay became routine, like the others, but when a young woman bounced into the room, pulled the curtain, and cockily said I should leave because it was bath time, Teresa's eyes sparked, and I knew there was no way she was going to let this student nurse give her a sponge bath. The girl, probably close to Teresa's age, was in training. What indignity, what invasion of her self-respect and privacy! Teresa's anger slowly rose, and she said her mother was not to leave the room, and furthermore she would be able to give herself a bath. When Teresa asked for the supervisor, the girl left, never to return.

Teresa was sorry for her outburst, but she could not handle the condescending and patronizing manner the young trainees addressed her. This was only one of many degrading experiences Teresa tolerated over the weeks to come. Nurses could not find veins to insert the chemo needle and would try over and over until Teresa could bear it no longer. But as her veins began to shrink, only the experienced nurses ever entered her room. I became an advocate for professional care on all levels.

Home at Last

Finally the latest siege was over, and we were able to take Teresa home for another reprieve. We knew the battle was not over, but it was a joyous family that welcomed Teresa home that day. As we passed Finley's cemetery on the way home, she had her head out the window just to breathe the fresh spring air. The sword of Damocles was gone for only a moment, but the sight of that cemetery put gratitude in my heart. Teresa was elated to breathe fresh air, go home, and see her horse, her room, and a few friends. She was home but had to travel back and forth to the hospital for a series of seven X-ray treatments to reduce the growth in her neck.

We had a black couch in the family room just off the kitchen. When Teresa was on outpatient treatment, she opted to sleep on that couch. Don and I would take turns sleeping on the floor, so we could be near to give pain medication or just comfort her. She was so very ill from needing both radium and chemo injections. Don would always take the Friday night watch. He would sleep close by and be in prayer most of the night. We were faithful to the doctor's instructions, as we truly felt the medical community was doing divine work for our daughter.

Would It Never End

However, we continued to get calls and advice from our charismatic friends. One of these friends came over when Teresa was lying in our bed and said we needed to stop all treatment, or God would not get the glory. We were beginning to sort out all the unwanted advice and thoughtless interventions by such people as the Petersen group. It seemed we were fighting a battle on many fronts.

That evening I was reading Jeremiah 39:18. In fact my Bible had fallen open to that verse: "Because you have trusted me, I will preserve your life and keep you safe." I was encouraged, remembering the night when Dr. Glass had said we almost lost our daughter. And indeed Teresa was feeling better, still drinking our concoction of carrot juice and garlic. In fact she was well enough to take part in her friend Kathy's (one of her horse-riding buddies) wedding—and so far she did not have any hair loss from the radiation. Teresa had to wear a patch over her neck where they had done the biopsy, but somehow she camouflaged it with jewelry and her smiling face.

With a mixture of joy and fear, we awaited the next hospitalization. We took Teresa to Dr. Glass following the weekend of the wedding. He did another bone-marrow test and sent her home. We were waiting for the blood counts to rise so the next series of chemotherapy could start. The doctor soon called, and Teresa went back into Kaiser for more chemo. This time it was even more difficult, and she suffered much pain and bleeding.

Dr. Glass took the blood cells further and further to zero, which opened Teresa to more blood infections. On many nights she would bleed from every organ in her body. Even so, she still maintained a positive attitude and wrote songs from the love in her heart.

Further Treatment

Whereas the first round of chemo seemed to leave no ill effects, no hair loss, and no weight loss, the second round was to leave us fearful. By Dr. Glass's decree, I had been allowed to spend nights with Teresa. She was so sick throughout the night, often needing platelets and red blood cells late into the night or early morning. I usually knelt by her bed praying or sitting quietly, pleading with God to give her relief. Her fever would rise to 104 degrees, and I would sponge her off in an attempt to bring it down. Early one morning her nose began to hemor-rhage, and when she was taking a bath, she said she could not see well.

Dr. Emerick, an ear, eye, and nose specialist, came to see her. He was a gentle man, a member of one of Portland's Presbyterian churches. He had been a mis-sionary to India, and it was again instant love for Teresa. When he saw her Bible on the stand beside her bed, they had an instant rapport. However, when he diagnosed her eye, he said it would take six months for her to regain her normal sight. The eye had hemorrhaged along with the nose. Her nose continued to hemorrhage for two days. I was at the hospital around the clock, and dear friends took Cean Michael until Christine and Michele returned from school.

The hospital staff continued to take blood for cultures. They had to put Teresa on strong intravenous antibiotics to make sure they attacked the right bacteria. To make it worse, she had severe reactions to the antibiotics, including a full-body rash and pounding headaches. She began coughing up blood and phlegm again. Dr. Emerick watched her closely. She was unable to eat anything but popsicles and Jell-O.

Teresa told us she felt she was being refined as pure gold. I was over the hill emotionally, but I tried to say only positive comments and not allow any negative comments from others either. I noted that Teresa was only another patient to the staff, but to Don and me she was our daughter. The staff often became impatient with her.

Once it was ten o'clock at night, time for a shift change, when we rang for the young nurse. She hurriedly gave Teresa platelets, and then it was time for her to be off her shift. In her haste she had spurted the platelets all over the curtains and onto the floor. Teresa began to cry and tremble with the chills. The young nurse said, "Oh, what's your problem now?"

Since the young nurse was anxious to get off her shift, she asked a head nurse to come in and take over. The night staff worked all night to get Teresa's fever down. This seemed to be the critical time in the chemotherapy, and I stayed with her constantly over the next twenty-four hours, getting Kleenex, ice packs, salt water, Jell-O, and popsicles; taking her to the bathroom; and just loving her with all the love any mother could give. I noted when taking her to the bathroom that she was bleeding internally as well.

I tried to recite the prophecies that had been given to us, and a song came into my head that I had sung as a teenager: "I believe the answer is on the way… cast not away your confidence." I really felt I heard the Lord say to me, "My promises are true. I have touched her and will continue to touch her." I vacillated between fear and faith, simply claiming that God would heal our daughter just because He loved us and not through manipulation. All the while I was fasting up to eleven days at a time. Was that manipulation?

When Teresa could, she read *Hinds' Feet on High Places*, a type of allegoric prose. The essence of the book was that as you go through suffering and sorrow, it will turn into peace and joy. Teresa's faith and ability to fight this battle blew our minds, for often it was she who lifted our spirits and faith.

In the interludes when Teresa was home, she was continually being asked to give her testimony at Christian coffee shops and churches throughout the whole metropolitan area. She had been fighting this disease since December, when she'd had the appendectomy, which we believed to be the start of this saga. Six months had already passed; she had maintained an active life in between hospitalizations, never once doubting her Heavenly Father's healing.

One night Teresa's dad and I sat on either side of her holding her hands, so great was her pain. Her father prayed, "In the name of Jesus, we push back the enemy. In the name of Jesus, we claim the victory." We started a new routine while she was taking the chemo: Don would leave late at night, and I would stay beside Teresa. Then I would go home early in the morning to get the children off to school. During that early morning period, Don would go back to the hospital to be with Teresa. Then he would go to class for a full day of teaching students.

During most of my waking hours, I tried to imagine a ball of fire circling throughout Teresa's body, bringing healing. Don, on the other hand, had to keep a dual track. I believe sociologists are programmed to be able to exist on two tracks, and he had to set his horror aside so he could minister to his students and maintain his job. No wonder we had no time to work out the chasm that was building. This stint in the hospital had been so difficult, and Teresa's high school graduation was near. We were still in the midst of this medical fight... How abnormal, how absolutely unthinkable!

Some Laughter in the Midst of Pain

Teresa had a roommate at the hospital who had formerly been a doctoral professor, Dr. Turner. When Teresa felt like it, she would put her makeup on in the early morning. Dr. Turner would say, "A sweet little Christian girl like you shouldn't wear all that war paint!" It amused Teresa, and she would just continue to listen to Dr. Turner chatter and tell her she loved her for entertaining her.

Dr. Turner did provide much laughter. She was loony most of the time and would throw her bedpan on the floor when the nursing staff ignored her alarm bell. As Teresa felt better, she would get up and take care of Dr. Turner's needs. Dr. Turner had a pair of slippers, which—she told Teresa in a more lucid moment—were her golden slippers to wear to heaven.

In spite of the unimaginable horror we were going through, we appreciated those moments of laughter that we so needed. Teresa had always had a sense of humor and had often seen the humorous in the macabre. Early on, when she wasn't nearly as sick, she had said in jest to put her in a red casket and bury her upside down. I did not laugh or even see any humor. She had read too many Agatha Christie books that had colored her sense of humor. Teresa, with her innocent faith, had no idea the fear she put in my heart. But once again she rallied enough to be sent home.

Graduation

Teresa's high school graduation fell during one of her reprieves from the hospital. The morning of graduation, June 8, we still did not have the good news we were waiting for. Teresa was running a 104-degree temperature, and we feared she would be unable to participate in graduation. We fixed the usual carrot-and-garlic-juice combo—a whole quart. She was in bed all day but was determined to go through the ceremony with her friends. Her fever did come down, and, still feeling horribly sick, she attempted to make herself presentable. We felt she put on way too much eye shadow and makeup, which—given the pallor of her skin—made her look even more pathetic. The pictures taken that night show how very ill she was.

She stumbled through the graduation march and received her diploma with glowing remarks. In spite of her illness, she still graduated at the top of her class and was on the honor roll and in honor society. She was also given an award by the cancer society. I looked out at the rest of the graduating class and wondered if they knew the pain and anguish we felt. This graduation was anything but a joyous occasion…not like her brother's the year before. All of her friends were able to go out that night and celebrate. Teresa had to go home crying from the intense pain throughout her whole body and heart! No joyful graduation party was planned to celebrate her accomplishments…just a pleading with God to heal this jewel.

It was late June, and we had put the night of graduation behind us. Teresa seemed to be bouncing back once again when Dr. Glass gave us a call. We knew the chemo had taken her blood count down to almost zero. In the treatment of this dreaded disease, all blood cells are destroyed—the good along with the bad. When Dr. Glass called us that afternoon late in June, he said her blood counts were looking pretty normal. Teresa was feeling good, had gained back weight, had lost no hair, and seemed to be ready to enjoy the summer. He seemed pleased with the report of good cultures.

Long-Awaited News

A few days later, Dr. Glass called us to come in for more tests. When Teresa came in, he said, "You look damn good!" He said to give him a call later that afternoon, around four o'clock. I told him I didn't know if I could, fearing what I would hear. So Dr. Glass said he would call us!

When the phone rang late that afternoon, Don answered. It was Dr. Glass. He said, "Mr. Gibbs, I have good news. We have a beautiful remission. I can find nothing anywhere." He later added, "It doesn't mean there isn't any hiding and that it won't come back."

We were jubilant, and I refused to hear the later statement. I was so full of thanksgiving. Teresa was gaining weight, had just finished a three-week booster series of chemo, and was looking beautiful. Our joy was indescribable. As I looked at her, I could not believe what we had been through, for she looked the picture of health.

That was June 22. After fighting this disease for seven months, yes, God did heal our precious jewel! We spread the word, and so many friends as well as the charismatic groups were praising God. Don and I were so thankful for this Jewish doctor that we sent him flowers in gratitude. We wondered how we could thank hundreds of people who had donated blood so Teresa could have those lifesaving transfusions.

Teresa's Account

This is how Teresa briefly described her harrowing experience:

> Going into my last year of high school, I was expecting a great year filled with fun and involvement! But to my dismay, that was not to be. In the fall I was diagnosed flu and strep throat. Then, the day after Christmas, out came my appendix.

> With that behind me, I was determined to gain the good health I had always known, only to acquire this time what was diagnosed as pleurisy. What an experience that was; every breath brought excruciating pain, every movement another tear. But as strong willed as I am, I bounced back for a short period—only to start a new episode.

> Early in March I developed extreme pains in my back. I could barely move without pain. Intermittently I carried on my busy school activities, my job in a fashion shop, and my church activities as best I could, still trying for the senior year I dreamed about. I had a few days of relief, and I determined to start living again. But wouldn't you know it, the

Friday before our spring vacation started, I woke up to the bright blue sky, the warm sun, and indescribable pains in my pelvic and leg bones.

Everyone had gone to work except my brother and his fiancée. I tried resting and found I couldn't lie still. I tried sewing but couldn't sit still. I tried lying in the sun, but the pain grew still worse. My brother's fiancée was a student nurse, and she gave me two pain killers, which she said would knock me out. Instead the pain grew more intense, and all I could do was roll on the bed in anguish.

I called my father, and as soon as he could free himself from his teaching job, he rushed home. He called my mother at the hospital where she was doing volunteer work, and she rushed home. They took me to the clinic only to have three doctors say they couldn't find anything. They concluded it must be a muscle spasm! One of the doctors had given me a shot of Demerol, so with some relief I went home to rest, only to grow continually worse.

Finally, that evening, my mother and father took me to a friend of ours, Dr. Ramsthal. By that time I was nearly unconscious from the pain. The doctor shot my pelvic bone with Novocain to localize the pain. After his examination he suspected some kind of blood disease and gave me a shot of morphine to knock me out for the night, until I could be admitted to the hospital the next morning.

So on Saturday morning, I started my spring vacation in a hospital bed, and a series of tests were begun. That evening I was to have a bone marrow test done in my chest. The pain cannot be described, only experience can tell. Although I did not know it, the first test was not successful, as the bone marrow cells were so packed those doing the test could not draw a smear. Out in the hall, the doctors were telling my parents what they suspected, but they could not make a final diagnosis until Monday, when they could do another bone marrow test in the pelvic bone.

From Saturday until Monday morning, I had my mother beside me, rubbing my legs to help ease the pain, and my father, being the priest of our family, praying to Jesus. When Monday came I was so afraid for another bone marrow test, but needless to say that didn't stop it. I think I scared my roommate to death with my screaming bloody murder. When it was over, tears streaming down my face like a huge waterfall, I wanted nothing more than to crawl into Jesus's arms.

After the doctors had made their final diagnosis to my distraught parents, my father came into my room to break the news to me. The bone marrow test had shown acute myeloblastic leukemia, which is common in teenagers. The pain was because the white cells in my bones were expanding at such a rapid speed as to cause pressure on the bones. My father said that night I would be receiving a blood transfusion, and then they would start some chemotherapy.

Strangely enough, as my father was so carefully explaining this to me, Jesus took me in His arms, and tears of joy streamed down my face, for He assured my spirit all would be well. I knew the minute I heard that, I would not die. Jesus allowed my faith to be such that I rejoiced at the moment when my world should have been caving in. From that moment Jesus never left my side.

With my family I went through some very trying times, much heartache, pain, loneliness, and despair, but through it all my faith still remained. Even until June 22, when further tests showed my bone marrow to be perfectly clear. That was a day of rejoicing and thanksgiving for us all, even as I still rejoice for the wonders of His miracle.

Our Miracle Had Come

We spent most of our summer on the water, in between Don's eight-week summer classes. Dr. Glass had given Teresa permission to waterski if she did not do it with a carrot in her mouth! Teresa and he had developed a rapport with each other. Teresa said when he worked on her; it was like Jesus working on her. Dr. Glass was a giant of a man, not in stature but in spirit, and had a blasphemous sense of humor. On one occasion I was reading *Healing Light* by Agnes Sanford, and he asked what I was reading. When I told him, he switched on the overhead light and said, "Let there be light."

My quest to polish my jewels continued, and we celebrated the rest of the summer to the max. One night while I was waiting for Don to get home from a night class, I was reading my Bible. It was late; Don Ralph and Teresa were out. The younger ones were in bed, so I took a warm bath, crawled into bed, and opened my Bible.

The fifty-fourth chapter of Isaiah literally leaped from the pages: "Enlarge your house; build an addition. Spread out your home…For you will soon be bursting at the seams…" (Is 54:2–3, NLT). My heart pounded within me, and I pondered the meaning of what I had read, for I saw no possible means of enlarging our home. I believed it already was bursting at the seams, but I had such a strange feeling. I underlined the scripture, shared it with Don, and simply tucked it away in my heart.

More to Come

Father Truehella and Teresa had met for lunch during her times at home as well as spending much time together at the hospital. Father T did not need to do this, as he was the chaplain at Good Samaritan. But the bond had grown tight. Now, with Teresa displaying healing, he still wanted to have lunch with her. During one such luncheon, Teresa mentioned to Father Truehella that we were ready to adopt another child. We had only casually mentioned in passing that it might be time to adopt again. With a stunned expression, Father Truehella told Teresa he had just talked a young woman out of an abortion that very morning. He further stated she had given her heart to the Lord and would give her child to the Lord as a gift of thanksgiving.

Teresa could hardly wait to get home to tell us of this possible miracle in our lives. Something leaped inside our hearts, and we wasted no time in talking to Father T and putting in our request for this jewel. When we called, he shared with us the family's history. He was excited that we were interested and said it would be a private adoption. In that moment it all seemed so natural that this child was to be our child. We felt it. Father Truehella felt it. It was the same feeling you have when you discover you are pregnant with another jewel. However, the delivering doctor did not agree. He felt the child should go to a family who had no children, not one who already had five. But it was determined…It was set in stone. We were to have another baby.

Somehow we were so sure it was to be a girl that Teresa and I went shopping for a darling little blue dress on the same day the adoption was confirmed with

Father Truehella. The decision lay in Father Truehella's hand alone; no one else was to make the decision. So in spite of our mental and spiritual fatigue, we had a daughter who was healed, and we were to become new parents! Would this erase room 101? It really did seem God had heard our desperate plea for healing and was now giving us a new jewel.

In the midst of these strange happenings, Don had an unusual dream. He saw an embryo growing and a little blond girl with a ponytail holding his hand. Very strange indeed! What was the meaning of these strange happenings? We simply pondered them in our hearts.

CHAPTER 16

Interlude of Miracles

> Enlarge your house; build an addition. Spread out your
> home…For you will soon be bursting at the seams.
> —Is 54:2–3, NLT

Miracles and Heartbreak

The prophecies and comments continued to come our way. The charismatic people were so glad to claim this mighty healing, as though they had brought it forth. I did not care, for our daughter was healed. Our joy was uncontainable! We still pondered the meaning of that scripture that had jumped off the pages. And now to hear of our newest jewel to arrive…Oh my… Life was good again!

Cean, Christy, and Michele were so glad to have their sister home. Teresa started hosting parties for her friends. Some of my foreboding had left, but only because Don seemed so sure that all was well.

Don Ralph (now sometimes simply going by Ralph) finished his first year at Lewis & Clark, completed the training in Washington, continued working at McDonald's while doing training at the National Guard in Portland…and broke off the engagement with our darling Susan. It was difficult to carry on a long-distance romance, and the trauma of Teresa's illness took its toll on Ralph as well. We were sad to lose Susan as a future daughter-in-law, but what could we do?

Don and I continued to fast and believe and declare the miracle of Teresa's healing in our lives. I was given a book, written by John Osteen, entitled *A Miracle in Your Mouth*. The essence of the book was that we could just speak what we wanted, and it would be done by the authority given to each believing Christian. How I declared Teresa's miracle over and over. I was being faithful in prayer and Bible study daily. Our daughter was healed, and now we were expecting another blessing from the Lord. We truly believed that the scripture Isaiah 54 was a word from the Lord as we anticipated the new baby. We really would be bursting at the seams! We had gone through a horrible experience, but yes, we would go through it again for Jesus when the ending was so joyous. Teresa seemed in such good health. She had bounced back with full energy and joy, and she was again in much demand to give her testimony weekly. Her schedule picked up speed.

What Else?

It was a balmy Saturday on September 23. The summer was too soon over, and Don Ralph was now in Alabama. He had switched from the air force to the marines, as they had offered him a flying slot. He was so anxious to fly that when he heard of an opening to do so in the marines, he jumped at the chance.

I had the strange feeling I was pregnant but said nothing. Surely it was my imagination as I anticipated our new baby girl! I certainly did not have the intense pains I had experienced a year earlier. I had no morning sickness or obvious medical reason, just a feeling. Could this be the embryo Don had seen in his dream? It was probably just an upset stomach, so I set the feeling aside. Besides, I was soon to be forty years old. Stories of babies born to older mothers indicated it was risky to have a pregnancy at that age.

Teresa was sitting on the kitchen floor painting one of her gorgeous pictures. She was anxious to give some of her paintings to the various doctors who had cared for her. Christy was on the living room floor cutting out a pantsuit pattern for an outfit she planned to sew. Michele was making caramel apples. Cean was playing in the backyard on his little motorized car. Don was winterizing our boat in the garage. (He had been fasting for several days. This had become a ritual for both of us—at first to request healing and now in thanksgiving for that healing.)

As he was draining the gas from the boat, some leaked from the gas can onto the cement garage floor. Don grabbed a blanket to soak up the spill, and the blanket pushed the gas fumes into the gas water heater...and instantly everything was aflame. He ran through the garage door to the kitchen and out the sliding doors to the backyard, and he grabbed Cean. Then he ran back into the house and told us all to get quickly outside. He called 911 before joining us out on the street in front of our house.

The fire engine was there almost instantly, as the firehouse was only a little more than a block away. We stood out front watching our beloved house burn while firemen sprayed water into every window of the house. The older children were weeping; Cean was on Don's shoulders, his inquisitive two-year-old heart enamored with the excitement. Teresa's poodle (whom Ron had given her) was cowering in her arms; neighbors were beginning to gather, offering their condolences. All I could say to them was, "What is a house when you almost lose your daughter?"

When the fire was under control, the firemen pulled the burned boat and garage contents out onto the driveway. It was a pile of devastation…My boat… Our family's favorite sport. The firemen boarded up the house and told us to go to a motel and call our insurance company. They told Don he was a very lucky man to escape. Since there were paint cans in the garage, it had all ignited almost like combustion. Many neighbors offered to take us in, but we opted to go to a motel—after all, there were six of us! Don Ralph was the only one missing.

How the news traveled so quickly, I will never know, but our pastor, Bob Davis, showed up at the motel. We had barely arrived, but he had already heard the news and was there to encourage us. He said he thought we'd had enough tragedies. We so loved that man. His sermons always ministered to our hearts. In fact we often felt he had peeked into our hearts to see what we needed to hear. He had kept in touch as we had fought the cancer battle. After he left that night, we saw some cash he had placed on the counter. How grateful we were. We wondered together what we should do next. But it was the weekend. We could do nothing until Monday, so we called Don Ralph in Alabama to tell him about the house fire.

We had difficulty going to sleep that night. After baths we huddled together, giving thanks that no one was hurt. I truly imagined myself kneeling before God's throne. I was inquiring how much more we could endure. We needed His wisdom now! We needed His protection now! At times we felt that the last ten months had been a journey through hell. How could a literal hell be any worse? The children shed tears for their newborn kittens lost to the fire. We were not sure about the mother cat, whether she had been in the fire or had run. We could not find her anywhere.

We did not go to church the next day, as we had nothing to wear but the clothes we had been in the day before. Don still smelled of gas from the boat. But one must eat, dress clothes or not. We went to breakfast at our favorite pancake house and just praised God for protecting us from the fire. Our meals out were always full of laughter, no matter how dark the circumstances. So it was a bonus to eat all our meals out over the weekend—something our whole family loved. People were so gracious and sympathized with us about these horrible happenings in our lives. I remember Teresa saying she would go through her illness again for Jesus. Would we? Could we?

Must Get to Work

On Monday we put into motion all the necessary things one does after a house fire. We called the insurance company; a company to haul away the burned, mangled mess in the drive; a company to clean the burned objects that could be saved; and a company to remove the fire odor. We also called around to find an apartment to live in until the renovation and restoration were complete. We were told it would take three months.

We wrestled through all the things that needed to be done, including Don's responsibilities to teach both day and night classes. We had only one car at that time, and the children would need to be taken to their schools. Teresa was taking classes at Portland Community College. I would need to take Don and her to class in order to do all I needed to do in regard to this latest scenario. It was good to be busy, and we even found joy in being able to "enlarge our house," as the scripture had stated, for we decided to enclose the garage and make a big twenty-by-twenty-foot family room—a place for fun and entertainment! It seemed I was always living on a dual track of emotions: joy and fear.

The apartment we rented was on the second floor. It was crowded, but it was another sanctuary for our family. Cean had been used to playing in his big back-yard with his little motorized car. He grieved because it had burned beyond use. We did buy him some new house toys, hoping it would appease him while he was stuck in this upstairs apartment. We had to watch him closely, as he would try to open the door and head down the stairs to who knows where.

There were adjustments to this new experience. We were so very busy working to refurbish our home. And yes, I was pregnant. I said nothing but wondered how I could deal with this news as well as adopt a new baby, who we were sure was a girl, and keep my sanity. Don's dream had it right: an embryo was growing as well as the upcoming little girl with a blond ponytail, as his dream had shown!

In addition we were barely settled in at the new apartment, busy building and planning, when we noticed that Teresa seemed a little less upbeat. She declined some singing engagements. We took her to the doctor, but the blood work was still fine, so we decided the change we saw was due to stress. Some of her dearest friends had gone away for college, and her doctor wanted her to stick close to home.

It was taking longer than promised to get back into the house. Some of the work done was extremely inferior, and we continually insisted that the workmen redo it. We wanted professional work. We selected red carpet for the family room and blues for the kitchen and living room. The downstairs had not been destroyed in the fire, so it was mostly the family room (garage), kitchen, and living room that had to be completely renovated.

Besides my boat, I had lost another treasured item: something Marie Stara had given me. It was a pressed-glass bowl that I had prominently displayed. Marie had given it to me when we'd moved from Aberdeen. Pressed glass, sometimes called molded glass, was introduced as a substitute for costly European cut glass, and I was extremely fond of it. Marie said the bowl was a token of her admiration for me. But here again, what is a boat or valuable antique dish when you almost lose a daughter?

We had been in the apartment for a month when Don Ralph returned home and moved into his old room downstairs. (There was no room in the apartment for him, and the downstairs of our home was undamaged.) He completed the next six months at the National Guard unit in Portland. It was good to have him home. He and Teresa picked up where they had left off, attending the Assembly of God church together.

Teresa had completed a term at Portland Community College. She took her father's sociology class and loved being in her dad's class. She said she felt quite proud when she walked around campus with him. She had a habit of quoting her father when most of her associates at that time were calling their fathers their ol' men. Teresa would say, "My father is a sociologist and the smartest man I know!" For her that was the end of the matter. How blessed we were to have this kind of respect.

A Trip South

It was soon to be Thanksgiving, and our home was nowhere close to being finished. We decided to go to California to spend Thanksgiving with Don's brother and family. Don Ralph was home, and we wanted a little holiday celebration of all our good fortune that included the whole family. We also all needed a reprieve from the crowded quarters and demands of remodeling. We knew that our baby girl was due around the end of Thanksgiving, so we let Father T know we would be gone over the weekend and said we would keep in constant touch with him. We had to be back on Monday for Don's classes anyway.

I knew for sure we would not disclose that we were expecting two babies. Announcing that I was pregnant would bring on a tirade of "what are you thinking?" Don's parents were still trying to control our lives. They had not been supportive when we had adopted our little son, and we were sure they would not be supportive of our adopting another child! If they knew we were to have two babies...oh my!

It was wonderful to jam all of us in the car and take off. Cean was not a good rider, so we had given him a bit of phenobarbital. Mistake or not, he slept most of the way to Central California, where Don's brother lived. Since Don's parents were to be present as well, I was determined it would be a joyous time without unwanted advice, and I wanted no stress for Teresa. Don's parents had made a trip to see us earlier, during one of Teresa's home reprieves, when she was still very ill. As Teresa lay in our bed upstairs, they began talking loudly about their cemetery plots—for what reason we did not know—but it greatly disturbed Teresa to have such a spirit of gloom in the house. We wanted none of that. It was difficult enough to be continually upbeat—accentuating the positive and eliminating the negative, as it was.

An Unbelievable Gift

On the way down, we stopped at a pay phone to make a call to Father T, and we found out the young mother was already in labor. We called every two hours after that. When we finally stopped for dinner, we called and finally heard the news that our baby had arrived. Father T said he did not know whether it was a girl or boy, but we knew. Tears filled my eyes as I tried to eat dinner. I kept thinking of this young mother who was making a horrendous sacrifice in giving up her baby. I wondered how any mother could make such a sacrifice and surrender such a priceless gift. I had an overwhelming love for this young mother whom I knew not, but I would receive her gift to the Lord, even though my heart grieved for her. We all left the restaurant with joy in our hearts and extreme sadness for the young mother. We continued our trip and had a pleasant time with the relatives without incident, but we were anxious to return home.

Early Monday, after Don finished a morning class, we gathered up a darling pink sleeper outfit and diapers. We also had the blue baby blanket the young mother had knit for a baby she would never hold. We went into Good Samaritan Hospital, where Father T was the chaplain, and took the elevator up to the nursery floor. We went into a vacant room, and our new baby was brought to us. She looked up and smiled with dimples as though to say, "Here I am! I'm yours, born in your heart." We instantly bonded with this new jewel for polishing, and we fell in love at that moment. There is *no* difference in mother love for an adopted child! We dressed this sweet little bundle of blessings and were ready to get out of that hospital promptly. But as we were about to leave with our baby, a nurse came in and said, "I'm sorry; you cannot take the baby before your pediatrician checks her out." We had not counted on this and had planned to schedule a doctor appointment later when we got her home. We called Dr. Glass, who was not only Teresa's cancer specialist but a pediatrician. He was unable to get away from his practice until later in the day. Therefore we had to leave our new jewel and go back after Dr. Glass had checked her out. He called to tell us what time he would be there, and we left very unhappy.

I was now three months pregnant, and we had told no one—not even the children. I lived with a fear that if anyone found out, we would not be considered for this adoption. I also feared the crazy comments that would come our way. In fact a gentleman in our Mariners group had already said he did not know they had any Catholics in his Presbyterian church (referring to us because of our large family). This was the beginning of the era when it was not popular to have more than two or three children—especially at the age of forty!

I dropped Don off at class and then waited until the afternoon when we would finally get to bring Danielle Marie home. We had named her Marie after our dear friend Marie Stara. Marie had been so faithful to walk beside us, always supporting us. She had prophesied about our home of promise with all the flowers and had also predicted we would have a child of promise: Danielle. She missed the prophecy about the embryo growing, though! Her spiritual insight was so balanced and accurate that we cherished her friendship and wanted to honor her by naming this little jewel after her. The name Danielle is a derivative of Daniel, which means prophet. Marie Stara had been our prophet in many areas. And as God would have it, Danielle Marie was to have the same qualities.

It was with joy in our hearts that we met Dr. Glass at Good Samaritan Hospital that afternoon. Don always felt like he was going home when he walked into this hospital, as he had been teaching nursing students there for several years. Dr. Glass tenderly checked out Danielle and told us we had one healthy newborn baby girl. He was all smiles and encouragement about our decision to take on more responsibility in the midst of our journey with Teresa. The nurse placed this bundle in my arms, and I wanted to get out of there as quickly as possible. I wanted to run with our new jewel for fear something would go wrong!

Since we were still in a crowded apartment, we placed two fluffy pillows on either side of our new baby in our king-sized rented bed. We wanted to be able to reach over and touch her and let her know we were there. Everyone wanted to hold the baby, especially her new daddy. She kept opening one eye and looking up at him a trait that would stay with her. So here we were in an apartment with part of our enlarged family. Cean Michael had a new four-day-old baby sister to love. He did not seem to mind that he would no longer be the center of attention as the baby of the family.

Still Celebrating

Soon it was December and Michele's birthday again. She would be twelve and entering into the puberty years. Celebrations were always important time for our family. We went to Grandma's Table for a birthday dinner, with our new baby in tow. Grandma's Table is a restaurant in downtown Beaverton where they serve dinner family style: golden fried chicken mashed potatoes, carrots, salad, and of course blackberry pie, just like grandmas make. The oohs and aahs at this darling baby—who was all secure in a BabeeTenda by my chair—pleased us all. The newest family member was wrapped in her blue blanket that her birth mother had knit for this gift she was offering to the Lord. We were so grateful to have a healthy daughter, Teresa, in remission and Christy, Michele, and Cean all sitting at the table. What could be more perfect? Only Don Ralph was missing, but all was going well with him. We had reason to rejoice! After the smoke of battle had cleared, this family was still intact. How grateful we were. My desire of many years before, after reading the Bobbsey Twins series—to have a baby dropped on my doorstep—was now a reality two times over. I thought about God uniquely weaving this baby together in another woman's womb and carefully selecting our family to love and cherish her.

We continued to watch the renovation of our new home of promise. We had to buy new furniture and pick out interior paint, exterior paint, and carpeting. We also had to refinish our badly burned dining-room table. We anxiously awaited the time when we could move back home. The expenses were rising. Farmers Insurance canceled our policy—a policy Don had had since he was a teenager. We thought that was odd, but we found out it was typical procedure.

We celebrated Christmas in our little apartment with much joy, and we patiently waited and waited for the builders to say, "It is time!" Danielle was such a happy baby and seemed to thrive on all the love given her…that was, for a few more short weeks. Finally we were able to move back home, with much stuff in tow, and we were so very happy to spread out.

CHAPTER 17

We Did Follow the Yellow Brick Road

> Courage is the art of being the only one
> who knows you're scared to death.
> —EARL WILSON

We concluded our adoption quickly in a Hillsboro courtroom, with a judge who sensed the miracle of it all. He said Danielle was a very lucky little girl, and we were very lucky parents. We agreed. I was relieved, for I continually feared if anyone found out I was pregnant, Danielle would be snatched from our home. As of yet even the children still did not know they were to have two babies to love.

Broken Again

Life did seem perfect and back to our normal, but as we celebrated the new miracle in our lives, Teresa continued having pains throughout her body, and finally the blood cultures *did not* come back clean. She would need more chemotherapy. Rumors flew. Many of the charismatic believers said she'd lost her healing because she had not been following the Lord closely enough. How those words devastated Teresa…and Don and me as well!

Some said we did not have enough faith. Some said we must not have God at the center of our lives. Some said the Lord was trying to teach us something. Some just ignored us now, not knowing what to say. How quickly people can turn on you. When everything was going well with us, they were knocking on our door to learn the secret of our success, but when the axe fell they did a disappearing act. Some of the other self-made prophets were painfully silent. We became a threat to their pious religious formulas. If you do what God wants, then He will answer your prayers. If you have enough faith, then He will heal your child. They had wanted to hook their wagon to our star. Then they turned on us, suggesting we had done something wrong for God to take back His healing.

Always Someone to Hold You Up

I was stretched beyond human endurance. We had hardly recovered from the last siege—leukemia, a house fire, pregnancy—and now we had to face another series of chemo. To top it off, Danielle had pneumonia. I did not know what to do! Teresa needed to be admitted once again for the initial chemo treatment. I called a friend and asked if she could stay with the children until Don got home, so I could stay with Teresa. She said, "Can't you get someone else who could do it? I have a luncheon engagement." I was crushed. It was so difficult to ask for help anyway, and now I felt deserted and left to fight this new battle alone.

Christy and Michele stayed out of school to care for Cean and our new baby, Danielle. The next evening I got a call from my sister, Dorothy, in Seattle. When I told her of our renewed battle, she said, "I'm coming down! I'll be there in three hours." She left her own five children in the care of others, took time off from her job as a nurse, and came to our rescue immediately. My younger sister's help blessed us beyond words. Her heart was so caring. She stayed as long as she could be away from her job. To me that is putting legs on your prayers.

Don had gone to the hospital right after class and intended to spend the night. When my sister said she was coming, I decided to go back to the hospital as soon as I made up a bed and did a load of laundry. Having a two-month-old baby had added a new wrinkle to this next series of chemo, as we tried to keep one of us at the hospital around the clock. We never left Teresa alone unless it was for a brief period.

I did go back up to the hospital for a little while until I was sure all was OK. I left the hospital at about eleven o'clock, when I felt Teresa was resting. I walked out the back door of the building in a state of shock, not comprehending the magnitude of this new battle that was raising its ugly head. This series seemed to be far more severe, and the bounce back was not as strong. I drove home in a stupor, crying to God, "Lord, I have these promises of healing squeezed in my hand, and I will not let them go!" All the while my whole body screamed with fear.

Once home I walked in the door and my sister took one look at me and said, "You are pregnant!" Don and I still had told no one of our upcoming jewel to be added. When she said that, I burst into tears. It was like a floodgate was opened, and my emotions were released. I was five months pregnant and had tried to conceal it with loose-fitting clothes; such was my fear of losing our baby girl. After the tears subsided and my sister unpacked, I literally slumped down on that lovely new plush blue carpet and went to sleep. I was too tired to remove my clothing. My sleep was fitful, and I dreamed Teresa did not make it.

I woke up with a start to the telephone's ringing. It was only 6:00 a.m., and I was terrified after my dream. It was Don, and he said Teresa was resting more comfortably, and he needed to get to class. I freshened up and went immediately to the hospital, so Don could make it to his seven o'clock class. How either of us kept going can be explained only by our passionate love and commitment to our family—or was it supernatural strength from above? I wondered how Don could keep an all-night vigil and adequately teach the next day.

Teresa's new battle continued to rage. She battled surging temperatures and was in and out of the hospital. We continued to make our carrot-garlic juice with the same successful results. We had a darling new baby to care for at the same time. Even though I felt we were in a fog most of the time, we continued our prayers without ceasing.

It was shortly after we moved back into our house that Danielle began to have colic every evening from nine to twelve o'clock. I would rock her in our old-fashioned rocker for those three hours—half awake, half asleep, wondering what the baby growing within me thought of all this crying. If I were at the hospital, then Christy would rock her.

Though Danielle had not had colic in the apartment, I believed she had developed an allergy to the different formulas we tried. Whatever the reason, we would not leave her in her crib crying. I remembered how Teresa had been so colicky. She had needed to be held close to my heart. So we felt Danielle needed the constant closeness to ease her distress. At almost midnight each night, the colic would be over, and she would sleep soundly until around six in the morning.

Teresa would have short stays at home, and then she would have to spend another week or so in the hospital, fighting the infections and needing platelets and transfusions. The younger girls had to become surrogate mommies, cooks, and housekeepers and keep up with their homework. If Don and I were home, we would lie in the living room, so we could hear both Teresa and Danielle throughout the night. It was difficult to be pregnant and sleeping on the floor.

The family fabric was being stretched to the limit. I became exhausted, but I kept saying, "Must hold on, must hold on!" I kept remembering hearing Teresa say she would go through it all again for Jesus. The memory made me cringe in horror, yet we knew only too well that she meant it from the depth of her being.

Provisional Care

On one occasion I rolled into a service station on the last fumes of gas. It was very early in the morning, and I was on my way home from spending the night with Teresa. I had not looked at the gas register, and I literally rolled into the gas station totally empty. That was just one of the many incidents when we felt God's overseeing protection and mercy. I would have been an odd sight on the side of the road—pregnant, alone, and needing assistance. Who would have believed I was coming home from the hospital?

As before, Teresa would go through hell and then bounce back. Many times during the long nights, she would say to me, "Mom, you won't let me die, will you?" I would assure her that nothing could break through my watch nor touch her. Then, a few days later, she would be sent home. This pattern repeated itself many times over the next few months, and school had to be put on hold.

On one of our home stays, as they were called, I was already up very early in the morning to catch up on domestic needs. Teresa got up early in the morning that day too. She found me in the laundry room, lovingly put her arms around my neck, and said, "Mom, if God were looking for a mother for Jesus today, He would pick you." She always brought sunshine into my life, saying things that melted my heart, and she never failed to continue to tell Don and me how grateful she was for our around-the-clock care.

I pondered the thought in my heart that if this was what Jesus's own mother had gone through and felt in her heart. I had a new appreciation for her. His excruciating pain was short-lived—not of the duration our daughter was enduring. However, Jesus's suffering was from violent men, and Teresa's was an internal battle. And even though Christ was thirty-three at his crucifixion, a mother is a mother no matter what the age!

A Giant Blessing

Soon the month of May arrived, and I thought it was time for our newest jewel to be born. I was having contractions and passing blood, so Don took me to the hospital. Teresa had just gotten home from the hospital the day before, and I had been with her, heavy with child, to the nurses' surprise. We had become an item in the hospital, so even though I was not on the cancer floor, the whole hospital knew who we were. But the birthing process did not continue, so they sent me home. I went home for a week before it was definitely time to deliver early on a Friday morning.

Don stayed with me until he had to leave for an eight o'clock class. I was rolled into the delivery room, where I gave birth to the most beautiful little blond-haired baby boy. On an earlier evening, since Teresa had been home, we had decided we should pick out a name for this upcoming jewel. We were so sure it was to be a boy that we just skimmed over girls' names. We picked out the name Taylor for the middle name with no objections from anyone, but we tossed the names Jeremy and Joshua back and forth before we finally said, "Why not Jason Taylor?" Everyone had agreed, and now here he was. Later I read that the meaning of Jason is "healer." How true that is! He was the cherry on top of the pudding.

When his daddy came back from class and was able to see him in the nursery, all Don could say was, "What a goodly child." And that he was. When we took Jason to the church nursery two weeks later, people were aghast that we had been able to keep our growing family a secret. There we were with a six-month-old baby girl and a newborn baby boy...quite unusual. But we felt extremely blessed. Our house was enlarged per the scripture given to me, our daughter would soon be in remission again—we were sure—and we had these two darling jewels, just dropped out of heaven it seemed!

The House of Shekinah

My fear was often overpowering. But now Teresa was home again, and another series of chemo was completed. She seemed to be her old self, was out on dates... oh, the joy! It seemed right with both of us home, we should begin preparing to have this newly renovated house blessed.

We asked Father T to do the honors. He had been so faithful to journey with us through Teresa's illness, and we had such gratitude for the way he was instrumental in the adoption of our new jewel. Even though he was a little surprised by the newest baby, he did not question us about the adoption. He agreed to bless our house, and we began making plans. This home blessing would take the place of Teresa's graduation party, which I was never able to plan. Remembering how we had described God's presence those many days in the hospital, Teresa composed a song to be sung on that blessed day: "The House of Shekinah."

Sing of Shekinah and the glory of our God
For He has made His dwelling here within our humble walls.
And He has promised love and protection for each one of us.
So you ask how it came to be.
Well, the answer, my friend, is really very plain to see.
We have found the one, Jesus Christ, God's only Son.
And we delight in Shekinah, the glory of our God,
The presence of our Lord,
Filling our home, ruling our lives with love and joy and peace.
Sing of Shekinah and the glory of our God
For He has made His dwelling
Here within our humble walls.
Because we delight in Shekinah, the glory of our Lord,
The presence of our God
Filling our home, ruling our lives with love and joy and peace
That the world may know here is Shekinah, the glory of our God
Illuminating our house, hovering over our home.
Thank you for Shekinah, the house of our love.
Thank you for Shekinah, the house of our God.

It was a glorious day. So many dear friends graced our home that day with encouragement. Teresa played her guitar and sang "The House of Shekinah" in the red-carpeted room. She wore a pink satin pantsuit that we had made for this special occasion. Tears were streaming down many faces that afternoon, as once again Teresa sang like an angel, giving praise to Jesus.

Father T gave communion as he blessed our home, and Priscilla carried little Danielle around. Someone else held Jason for him to observe these miracles. My dear aunt Vildy came down from Kelso with new little shoes for Danielle, such was her joy at our adopting two children. She and her husband had adopted two boys from Albertina Kerr many years before. She had not been told of Jason and— along with our many friends—she was very confused to see this new baby boy. Some wondered who this baby belonged to. We handled all the questions with grace. Our family was intact. What more could we want?

Our dear friend, Durwood, presented a gift to us: a sign he had made when he'd heard of the song Teresa had composed. The sign said, "The House of Shekinah." That sign graced the front of this enlarged dwelling that I believed had been given to me and was truly a gift from the Lord.

We lived across the street from an apartment, and so inviting was that sign that on occasion, we would have ladies knocking on the door in the middle of the night, requesting a place to sleep. They said their husbands or boyfriends beat them up. We did not mind when they knocked; we wanted our home to be a place of refuge.

Life Is Good Again

After that joyous occasion, Teresa seemed to gain more energy daily. Her schedule was full, and Don's and my identity became "Teresa's parents." She continued to write music and give her testimony, and she was spending much time painting and giving many of those paintings away.

Teresa was working again at the boutique in the mall. Her boss was so happy to have her back. She was never without boyfriends, it seemed. In spite of what she had been through and was still going through, boys wanted to be in her company. Her gentle testimony was so compelling; others wanted to know what she had.

She was able to work with her horse again, but she felt Kishan had been so neglected that she should consider selling him…but not yet. Teresa often brought him into our backyard and would put tiny Danielle on his bare back. Danielle's giggles were so infectious, and she seemed fearless, always pointing to do it again. Was this another little girl with a horse-shaped brain?

Don Ralph and Teresa had much fun that summer. They went to Kah-Nee-Ta Resort, a fabulous recreational camping and lodging site in the middle of Oregon, where the sun only shines. Together they put up their tent, went fishing, and just had time to share their love as brother and sister. When they went to massive swimming pools, crowded with teenagers, Don Ralph would ask, "Teresa, does that guy have as many muscles as I do?" These almost twins had remained so close over the years.

Hope and Doubt

Teresa was feeling more like herself, and it was with great joy that Dr. Glass once again announced a solid remission. It was now the middle of July. This time the announcement was met without fanfare, as it was tempered by experience. There was not the euphoria we had displayed with the first remission. Our joy was great, but there were not nearly as many charismatic groups boasting their victory. We were busy with the two babies and trying to hang on to our faith, which for me often wavered.

Teresa was so gifted in music and— with a heart only for God—she had heard of the excellent music department at Oral Roberts University (ORU) in Oklahoma. The music director at the Assembly loved Teresa. (She had taken care of his children.) He believed she was extremely gifted, and he encouraged her to go there. Also ORU had offered her a scholarship.

I was fearful, but after much discussion with Dr. Glass, I agreed, since he thought it would be fine for her to go if she kept close contact with a doctor. Dr. Glass referred Teresa to a doctor in Tulsa and confirmed the details with her and the doctor. Don and I finally agreed that a university that truly believed in healing might be a good place for Teresa to be.

Don Ralph had finished his technical training in Texas, and rather than go back to Lewis & Clark, he said he would go to ORU with Teresa. The thought of Teresa so far away gave me great fear, but wasn't Oral Roberts's ministry about miracles and healing? What better place would there be, possibly ensuring Teresa would stay in remission?

My faith was wavering, and Don seemed short with me when I kept asking him to tell me she would be fine. There we were with two babies and a preschooler to care for, two teenage daughters feeling left out when they so desperately needed a mother's care, two children leaving the nest, and a perfect marriage in need of renewal. The past two years had taken a toll on our perfect fairy tale. Would we ever return to normal? Or was this the new normal?

Trying to Be Whole

Our youngest three jewels were only a little over two months old, five months old, and three years old when we made plans to drive down to Oklahoma in Don Ralph's car, a 1966 Ford. We left these babies with my sister in Seattle and loaded up a U-Haul with Don Ralph's and Teresa's necessities for the year. It was August, so Christy and Michele were not yet in school.

It was a good trip but nothing like our former trips of the last eighteen years. It was the first time we had been back to visit Disneyland since our first three children were toddlers. Disney had captured our love years earlier, but this time there was not the laughter or joy. It seemed to me that everyone in this fragmented family had a mixture of tension, fear, and joy.

I was torn about leaving the little ones, but I desperately needed to be on this journey with Don, Ralph, Teresa, Christy, and Michele. Don and I and the girls planned to fly home after getting Don Ralph and Teresa settled. I would start out the day with such faith that everything would be fine and, throughout the day, watch it ebb away like a leaky raft!

When Raju heard we were taking Ralph and Teresa to Oral Roberts University, he flew down to be with the family. By that time he was working for DuPont in Delaware. It was a pleasant time being all together, as in the past, but again, it was just not the same! I thought maybe I was having postpartum depression, because there was no joy in my heart.

We had three days before we would fly home. We helped Ralph and Teresa unload the few possessions they had brought with them, met their dorm roommates, and drove around Tulsa, just checking out where we were leaving our two oldest children. The climate was very muggy that time of the year, but it was a beautiful campus. The staff was not present to greet us, just upper-class counselors.

It was time to leave, and, after copious good-byes among us all, Don gathered his eldest daughter in his arms and said, "Good-bye, daughter." Then we were ushered into the plane. Taking our seats, through tears, we four left our hearts there in Oklahoma. But we had barely arrived home and picked up our little ones when the phone began ringing several times a day. Don and I would often say, "Look, sugar, we have to cut down on these calls." But if Teresa did, we didn't. That was a good year for the phone company!

CHAPTER 18

Lord, You Stretch the Shoes

You keep track of all my sorrows.
You have collected all of my tears in your bottle.
You have recorded each one in your book.
—Ps 56:8, NLT

Empty-Hearted

We had flown home with great sadness and anticipation in our hearts that all would be well. After all, Don Ralph was there to look after his sister. Teresa needed to stay connected with her family at home. Was she ready for this after the hell she had been through? I did not know.

In spite of the phone bills, we would send cash for paints and pocket change for Teresa's needs—only to learn she had shared it with her friends in the dorm, such was her giving heart. She began painting pictures and giving them to all her new friends and sometimes selling them. She was always sending us little love gifts and letters. She kept up her grades and so enjoyed the music classes she was taking. Now and then she would send us a new song. She did sound a little weary, and we cautioned her to make sure she got enough rest. On one occasion when I thought she sounded extremely weary, she sent this song:

Garden of the Lord

We need some time to steal away from things
That vexes us through the day—
To seek somewhere a quiet place,
And talk with God there face to face.

That hallowed spot when once 'tis found is where
He changes things around; makes bird
To sing and flowers to bloom
Within our wilderness of gloom.
He turns each stalk of fret and care
Into a flower of beauty rare,
That we might store in memory's vase
A sweet bouquet of Jesus's grace.
Seek, ye children, the garden of the Lord.
That's where you'll find peace that lasts forevermore.
Come to it, children, the garden of the Lord.
That's where you'll find love that reigns forevermore.
Seek it when you're down and lonely,
When you're sad and in need of a friend
Or simply because you miss your Lord
And your relationship you want to mend.
Whatever the reason, whatever the time,
Come to this place and see the joy you find.
Seek, ye children, the garden of the Lord.
That's where you'll find peace that lasts forevermore.
Come to it, children, the garden of the Lord.
That's where Jesus is and lives forevermore!

Always on the Roller Coaster

I stayed on a roller coaster of hope and fear daily, waiting for the calls, listening for the tenor of Teresa's voice to determine the state of her health with each call. I tried so hard to release her into God's care, believing He did love her far more than I could comprehend. When I was most down, she would call and be totally upbeat with excitement about singing in some church or the paintings she was able to share and sell.

Once she sent me a pair of shoes, smaller than I wear. When she called she said they were so cute, she could not resist. She said, "Mom, we will just pray, 'Lord, You stretch the shoes!'" She knew how I loved shoes and dressing up. Her faith was so very innocent. Maybe she went overboard with a simple, trusting faith. She knew how I felt about white magic—slipping from faith onto the slippery slope of the occult. But I cherish her innocence and those shoes sent from a heart full of love! They remain in my cedar chest.

She continued writing songs, singing around the Bible Belt, and endearing herself to whomever she came in contact with. Giving her testimony was not the only gift she shared at churches, for she painted the nursery walls of one church she visited. The church members loved having her in their homes, this young jewel from Oregon. Letters would come telling us how much they enjoyed our children and how very gifted our daughter was.

Teresa did live a fulfilling life on campus for about six months. ORU's healing philosophy was totally absent on campus, and it was not long until the fundamentalist doctrine taught there began to gnaw at Teresa's heart. She would call home and say, "Is God really like that—a cruel taskmaster?" Her relationship with Jesus had been one of freedom and love. Don and I would put her back together, hang up, ponder why we had let this happen, and then desperately pray.

When Teresa was out on a date with one of the guys who was pursuing her, he could not keep his hands to himself. Many of the guys on campus would spout their fundamentalist beliefs of purity and then could not keep their hands to themselves. I still believed there was a fine line between spirituality and sexuality. Ralph and Teresa were not housed in the same dorms; in fact the boys' and girls' dorms were not coed at that time!

When the guys overstepped their bounds, Teresa would call her brother. At midnight Don Ralph—who was living in another dorm across campus—would quickly get dressed and meet her. One time they sat on the curb talking and then, in the early hours of the morning, walked around campus with Teresa crying. Don Ralph, who had many disagreements with the fundamentalists, would reassure her of her standing with Jesus before he would leave her.

These calls at midnight became a ritual, even though Don Ralph had to get up at five o'clock to play air force as well as keep up on his sociological studies on campus. On these occasions he would put his strong arms around Teresa and pour life and strength back into this delicate flower. Sometimes they would run around the track together. She became very dependent on his strong, free spirit that was able to lift her sagging spirit. It seemed to be two against three thousand in this fundamentalist university in the heart of the so-called Bible Belt.

Don Ralph would often take Teresa and her girlfriends out for pizza. Teresa needed her brother's protection, with her fragile state of mind. Don and I worried about her being so far away and in an unhealthy environment, but then she would call and tell us her brother—her champion—had solved her problems.

Don Ralph felt it was the needy guys who pursued Teresa, as they observed her emotional strength and devotion to Christ. He wanted her to date the more stable, less charismatic guys. Don Ralph said he could handle the fundamentalists but not his sister's pain. He said her depression became more and more apparent. They started meeting every Thursday at the Pagoda, a local Chinese restaurant, to talk and sort things out. This was a different side of Teresa that Don Ralph had never witnessed. The calls became more frequent as Teresa became greatly distressed. Her free spirit was being stifled, and we wondered if all was right with her health.

Interlude of Joy

Don and Teresa flew home for Christmas. She looked so vibrant and happy to be home. Teresa had four dates while home, but her joy was in seeing her family and friends and singing at coffee shops.

The babies were growing. Even thought it was winter, Danielle remembered the horse rides, and now the one-year-old wanted more. She and Jason cuddled with Teresa and Don Ralph in the family room, on the red carpet; Cean was so glad to see his sister that he trailed behind her continually. Christy and Michele started answering the phone once again as they had before: "Hello, this is Teresa's answering service."

Teresa slept in the red family room, as the little ones were occupying the downstairs bedrooms. In the middle of one night, she heard unfamiliar sounds, and Don and I were roused by the sounds of quick footsteps ascending the stairs to our room, giving us only seconds to move apart before she leaped in the middle of our bed. It was so good to cuddle this grown polished jewel when most of the time my arms were full of little cherubs. Two short weeks of joy, and my oldest two would be off again.

I was not able to be as involved in activities as I used to be, since the two babies kept me home, but we were able to catch a couple of dinners out with the whole family—such joy! Over the holidays Michele was in a play at her junior high. Teresa's laughter rang out through the gymnasium. On another occasion little Jason climbed through the missing glass into the fireplace (it had not yet been fixed, since it had been popped out by the house fire) and peeked through the remaining glass. This sent Teresa into hysterics, rolling around on the plush blue carpet. She was so joyous for these two weeks, and we could see her hesitation to leave. I wondered why we had ever agreed to let her go clear down to Oral Roberts University. I still had that foreboding when we saw her and Don Ralph off at the airport. Why had I given up this year?

Great Performance

The school had an excellent music program, which was the reason Teresa had chosen to go there. In one of their yearly concerts, Teresa was to sing her song, "The House of Shekinah," with her guitar. Her brother told us her five-foot-two-inch frame had trouble climbing up on the stool. But she glimmered in the spotlight, as her beautiful blond hair cascaded down around her angelic face.

She started to sing, but her guitar was out of tune, and she could not get it in tune. Finally she almost cried, "Help, Mr. Campbell!" While the choir director tuned her guitar, she seized the opportunity to share about her illness and her family with the audience, leaving her listeners enthralled. Once her guitar was finally tuned, she began singing "The House of Shekinah" with her heartfelt testimony. Her performance was a perfect example of her composure before an audience from infancy on, and she upstaged every other performer in the whole concert. She received a standing ovation. Waiting in her room were roses for our beloved daughter. That was all we could do to share in this evening. Don Ralph sent us the tape he had recorded at the concert. Over and over it reverberated through our home!

CHAPTER 19

Take Me Home

> I am worn out from sobbing. All night I flood
> my bed with weeping, drenching it with my
> tears. My vision is blurred by grief…
> —Ps 6:6–7, NLT

Love and Sorrow

Teresa had begun dating Doug. I believe there is more pressure in a religious college setting to find a mate. It is almost an insatiable push. All I wanted was for her to be perfectly well and for the fear in my heart to vanish.

Doug was a trumpet player, drove a Subaru, and was crazy in love with Teresa…or was enthralled by her free spirit. He came from an extremely dysfunctional family and hated his father. Evidently he saw strength in Teresa that he wanted. Teresa's brother was not in favor of this relationship at all, but she believed she was falling in love. Don Ralph told her Doug was drawing too much out of her. She needed to preserve her strength. But when does love listen?

When Teresa called she sounded more and more tired and unsure of everything. She said Doug was not always nice to her. She even seemed irritable with us. What was going on? We encouraged her to go see a doctor. She said she had seen the doctor Dr. Glass recommended, but he said her blood work was fine, so she had not been back. When we insisted, she said she would make an appointment and go.

When she finally went, the doctor found she was running a high temperature, and he put her immediately in the hospital. The doctor then called Dr. Glass and said there were a few stray leukemia cells, not many that could be disposed of in a hurry. This was the hospital Oral Roberts had built as a healing hospital, as he called it.

The university staff was made aware of Teresa's relapse, and plans were made for her to come home immediately. Don and I agreed she must leave ASAP, although we did think it a bit odd the way it was handled. We believed that a student who had been diagnosed with leukemia, with reoccurring symptoms, would not be good publicity for a school that was built on miracles and healing. I could not wait to have Teresa back under the care of Dr. Glass, but I wondered why he had agreed to let her go off to Oklahoma knowing she might have a relapse. We had been so blind to reality!

Good-bye to Friends

When Teresa was preparing to leave her friends at college, they all gathered around her with sympathetic good-byes. Distressed by the unwanted sympathy, she excused herself. She crawled into the tub for a bath and started singing loudly. She could not tolerate being the object of sympathy. Her friends were aghast at her ability to sing at such a moment! Many tears were shed, for everywhere Teresa went she endeared herself to all, but sympathy stifled her free spirit.

Her faith had been shaken, and Don and I were scared—really scared—but we quickly made plans for her to come back home. We were alarmed that at Oral Roberts University—supposedly a campus that believed in miracles—no one offered to pray for her. It just seemed the school wanted her out of there pronto. Was there no integrity to the charismatic movement? Were they always in denial of reality? Here again my angst with the charismatics arose.

Home Front Not Much Better

Things at home had deteriorated, and my mind was not working correctly. My renewed fear cast a shadow of unbelievable fear over the whole household. I believe Don and I were both skirting the reality of the situation. Our marriage was explosive with conflict. Stress was just in the air. We'd had such a happy and healthy marriage for almost twenty-two years. What was happening to us? I would retreat into my inner thoughts, often reading the songs Teresa had written just to feel her spirit and commitment. I continually tried to find solace in something…anything!

Horror Again

Even in the midst of her new battle—and with the disappointment of losing her dreams of attending Oral Roberts University—hope and faith were still the essence of this modern-day martyr, this angelic St. Teresa, this daughter of our love! She planned to come home, get well again, get a job, and plan a wedding.

On the way to the airport to pick up our daughter, I'm not sure if Don and I even spoke, so distraught we were in our uneasiness. When the plane arrived, we expected Teresa to run into our arms, but she was wheeled off the ramp in a wheelchair...such an unbelievable sight. We could tell she was embarrassed, but the flight attendant was following the instructions he had been given.

We took Teresa to see Dr. Glass immediately. It was April 11, 1974, two years after her first series of chemo. New testing began. Her bone marrow was again 95 percent packed with leukemia cells—not with the few stray cells the Oklahoma doctor had told Dr. Glass.

Connection with Wholeness

Teresa said that before she started any more chemo, she wanted to go see Judd Kilpack. About two years before, Teresa had moved her horse, Kishan, to Judd Kilpack's barn and pasture, and she and Judd had become good friends. Horse people seem to have innate connections. Teresa had sold Kishan to a young girl during one of her good times at home. She did not feel it fair to keep him and not be able to ride and care for him. Even though she had sold Kishan, she was free to ride Judd's horses, which she did as often as her health allowed. Judd was so glad to see her and told her one of his horses was about to foal. He said if it was a black filly, it was hers. Teresa said that when she was riding, she felt perfectly whole. She loved the wind in her face and her hair flowing in the wind. She felt so free!

Don and I tried to celebrate her coming home, even with our bleeding hearts. We encouraged her to see her friends who had not gone away to college. But before anything else, she wanted to go ride Scarlet, one of Judd's horses

Trying to Be Normal

Doug Wilson, who was newly Teresa's fiancé, planned to visit when school let out. He would follow Don Ralph, driving his own car. Teresa and Doug's relationship definitely seemed serious. Unrealistic as it was, Teresa started looking for work and making plans for an August 10 wedding. We were all trying to ignore what lay before us.

She went looking for a job, sure that everything would be OK again. She secured a job—working the night shift in the proof department of a local bank—after her first interview. And she waited for Doug's arrival with great anticipation. Both Don and I were panic stricken in this strange world of unreality. We were planning for a wedding when more chemo was about to take place. Had we lost control of our minds?

After allowing Teresa a short time to catch up, the chemo began once again, with another induction of cytosine. How does one maintain the emotional tenure of one's psyche when dreams have crashed? Don and I had clung to such hope, but that hope was dashed before our very eyes.

It was soon after a series of chemo that Don and I were invited to a wedding shower for a dear friend. Sonja and I had been in a women's Bible study at Valley Presbyterian Church. Her husband had recently left her, but she refused to let it ruin her life and kept a positive outlook. When Don and I had our little ones baptized at Valley, it was Sonja who invited us to lunch for a celebration. She later asked me to go to lunch with her so she could talk about Lowell, a former pastor who was in pursuit of her. A romance had ensued, and now they were to be married. (Lowell's wife had left him as well.) In the church where he had served, divorce was almost the unforgivable sin, and his heart was traumatized from the whole situation.

Pretense

Don and I had become good friends with Lowell too and had many coffee outings together, discussing our painful experiences. A mutual friend was having a shower for the new couple. Emotionally crippled, Don and I still attended, hoping no one noticed the sword of Damocles hanging over our heads with our every movement. It was a lovely April day, which enabled us to sit on the deck. A dear senseless lady began going on and on about all the miracles occurring in her life daily. What was she thinking, with us sitting there, blood oozing from every pore of our hearts?

Don and I had been waiting patiently for the results of a bone marrow test that had been performed the day before. While we were at the party, Teresa called from the hospital to tell us the recent chemotherapy had not brought about remission. We knew we might get a call while we were at the shower, announcing another remission. When we would get that call, then we could lighten up. This party was to be a joyous occasion for these two dear friends! However, the call we got was not what we wanted to hear. When I hung up, I could hardly hold back the tears, but I felt like I needed to rejoin the party like nothing was wrong.

A few minutes later, Michele—twelve years old now—called and needed a mom to be in her court. She had just gone to have her hair cut and was not happy with the result. In fact she hated the cut and was crying out to me over the phone. I should have been with her. Actually it was a darling cut, but this was the frame of mind each of us was in: Nothing looked right to us. The whole picture was lopsided. Numbness and despair hung in the air.

Please, No More

Fatigue and rushing adrenaline were constant companions. Friends were not as eager to help as they had been initially. The battle had become too long for them. The news was never good. By May Teresa's bones were 99 percent packed so more treatment was needed. By the end of May, they were still 95 percent packed. On June 3 Teresa had to have blood transfusions and platelets. By the twelfth of June, her marrow was 104 percent packed. She was given massive amounts of drugs, with no apparent effect.

On one occasion at midday, during one of Teresa's lowest ebbs, I was alone with her in her hospital room. The hospital chaplain came in and began to tell Teresa she needed to prepare for her demise. If she had anything she needed to make right, now was the time to do it. I was livid, and Teresa was devastated. His advice was so uncalled for.

When I saw Dr. Glass later that afternoon, I told him that a ten-minute visit from that chaplain had undone everything he had so diligently been trying to do for Teresa in the last two years. Further, I wanted it known that the chaplain was never to come back into Teresa's room. I spent the rest of the day reassuring Teresa that God was a loving God. Later a social worker came in with the same agenda. She filled the room with her garbled attempt to make conversation. Everything was totally out of sync!

From April to June, there had been no significant reduction in leukemia cells. If we were told this, we did not hear it, or we blocked it out of our minds and hearts. Teresa had experienced two previous remissions. We had suffered through people telling her she had lost her healing because of sin. We had survived those attacks. We would lick it this time as well!

I began going down the "what if?" road. I wondered if, we had never left Colfax or become mixed up in the charismatic movement, life would be different now. Our resilience was lacking. Teresa's resilience was lacking. Even so, we would continue to fight with sheer will once again. I was guilt ridden. I was spent. I was heartbroken.

As Teresa was able, she did keep riding Judd's horses with great delight. Those times were brief, but it seemed at those times she was pain-free. However, on one occasion she was with several horses in the pasture when they stampeded. She came home with her clothes torn and in much pain. This was such a surprise, as most horses crept up to Teresa as though she were the horse whisperer. I wondered if now those horses sensed her weakness.

Nothing seemed right. Teresa continued to work at her night job, take chemo, and receive transfusions and platelets, but she was not bouncing back as she had in the past. Her spirit seemed to be broken.

Still Turning Over Stones

Kathryn Kuhlman, the evangelistic healer, came to town, and we took Teresa to see her. We were still trying to turn over every stone for an expected miracle. Dr. Ramsthal, our friend, was the doctor onstage who was checking and verifying the healings. I wondered how he could tell a healing just by looking at a person, but he indeed pronounced healings.

As three different ladies came up on stage, we recognized them. We had met these ladies at the Wednesday night Baptist healing service. They had been up on the stage claiming healing, which Dr. Ramsthal had verified. (But all of them later died!) It was such a conflict of hope and fear. Afterward Teresa told us she would have felt much closer to God if she had been riding through the meadows on Judd's horses. I had really had it with the charismatics, but I did not want to close the door on any possible miracle. What should I have done?

Too Much

Teresa had misgivings even though she was still planning an August wedding. While waiting for Doug, she had received letters from his mother and grandmother. Doug had told Teresa he came from a dysfunctional family, but both his mother and grandmother warned Teresa about his temper and hostility. When Teresa shared some of his background with Don and me, we were extremely concerned, but how do you deal with that when your only concern is to see your daughter whole once again?

Teresa said she just wanted Doug to be around her father for the summer—after all, look how well her brother had turned out. She told us she was sitting on a dynamite cake, and she could not fight his relatives all by herself. She needed God's help. She felt the strain would kill her.

Teresa was still doing her night shift—5:00 p.m. to 1:30 a.m.—at the bank and taking chemo during the day, but that schedule would not last long, with another series of chemo coming up. We were on a dual track, trying to be normal and dealing with a deadly disease.

Eventually Don Ralph arrived home, with Doug following in his own car. Teresa said her first week having Doug there was glorious, but she was beginning to have serious doubts about their mutual values. Her diary noted: "I've been in the hospital since last Sunday. The turmoil I was going through caused me not to be able to fight. I lost all desire to live to fight or anything else. Douglas so drained me."

At that point Father T, Don, and I told Teresa and Doug they could not even talk about a wedding. Teresa's health was all that was important now. That seemed to relieve Teresa somewhat; however, another diary entry said this: "You see, diary, since Christmas I've been slowly dying inside. Especially since I got sick at school and took up with Douglas. The trouble came when I tried to be normal. I am so tired of loving unstable people."

It seemed when Doug was around, he wanted to wrangle, even as Teresa lay in a hospital bed. His negative spirit was leaving Teresa confused and depressed. Her tender spirit was being crushed. Since she was unable to give her testimony and sing, she said she felt stagnate. There was tension in the home. We had all lost our way. Where was the joy? Where was that fairy-tale life? Don and I didn't know what to do, but Father T told Teresa that Doug must go home.

Everything about that summer was unreal, full of pathos and despair. Doug could not comprehend the gravity of the situation. He just continued to pour out his sordid background to Teresa, draining her and crushing her spirit. We would see her with a lilt in her spirit in the morning, and after a day with Doug, she would be totally undone! She had never had such encounters. His language became very colorful—not good for the little ones to hear—and he became an exploding volcano. I encouraged everyone to be gentle—to be surgeons, not butchers—but when we learned Teresa needed more chemo, that was it. I was ready to bodily move him out.

Don and I watched Doug strangle our daughter's spirit for two months, and in our blindness—in the name of love—we did not lift a finger. She kept thinking he would grow on us, and in her compassion she wanted him to experience the same freedom she knew. Teresa said, "Where's all this love you've preached all these years?" And truly, Don did attempt to continually pour positives into Doug, but Doug was like a sponge soaking up Don's strength, which left Don physically and spiritually drained. Rather than ministering to the needs of his family, Don was wrestling with the demon in our home. Doug remained as pessimistic and defeated as ever. He would share strange hallucinations he was having, and still Teresa looked at him through the eyes of love and saw a little boy crying for help. Given her nature, she could not turn away.

When Teresa talked to Father T about Doug, he said at her age the maternal instinct was very strong to care for others and often overruled good sense. When Teresa shared a little bit of Doug's background with Father Truehella, he told us later, he went home thanking God he would not be around for the wedding. He should have told Teresa that!

On one occasion Doug said to me, "I hate to tell you this, Mrs. Gibbs, but your daughter is not that hot to look at!" I nearly swallowed my tongue, for this was the first time I had heard my daughter was not much to look at. I knew she was not five feet six inches with measurements of thirty-six, twenty-four, thirty-six, but this was totally inhumane from a supposed fiancé! What about all those boyfriends who had always pounded down our door? Does not genuine love see a beloved as a pure, radiant beauty?

Doug was even making passes at Teresa's younger sisters and commenting on any voluptuous female in his sight. Don and I were dumbfounded and knew not what to do to protect our daughter. Later Teresa was very angry at Father Truehella for not telling her his true feelings. Don Ralph, who was very angry at what he saw, said, "I've come home to see my sister get well!" So the atmosphere in the home was not good.

How could we think straight when we all felt like we were being stretched on a body torture rack? I was trying to blot out everything I was hearing and seeing and even participating in. For all our married years, Don and I had desperately tried to establish a utopia for our children, a place where peace, tranquility, and perfection had their domain…and here we were in a concentration camp of nature's making. Was this how those in concentration camps felt? Those who were about to enter the gas ovens, those burning at stakes, those being tortured at the hands of terrorists, or those tortured with terminal diseases?

Job's Counselors

During this drama every dollar was stretched to care for our jewels, and we were even being criticized for this. The battle of the last three years had depleted our funds. Some suggested Don and I should not have spent so much time at the hospital with our daughter. They also felt it was wrong to bring in food for the younger children who were left home night after night fending for themselves. We felt that purchasing food was the minimum loving care we could give. These supposed friends said we should have just let the Lord supply. In fact they complained that we were not giving *them* the attention we had in the past. All our attention was given to fighting the lethal battle before us, not to trying not to offend people who wanted our attention. Job's counselors (false friends like the ones in the book of Job) were everywhere, clamoring to get at us!

Oasis

Thankfully, in addition to these Job's counselors, there were dear friends who were ever ready to relieve a little pain. When our friend Durwood put legs on his prayers, he said we needed a little fun and took us down the rapids in his raft. Doug, who was still living with us, refused to go. Was it fear? He had no interest in any of Teresa's sports or desires, so he stayed home. The rest of us went, and Teresa had a grand time with our beloved friends. If Teresa was in pain that day, no one knew! That day seemed like an oasis in the middle of the desert. It was a day of laughter. Even bumping over the rapids did not seem to affect Teresa's joy.

Free at Last

Don and I suggested—as tactfully as possible—that since Doug would not be going to school in Oregon and the wedding was off, he would be happier in Oklahoma. He still couldn't see the gravity of the situation and continued to pour out his sordid background and his present needs to Teresa. We explained she did not have her usual stamina to meet his needs. Finally both Teresa and Doug decided he should return to Oklahoma. We took them out to dinner, and later Teresa bid a tearful good-bye to Douglas, the young man she had thought she would be marrying on August 10. Our hearts were breaking for many reasons.

After Doug left, Teresa said her spirit lifted, and she felt free once again. I thought it was a little unfair that he went home free, and she was left depleted to wage her battle. Thank God some of Teresa's old boyfriends continually called and wanted to go out with her, once again building up her self-esteem. Don and I filled every moment we could with what possible joy we could fake. The roller-coaster ride with Doug was over…briefly!

Reasoning Gone

After the fire had destroyed our boat, we had found a boat advertised. It was a fine seventeen-foot boat that had to be sold in a divorce settlement. The price was excellent, and this family who loved the water could not do without a boat.

Still trying to be normal, we decided to take the boat out one sunny afternoon. It was late in June, and Doug was gone. Teresa was getting a teeny tiny bit of her spirit back. But sailing across the Wilson River caused her to sob and scream in pain, and we quickly knew this idea was a poor attempt at being normal. Teresa had wanted to go out in the boat and thought she could do it. Where was that spirit? Where was that resiliency? She said, "Mom, I just can't bounce back." I pleaded with Don to go back to shore, which he did. We loaded the boat and went home with heavy hearts.

During one of Teresa's slight reprieves, still trying to play the normal card, Don and I left Teresa home with her sisters and left the little ones with our dear friends the Thomas family, and we took off for a seekers' retreat in Eastern Oregon. We had been working with the young adult group at Valley, and they suggested we needed to get away. Nonsense! I do not remember one thing about that retreat. What were we thinking? We just could not pretend to live in normalcy any longer.

We were riding with a young couple in the group, Mark Hilditch and his wife, so we could not turn around and go home. At every stop for gas, I found a phone to call home. In my heart I was begging to return. I so needed to know Teresa was OK. Even though we were gone only one night, I knew I had made a serious, damnable mistake leaving Teresa alone—and all the children, for that matter! I do not remember where we slept that night, only that I prayed all night, unable to sleep. When would we learn that we were dealing with an abnormal situation and should learn to say no?

After an agonizing thirty-six hours, we finally got home, and I vowed never to leave again. Teresa's reprieve lasted only a few days before a new series of chemo was to begin using a new experimental drug.

Ying and Yang

It was the Fourth of July. We decided to go out for breakfast and then take a drive up to Multnomah Falls. We took the scenic route along the old Oregon Trail Highway, and we saw a little parade on the way. It was such a simple thing, but it brought joy.

There was no way we would attempt taking the boat out on the water again, as we had done in past July Fourths. Teresa seemed to be so free that day and relatively free of pain. Her diary says it was a refreshing day. I think we were in a bubble of joy. I had such love in my heart for my husband and my family…all safely tucked into our car…Yes, that day was a bubble of joy!

However, we couldn't live in the bubble forever. A couple of days later, Don's aunt called and asked if he would marry her and her third husband-to-be. She wanted Don to do the ceremony in our living room. It was a day that should have been devoted to the family and to Lowell and Sonja's wedding, which was planned for that same afternoon, but Don changed his plans for the day, unable to say no to their demands! Don did the best he could, with pain crowding out good reason.

We all looked forward to celebrating with Lowell and Sonja. Our lives were so intertwined with our friends and their celebrations…How could we stay home? Teresa wanted to join us, and she wrote in her diary that it was a beautiful wedding, but I remember nothing except for the pastor being late. Teresa had painted an ethereal painting of doves, all in shades of blue. She had painted it for Dr. Emerick, the ENT who had ordered radiation for the growth in her neck, but she wanted to give a painting to Lowell and Sonja as well. What should she do? She decided she could do another painting for Dr. Emerick later.

Not the Same

Life was such a haze. We staggered through experiences that should have brought joy, thinking only of getting our daughter well. A couple of Teresa's best friends, Patti Pullin and Brenda Banford, were home for the summer, and Brenda was to be married. They called to have lunch with Teresa. Did they know? Could they tell how serious her condition was?

Teresa had made them necklaces, and she said it was like old times, laughing and being together. However, she was deeply hurt at not being asked to be in one of her best friends' weddings. They had been so tight throughout high school;

she had hoped to be a bridesmaid. Doug had gone back to Oklahoma, and there would be no wedding for Teresa.

New Drug

When it was time for the experimental drug, I asked Dr. Glass if Teresa should be hospitalized. We did not want to take risks. He told us he did not take risks. So, in spite of our fears, we put our confidence in his expertise.

On July 11 Dr. Glass started the new drug, called Azacitidine. Another drug that she had been on was called tioguanine. It was mild compared to this new drug. Teresa remained home, vomiting for five days straight. She clung to me as she lay in a fetal position, and I dared not leave her side. Don's and my constant touching and loving was all that could momentarily remove the pain. It was very hot, so Teresa usually stayed in her brother's bed downstairs, where it was cooler. Our house had no air conditioner, and fans did little to ease the discomfort, but Teresa also wanted to lie in our bed upstairs sometimes to be nearer to the family and activity.

Jason, now a toddler, would pat Teresa's head and smother her with kisses. He would look at me and say, "Mommy?" Did he understand the gravity of the situation? I prayed nonstop for a miracle. The air was thick with foreboding, and we felt almost as if we were in another time zone…one where we did not belong.

After the horror of that first series of the new drug, Teresa said, "I am not taking that drug any longer. It feels like they are dumping twenty tons of poison into my body."

And so I said, "Bring our miracle, Lord, please, oh, please! I am speaking it!" Isn't that what John Osteen said to do?

Teresa's words in her diary were as follows: "I'm just afraid to go back today. I feel so much better in the mornings, and then I have to get that junk. It feels like twenty tons of poison. Oh, Jesus, please be with me, please, I am scared!"

CHAPTER 20

Yes, Chicken Little, the Sky Has Fallen

She sobs through the night; tears stream down her cheeks…
All her friends have betrayed her and become her enemies.
—Lam 1:2, NLT

Where Is God?

On August 7 Teresa began running a raging fever, over 104 degrees. It was a Thursday evening, and Don and I were so frightened by her appearance that we felt she needed to be in the hospital. We were frantic! She was wearing her pink bathrobe and pink slippers because she had been too sick to dress for several days. We helped her lie down in the backseat of the car and made the trip across town to Kaiser, entering the emergency part of the hospital.

Teresa sat in a wheelchair but could hardly sit up she was in such pain. Why couldn't the entry staff hurry with all their procedures for admittance? When they finally completed all the paper work and had her in a room, they started doing tests right away. Don had to go home to be with the children and to prepare for several classes the next day, leaving behind his very sick daughter and bereft wife.

Teresa's blood pressure was low. She had sepsis in her blood, and her body functions were not acting right. If that was not enough, she had pneumonia. They gave her several units of blood and started massive doses of antibiotics. That seemed to pick up her spirits somewhat.

I was awake all night holding her. The pain was too intense to deal with rationally, and she dozed off periodically but kept saying, "Please, don't leave me!"

Hospital personnel came in throughout the night. The next morning she rallied only slightly, but by afternoon she had a seizure, and her kidneys had shut down. Doctors rushed in to bring her out of the seizure and to do a spinal tap to check what was going on. All the while I hovered, not really aware of my surroundings, knowing only I could not leave my daughter.

Over the Edge

After that first seizure, I was called out into the hall. Our young assistant pastor, Jim Mead from Valley, had come. He held me tenderly while I sobbed, unable to tell him what was going on. I have no idea what he said to me. But he did go in and pray with Teresa. She thanked him for coming. I had just witnessed her eyes roll backward and her body in seizure, and now she was already lucid and thanking our young pastor.

Don had been checking on us by phone throughout the day. He called again after a class to check on us before his night class. I did not want to sound like it was critical that he come, so I just said, "Why don't you come?" I could not bear to tell him of this latest crisis, and I did not want to alarm Teresa nor for her to hear me. I was not sure I could hold myself together after witnessing the seizures.

Whether or not Don heard the seriousness in my voice, he canceled his night class. He called Christy and told her to go ahead and feed the children, for he would be staying with me at the hospital. By the time he arrived, Dr. Glass had decided to move Teresa to the intensive care unit. They got her ready; she was hooked up to so many tubes. She did not want me to leave her side, but when Don came, Dr. Glass asked us to accompany him to an empty room. He had us sit down and said, "Mr. and Mrs. Gibbs, your daughter is not going to make it."

I looked at him and nearly shouted, "I have seven children, and I am not giving up any of them…Do you hear?" I have no idea what he continued to tell us. I wasn't mentally there.

Still the Saint

In a total stupor, Don and I joined Teresa in the intensive care room. The nurses wanted to give Teresa oxygen to help her breathe, but she refused. We stood at the foot of her bed unable to speak.

She looked at us and said, "Mom and Dad, I am fine!" It was ethereal. Her smile was unreal. She had not smiled in so long. Was it the morphine? Or was it a knowledge we knew nothing about? It chilled me to the bone! How could a smile be so heavenly and yet so soul chilling? I had to step out of the room to compose myself.

As I stepped back in the room, I heard Don Ralph, now very much a military man, stride down the hall with that military cadence. Teresa heard his footsteps also and was so elated to have him come. When he stepped into her room, she said, "You sure do look handsome in your uniform! I'm glad you are so free." He had just come from the National Guard unit across town. Don and I stepped out of the room again so Don Ralph and Teresa could have some time together. He stayed with her briefly, and they talked like always.

Damnable

Don and I were in the hall when Blanch, the lady who led the healing meetings we attended every Wednesday evening, appeared. She had come to see Teresa. We did not let her go in and invade Teresa's time with her brother, but before she left she had a comment for us. Her sarcastic comment to me was, "Too bad you didn't speak to that little girl about death." I wanted to vomit, for she was one of those people who said if you want healing, you must never ever say or believe anything other than healing.

I was in a fog! I was depleted and exhausted. It seemed like charismatics were lurking everywhere, ready to shoot the wounded. I had not had any sleep for the last thirty-six hours, and I had not been to bed for the past week, as I had been sitting by Teresa's bed, only dozing.

Don Ralph left, and Don and I went back into Teresa's room. She was becoming listless. I kept telling Don to pray, pray…Do not sleep!

Teresa said, "Stay close, and come up here by me." But there were tubes everywhere, seemingly attached to every part of her body. The tubes were mostly on her right side and near her headboard, so I had to sit on her left side, holding her hand but unable to embrace her. Her dad was sitting at the foot of the bed. She seemed to be talking to some of her friends. Once she said, "What are you doing here?" Was she delirious? And if not, what was she seeing?

Please, Oh, Please

At five o'clock that morning, Teresa said, "Dad, you better get help!" Don and I both rushed out to find help, and he went to get the nurses. Evidently the nurses who were continually coming in and out had already alerted Dr. Glass, who had stayed in the room next to Teresa, unbeknownst to us. He was there in a heartbeat. Then I heard a code ninety-nine reverberating throughout the hospital corridors. I ran. I don't know where I ran, but I ran, screaming for God to hear me.

Male nurses brought the defibrillator paddles and tried to revive Teresa, but at 5:15 a.m. on August 9, 1974, she was pronounced dead. The next thing I knew, Dr. Glass had Don and me in a sterile private room telling us our daughter had died. He said the previous day she had thanked him for all he had done for her. The sun was shining through the window, casting shadows on the floor, but as he spoke those words I felt like my essence left my body and floated down—from head to arms to legs to feet—and onto my shadow on that cold hospital floor. All life drained from us and into those shadows. This moment was never supposed to come, but here it was.

I experienced grief of such magnitude as it moved in and hovered over every room of my mind and heart. My life and personality were blown to bits. Every room of past hurts and past memories was crumbled into nothingness. The giant of disbelief filled the room. The events of the past twenty-four hours seemed to be compressed into this moment in eternity, and I was a jumbled mess of nothingness. "Please, let me wake up!"

The room was swimming dizzily around us. Who was this man before us saying these strange words: "Your daughter is dead"? Words…did we need to say any words back? *No!* That was it.

"No, it can't be!" I had to get out of what must have been a strange dream of unreality! I was in the hall alone when a nurse intercepted me. Where had that nurse come from, that lady in white? When had she intercepted me? Then I was outside. How did I get outside? Don was there too, with Dr. Glass, who was trying to console us. He asked us if we wanted to go back in Teresa's room. Did we answer? Dr. Glass called Don Ralph, who was home, because the doctor would not let Don and I drive our car home.

We had been so confident in healing, even though we were numbed by what our eyes beheld. We didn't become hysterical, but numbness covered us like a canopy, and our life oozed out. Ralph came, and like whipped children Don and

I climbed into the car, sitting in the front seat together. As we drove back across town for the last time, we were unable to speak. We could only sob!

I did not even go back into the room to see Teresa for one last time. I had been by her side for nearly three years, and she had been in our lives for twenty wonderful years…and now I was mad…mentally deranged with grief. I felt like a robot wound so tightly that the spring would break at any minute, and I would fall into a heap of tin, or like a victim of a car wreck, hemorrhaging on the side of the road and told to get up, but I could not get up.

Fly Away

Christy and Michele were waiting in the red room when we got home, expecting Teresa to be with us. The little ones were playing, oblivious to our tragic news. It was a beautiful morning, and when I stepped out to the backyard…I heard…I imagined…maybe I hoped…Teresa say, "Thanks oodles, Mom and Dad, for bringing me into my glory." Then she raced across the sky on a beautiful black stallion, glowing like she had so often. I remembered how she would say she felt normal and so very free when she was able to ride. But then that odd, fleeting thought was gone, and reality kicked me in the gut.

Sometime that day I saw Teresa's song, "Come Fly Away with Me," on the piano. It was one of her songs that she had sent home from college. At the time it had blessed me and left me shaking! Now here it was, leaving me shaking again.

Come Fly Away with Me

Come away and fly with me.
Leave your sorrows, come spread your wings.
Mount the air and reach for the sun,
Leave those problems in the past.
They're already done.
Let me hold you and ease the pain,
Let me give sunshine to dry up your rain.

Let the wind blow away those heavy cares.
Just close your eyes, and pretend you're not even there.

Think of me and the love that I give,
And you'll find how much you really want to live.
Life is made for you to conquer, my love.
Strength, I promise, will always come from above.

So when you're facing the problems that press you through the day,
Each time one comes along, the easier they'll drop away.
If you only knew how much I love and want you free.
I don't want that world taking your eyes off of me.
I just want you to be free, my love,
Free to laugh and dance and sing and smile, my love.

Come away and fly, fly with me.
Leave your sorrows, come spread, spread your wings.
Come fly away; come fly away, come fly away with me,
And be free, forever free, in me.

Unbelievable Grief

Friends began filling the house. I was given Valium. Dr. Ramsthal had given me this sedative many months ago, when tragedy first had begun to unfold. My friends JB and Shirley, whom I knew from my early religious connections, had heard of our loss somehow. They lived in Oregon City, way across town from Beaverton, but still came immediately to be with us. Shirley was a nurse and was glad to dispense the Valium when needed. Did I feed the children during those days? Did I talk? I really do not know. But I do know that those friends lay down on the floor with us and stayed throughout that first night. When we continually awakened to the horror of what had just happened, they held us! Don, who rarely cries, cried out with gut-wrenching sobs. Our grief was uncontrollable.

The next morning Assistant Pastor Jim Mead came to ask us if we wanted Teresa cremated, and I was horrified to think of my baby being burned up. I was unable to make any plans for a memorial service for our darling daughter. It would be up to whom? I did not know! I could not go to the mortuary. I could not possibly enter that nightmare. Don pulled himself together and went with Pastor Mead to the mortuary. He viewed our daughter lying there motionless, gone from us. He kissed her on the forehead and left. Teresa's own mother, after never leaving her side for all of those months, was nowhere to be seen.

Our home was full of people everywhere, but all I could do was cry. All was a blur. Bob Davis, the senior pastor, was in Canada backpacking with his family. He called us during that Saturday maze to give us his condolences. I wanted to say, "Please come home, Bob," but he could not. It was August, and even pastors need vacations with their families. It seemed the news of Teresa's departure had traveled the country in one day, as the phone was ringing constantly with calls from all across the United States.

The Thomas family came. They brought their girls, who would stay overnight and be with the younger children. I knew I would not take our younger children to a funeral service for their sister. I didn't want them to develop the same phobias I had. I am sure they felt the grief in the room, though. It was in the air. But maybe because we often had so much company, all those extra people made them think we were having another party.

They were such happy babies. Cean wanted to know where his sister was. I could tell the atmosphere did impact his little heart, though he did not really know what was happening. He just wanted his champion back. Was she still in the hospital getting well? At four years old, how much could he understand?

Hooray for Valium

The next day was Sunday, and Valley Presbyterian Church would have a memorial for our daughter, but she would not be there. Some years before, five members of one family had been burned in a house fire—the mother and four children. They had lined those five caskets up in front of a full church, and the church elders decided that never again would they allow any casket in a memorial after the anguish of that service.

Don's folks came to the house early that Sunday for their granddaughter's service. Their first greeting was to inform us that a clock we had given to them had stopped…they thought it was a sign of our daughter's passing. Later they went on to say we had lost our daughter because Don had left the ministry. At the time I was too stunned to respond or even hear. Later, though, their comment sank in, and I was crushed. Don's church ministry had touched people, but thousands of students had funneled through his classes in his more than fifteen years of teaching. His guidance and testimony to those students had been powerful; his students told him so. This dastardly comment would later give Don and the whole family great distress. Was this another one of those fundamentalist tactics? We hadn't obeyed, so the Lord took our child? What garbage!

Tapestry of Love

It was time to go to Valley for the final service. Someone loaded me up on Valium. I could hardly walk into the church, but dear friends were all around. I do not remember much, but I do know Jim Mead's sermon was about a tapestry. We can see only the underside with all the knots and weavings, but to God it is a wonderfully woven piece of beauty on the topside of one's life.

I heard our dear Suzanne New sing "In My Father's House Are Many Rooms." After Pastor Mead's message on the tapestry, Leonard Ranton, who I had sung with in the choir, sang from the choir loft behind us. I had never heard him sing more beautifully, although I didn't remember afterward what he sang. The music floated through the air with such beauty before Don Ralph—the only family member who was able to speak—went forward to share. Don and I wept silently as this loving brother spoke, telling tales of his beloved sister.

Then it was over, and many faceless people embraced us and shared their warm condolences. But it was one of Teresa's boyfriends, Tab Lahodney, lingering in the vestibule, waiting to give his regrets with hugs and tears, who made me crumble into uncontrollable sobs. He had been one of the boys from the Assembly church who had recently dated Teresa. He was very fond of her and had so built up her self-esteem with his gentleness. Why could Teresa's last boyfriend not care for her as deeply as many guys before him had?

Christy and Michele just seemed catatonic, not knowing how one acts when you lose a beloved sister. Some soul had told them they had to be strong for us... how absurd! The whole family was in a grief boat together.

During the service Don said he saw Teresa standing in front of the church. She was in a beautiful yellow gown, telling him, "Dad, I'm great!" Was it a dream? Was it desire? Whatever it was it touched him deeply.

Only Friends

The only relief in our grief-stricken home that night was friends. Our state patrolman friend and his wife—the one who had given Don the ticket for hitting a mudslide those many years before—heard the news and came immediately.

Over the years this couple had become such dear friends. They had been at the coast for a retreat. How they had heard about our loss, I do not know, but they came and sat on the floor with us and many other friends. They sang hymns and praise songs while I cried a bucket of tears. It was like a balm over my heart, and for moments the reality disappeared…there was just those beautiful songs reverberating throughout the house, which was to have had nothing but joy in it! But there was no joy that night or for many nights to come. The evening got late, and our friends all needed to leave. Again Don and I and our children were alone in our grief.

Dear friends from Valley continued to come with hugs, with no pat answers and no words, just embraces and food—legs on their prayers. Don and I had suffered such cruelty from the charismatics—and we were to receive so much more—that these embraces made us truly feel God's arms around us. But it was Monday. I wondered how I could possibly go to the cemetery and lay our daughter in the ground. Remember, I had grown up in a church that believed in soul sleeping. Father T, the undertaker, a couple of friends, and the children were with Don and me as we entered that cemetery. My legs gave out when I saw our daughter's casket draped in a green vestment Father T had given. One of the few things I remember about that black day was Mr. Springer, the mortuary undertaker, who had prepared our daughter for burial. He hugged my limp body so very tenderly. His daughter was one of Teresa's good friends at school. How could he be in such a heartbreaking business, I wondered. That black day is lodged forever in my mind. A part of me was buried alongside my daughter of twenty years.

Don and I went home to a house full of food, people, and friends who hugged us with tears in their eyes. But there were others there with not-so-welcome condolences, trying to convince us this was all God's will. One dear friend from my past brought frozen food. As she placed it in the freezer, she said, "Won't it be a glorious day when the Lord returns, our loved ones wake, and graves are opened?" Though I dearly loved this friend of my youth, I did not need to hear that, for I knew where we had just laid our daughter. I desperately wanted to believe Teresa had gone to heaven immediately. At that moment my deep hurt was slowly beginning to turn into anger.

There Is Love and Goodness

Soon Bob Davis returned from his vacation and came to us, showing us such tenderness. He had children the ages of our children, a daughter the same age as

Teresa. Pastor Davis gave us the keys to his cabin in Montana. He said, "Please, be my guest. You need some time away to recover from this blow." He had put legs on his prayers. Don and I appreciated his gentle generosity so very much.

Don Ralph was back in training, so he could not join us, but the rest of us crowded into our car for that trip. The little children joyfully ran naked around the cabin, and it made Don and I smile and giggle with them, but the pain was still thick in the air, and tears still flowed. Christy and Michele were grieving, and what could we do but grieve beside them?

We hated to return home to the reality of our future. We stopped at one of the new malls to shop, but there was no enjoyment in that. The girls and I used to love our shopping trips. We so tried to be upbeat but could not. As we continued to drive with our hurting teenage daughters and three little children, little Danielle kept saying in her one-and-a-half-year-old voice, "Hurry up, Scarlet!" When we investigated further, we saw she had a pretend halter and rope and was leading Scarlet the horse beside the car as we drove along. She had remembered those horseback rides on Scarlet that very summer. In her childish mind, did she know? Did this little jewel dropped from heaven have the same love of horses? We would see!

We stopped in Spokane to see our good friends the Hansens, who had been pastors at the Nazarene church in Colfax when we were in our Camelot. They now had a pastorate in Spokane, Washington. Typically Shirley put on a spread of food that glowed with love and warmth, and they simply poured healing oil on our hearts…no clichés, just love.

Then it was time to go home. Don and I returned the cabin keys to our beloved pastor with gratitude for that brief getaway. Our first Sunday back in church, Pastor Davis preached a sermon straight to our broken hearts, entitled "Utterly, Unbearably Crushed." How true this message was for us!

Our friends from Colfax, the Dotys and Culbertsons, often made fall mini trips to the coast after they had finished their wheat harvest. Don and I had not been home long when we got a call from Dale Culbertson. He asked if we could please meet them at a certain restaurant for lunch. The only catch was that it was in Lincoln City, Oregon, on the coast. We made arrangements to leave the three small children with the Thomas girls, as we could not refuse time with our Colfax friends. They surprised us by providing us with a catered room at their motel as well. Though our hearts were still breaking, these friends did not coddle us or us give empty-minded clichés. They just loved us with lavish dinners and healing balm. The two Colfax guys told jokes nonstop that made us laugh in spite of our bleeding hearts. All they did was pour the same love on us that they had when we served as their pastors. It brought a small measure of healing. We did not know what awaited us back home!

CHAPTER 21

Barnyard Care

> Singing cheerful songs to a person with a heavy
> heart is like taking someone's coat in cold
> weather or pouring vinegar in a wound.
> —Prv 25:20, NLT

> They wept until they could weep no more.
> —1 Sm 30:4

> It feels like being mildly drunk or having a concussion.
> There is sort of an invisible blanket between the world and
> me. I find it hard to take in what anybody says. Perhaps the
> bereaved ought to be isolated in special settlements like lepers.
> —*A Grief Observed*, C. S. Lewis

Barnyards Are Messy

Don and I found that people became like chickens in a barnyard. If chickens find a weak chick, like vultures they peck it to death. In the same way, we became the target due to our own vulnerability and wounded state. A lady from the Wednesday night healing service called me shortly after our loss, and, hearing the grief in my voice, she said to me, "When you get to feeling better, you sit down and ask the Lord what you did wrong, and He will tell you." Words defy explaining how that kind of counsel affects one in grief. She herself had a deformed arm from birth. What had she or her parents done wrong? She had called many times over the past two and one-half years, assuring us the Lord had told her of Teresa's healing.

Don and I had been in ministry for the first ten years of our marriage in small churches of pure happiness, and those were blessed years. But when Don's relatives, strong fundamentalists, said, "If you hadn't left the ministry, this would not have happened," the anguish was unimaginable. In times of grief, logic goes out the window. My husband had been teaching on college campuses for fifteen years and probably influenced thousands of students, as compared to what he could have influenced in a single pastorate. It spite of that, it seems people always look for someone or something to blame in times of crisis.

Our youngest son was now one year old, and it was past time for me to have a yearly checkup. So, soon after Teresa's demise, I went to my doctor's office. When I began to cry—which I was doing most of the time—at the appointment he said, "Snap out of it, and get on with life. Others have faced calamities and tragedies!" I wondered if my pain would be any less if I lost an arm in an accident, knowing my neighbor had suffered the same accident and lost his arm. The wounded are hemorrhaging on the roadside and are told to get up and walk. There is no healing balm poured into the wounds, only salt.

Another charismatic friend said, "If you don't praise God for this, then you are rebellious!" (This was this person's favorite phrase to lay on the guilt.) Another friend—at least I had thought this person was a friend—stopped in shortly after the funeral one evening. Don was at class, and Christy and Michele just needed to talk. I had boxes of cucumbers and peaches waiting to be canned, but the girls and I were sitting at the table talking when we heard a knock on the door…no warning! As my friend came in with her daughter, she incorrectly perceived me to be immobilized with grief and said, "Why don't you get with it and can your pickles and peaches?"

In my defense Christy said, "It is pretty difficult to concentrate on anything."

The friend's daughter said, "Oh, it can't be that bad!"

Another friend stopped by and, seeing Teresa's graduation picture on the fridge, said, "Take that picture down, and get rid of all her stuff, including her clothes. It will just remind you of her. Stop thinking about her, and get on with life!"

I wondered if one could really forget twenty years in one day. Another friend from out of town came to console us with these words: "In five years you won't even remember her!"

As difficult as it was to understand, some of the Christian community continued to attack us as the weak chicks in the barnyard. Another friend from Colfax called to tell us of a father in their community who had just accidentally shot his son while hunting. Our friend said the family was in church the following Sunday praising God, and we should do the same. "It was God's will. Christians should not grieve!"

Others said, "She is in a better place." But we had visited the grave site where we had last placed our daughter, and we could not make that transition.

When we heard the statement "you have all these other children," we wondered about Jesus telling the story of the shepherd leaving the ninety-nine in the fold to rescue the one lost sheep. Would Jesus have said that to us? All of our children were our jewels. There were no rubber stamps; each was unique in his or her own right. They could not replace the one lost—nor did we want them to.

Another charismatic said, "She died because something a lot worse would have happened to her. She's being saved from that!" What could be worse than the ravages of leukemia?

And then there was the person who commented, "You lost your daughter so you could minister to others." I felt I was already very empathetic and tender hearted to those in grief. Although this woman's statement may have been partially true—out of tragedy, one is able to enter into another's grief and journey through it with that person—we knew we did not lose our daughter so we could minister!

Friends fled. We were a threat, for if it could happen to us, it could also happen to them. They no longer wanted to hook their wagon to our star.

One evening I met a former friend, a pastor, in the local Payless Drug Store. I was trying to make a decision about buying an item, and I could not. I was immobilized with grief and indecision. He spotted me and hurried over. He gave a quick greeting and then began a long exposé of all the Lord was doing in his church and all the people who were being healed of simple ailments—such as stretching a shortened leg. He never once asked how the family was doing. He knew not how to enter into another's sorrow.

Don and I didn't dare to voice the hurt and turmoil within when we were around these faith-healer followers, for if we did we would be questioned about the quality of our faith. No matter what we did, we were in error according to what their current prophesy was: "You're not releasing. You do not believe strongly enough. You have too much fear. The symptoms are satanic. Ignore them; they'll go away."

Two doctor friends who had claimed Teresa was healed had suggested no further oral treatment be taken. "If you are taking medication, the Lord will not get the glory!" On and on and on. The worst comment of all was that we had not put the Lord at the center of our lives. We were bad publicity for the charismatic movement. When Teresa had been in remission, they had been knocking on our door for answers, but when the ax of tragedy fell, they did a great disappearing act.

The What-If Highway

Don and I believe that when a person experiences any such loss, he or she goes down the what-if road, and indeed we searched our hearts to locate our error. We wondered: What if we had not moved to Portland? What if we had listened to those who said not to take the medicine? What if we had taken Teresa to Mexico or to a doctor out of the country? What if we had sent Doug home sooner? What if we had stayed in the ministry rather than going into teaching? All of these questions led to a dead end, and nothing could be changed.

What person can stand faultless and claim God's protection for being sinless and making all the right decisions? And if we were punished for wrong choices or sin, we would have reaped the consequences, not an innocent victim, our child. Father T said we were being slugged in the gut. He said it was like going over Niagara Falls and that it was a miracle any of us survived.

Good Samaritans Still

This is not to say that no one ministered to our grief, for many friends simply put their arms around us and were present and available. There was the couple who had brought their sleeping bags that first night after our loss and slept on the floor beside us. Dear friends continued to check on us, calling on birthdays and on anniversaries of our loss. These friends continue to give encouragement. There were those who simply continued to come with food and who sat with us, listening to us vent. It seemed we needed to go over and over our loss in order to wrap our minds around it. Their concern was like pouring warm, loving ointment on our wounds.

Our friends Lowell and Sonja were always available, and they would go out to coffee or dinner with us, and we would cry together, for they were still in pain from their own past hurts. As Lowell described it, "We just need to sit down here on this curb and cry together!" We never judged each other.

My theologically liberal college roommate and her husband, Jane and Vance Shepard, were now living in Portland. They picked Don and I up one day, took us to their bank, and withdrew five hundred dollars to help us meet our needs. We were overwhelmed with gratitude. Dear friends like these were always interspersed with those who were butchers.

If we could have eliminated those barnyard tactics, perhaps we could have healed sooner. The physical and emotional exhaustion of the past three years added to our depression. We turned to Teresa's doctor and to books for consolation. We withdrew into our own reflections. The negative and cruel comments were driving our pain and grief to a dangerous level. I believe people remember the bad comments and minimize the tender care. We allowed this to happen to us. The wounds were gaping.

The Jewish Healer

We decided to go see Teresa's doctor, who described himself as a Jewish, amoral nonbeliever. It was he who brought healing balm to our souls. First Dr. Glass said to me, "Mrs. Gibbs, I hate to tell you this, but you are not religious. You are more like me." He continued, "Should I be gone, I would want my family to grieve for me as you are grieving for Teresa and to have loved me as you have loved Teresa." He also said those who do not grieve come back to him years later to be put back together. Trying to abort the grief only drove it deeper. This beloved doctor of Teresa's opened a floodgate, for future healing, but not yet!

For the first time, Don and I felt we had been put into an incubator of love rather than on a bed of hot coals. Teresa had said that when Dr. Glass worked on her, she felt like Jesus was ministering to her. I felt that was true that day. We knew that the Jewish tradition was to hire mourners to weep and wail at someone's death. I needed that. We knew that when Christ was crucified, there was no glory in standing by that cross. All Christ's so-called friends scattered. And that did happen to us in small measure, but in my idealistic belief of what our lives were to be, I was unprepared for the devastation death caused in our hearts.

Encrusted in Tragedy's Grip

I wanted to scream to all, "Don't you know the world has stopped?" Would we ever heal? It was only the laughter of the little children in our home that brought any joy. When people grieve they must relive the event over and over, trying to grasp the reality of it. Pain and suffering are packages nobody wants. Don and

I tried to abort the pain. We ran from it in an attempt to minimize it. Going through such a tragedy had blown out the seams of our personalities. Over the years we had learned to pile layer upon layer over our real spiritual selves. Some of the layers of our false masks were laid by our own hands, some at our parents' hands, some by religion, and some by school and society at large. Now we were gaping and raw but also encased in grief. Somehow we had to hack open this new crust of pain that had encased us. Our hearts were sealed up, and we did not know what to do.

Our tragedy had stripped many layers away, and we stood naked, with dangling masses of raw matter dripping from our souls. Character and mental disorders surfaced. We were no exception to grief's devastation. In the initial stages of pain, we screamed, "Why me?" And our anger intensified the pain. Then we tried to ignore the pain, and that drove it deeper. The alternative was to embrace the pain, but we could not! We had only perceived our tragedy as a call to show God's power in healing.

No one who has not lost a child could comprehend the division that creeps into a marriage. We were living in the pain of the tragedy together, yet this did not create a tighter bond. Instead of making us closer, it blew us apart. We learned that 90 percent and higher of grieving parents who have lost a child experience serious marriage difficulties, and many divorce. We were no different. Two educated people should have reckoned with the situation, but rational thinking goes out the window when you are grieving!

Besides those facts I believed God knew that my greatest joy in life was to polish our jewels. As we lay beside the road bleeding, the comments were endless: Keep your chin up and be happy. It's time to move on. She wouldn't have wanted you to be sad. Be glad you had her for as long as you did. It is God's will; she's in a better place. Now you have an angel in heaven. These clichés were damaging to the healing process. But the days droned on, grief weighed heavily in the air, and the clichés were endless!

Healing Oil

Don and I also discovered our grief was unlike anyone else's. Grief is a very individual experience. Even though psychiatrist Elisabeth Kübler-Ross established the stages of grief, and some ministerial personnel insist you must go through each stage and at what point, I disagreed with her on this point. No one grieves exactly the same way. Grief is contingent on relationships, circumstances, and cultural and religious backgrounds. But the pain did become a metamorphosis to new freedom and new beginnings—a new and more real self started to emerge.

A broken vessel lets off the fragrance of what is contained within; a closed and sealed vessel cannot. At that point, though, our vessel was closed tightly. We were to walk through much pain, many bad choices, and a lot of struggling and were to find out that aborted grief makes pain and recovery almost impossible. We were on our way through the garbage dump to healing!

The cards from Teresa's friends, hospital staff, the high school where she graduated, Oral Roberts University, the radio station, and those who had heard Teresa's testimony kept our dear postman busy daily. He often had to knock on the door to deliver a stack of cards. The kind words in those cards did drip some healing oil on our aching hearts, but we still woke daily with the thud of reality and our cries to go back and change something…anything! Here are just a few excerpts from those daily letters we received.

- **Hospital personnel** (where Teresa spent her last three years of life): "I wanted to tell you how many hospital people knew of her testimony and the influence her life was. Praises for Teresa…"
- **Voice teacher**: "Teresa's 'ray of sunshine' smile in *Amahl and the Night Visitors*, her beautiful music and lovely inspired and inspiring poetry, her sweet and so gentle voice and her strength are eternal. She brought to me great joy and great love and I am grateful for those beautiful shared years. Thank you both for letting her life be a part of my life."
- **High school teacher**: "As a student of mine, she always was a moment of happiness. It was indeed an honor to have been associated with her as a friend and a teacher."
- **A friend** (representative of many, many more, but space limits listing them here): "I realize there are no words—just the greatest love and affection that I have ever felt for anyone in my short life. Teresa has made the best contribution to my Christianity as anyone ever will. She showed me the most free and loving Father, our Lord, and His son, Jesus Christ, that I could ever hope to know…"
- **Dr. Matthew Shariah, Outreach for Youth International Broadcast Station** (in Tulsa, Oklahoma): "Teresa shared her testimony with me in such a way I never will forget it. It was a blessing to hundreds of people around the world for those who heard her testimony. She told me about having such a wonderful Christian home and such blessed Christian

parents, which I never will forget. She had a beautiful song about the Shekinah Glory, which means the House of the Lord. Everyone here at the radio station was so impressed with her blessed talent in music. They played her song for many months over the air…"

- **Patti (Pullin) Dilworth** (one of Teresa's best friends; she sent this note some time later): "I continue to thank God for the gift of Teresa's friendship. It is only as I have matured in my faith that I have realized how much she had to do with the direction my life has taken. She was with us such a short time, but, oh, how God used her! Love, Patti."

Don and I continued to receive countless letters from churches, coffee shops, and different organizations where Teresa had sung, painted murals for church nurseries, or displayed her angelic persona. She was embraced in lives wherever she went.

After Teresa died, Lowell, who had received the picture she had painted for one of her doctors, made copies of it. Therefore we were able to give the original to Dr. Emerick, and we hung a print next to her picture on the wall of our home. Dr. Emerick later shared with us that he was teaching a class on people's transitions before death. He used Teresa's last painting of the doves in different shades of blue as representative of how painters move from brilliant colors to light blues as they near the time of their earthly departure. We did notice that her last painting was almost ethereal compared to her former paintings.

Many saw Teresa as an unusual young woman with a pure spirit. Hearing Dr. Emerick share this, I thought of the hippie group that had invaded her space to tell her she had sin in her life and appeared as "an old man with sores all over his body." She was indeed a pure soul—not perfect, but she had no guile within!

CHAPTER 22

Grief Is a Long Journey

> Nevertheless, that time of darkness and
> despair will not go on forever.
> —Is 9:1, NLT

> To weep is to make less the depth of grief.
> —WILLIAM SHAKESPEARE

> He, who lacks time to mourn, lacks time to mend.
> —HENRY TAYLOR

New Normal

Remorse had become a comfortable blanket of protection for Don and I against future success, productivity, or even failure. We also had conflict within our souls, with joy and pain vying for prominence. The little ones gave us great joy, Christy and Michele were such sweethearts, and Don Ralph—now a proud marine—would come home in his uniform with class, striding out of the plane to his proud parents and siblings who awaited him. Christy was about to graduate. She had become such an accomplished dancer and artist. Both Christy and Michele were so tender in the home with the little ones, but they were often in tears.

Our lives were still full and very, very busy! Cards and flowers continued to fill our home with love from caring friends as well as letters from our former church members and the churches where we had served. Our charismatic associates fled after their initial comments. They saw us as only bitter and rebellious.

When I was growing up, my mother had told me bad language shows bad breeding. Theretofore I had rarely used the slang words of the day. Even *darn* and *gosh* were rarely heard in my vocabulary. But on this new path of pain, my vocabulary became full of *damns* and *bullshits*, as only these words—and worse—could express my pain. I am sure my colorful language reflected badly on my faith and my testimony at the time, but I felt like I had no faith left. I did not care about testimony! I cried out to God that I hated Him and did not even believe in Him, so deep was my hurt and anger. Those who had wanted to hook their wagons to our star were stunned, and for that I am sorry.

Wrestling

As I raged against God and wrestled with Him, as He told us to do in His word, ["come now, let us reason together" (Is 1:18, ESV)], I began to trace Teresa's life. She began from our egg and sperm—unexpected, uninvited—and emerged into our lives to grace us for twenty years…how miraculous. I looked at the stages of her life as a toddler, a happy little girl, and growing into a beautiful young woman in love with life as well as with her Savior. All of her stages of life gave us great joy. My private journey into her past was healing. The same spirit had remained in Teresa from her birth and throughout her life.

Christy was to graduate later that year. Some of her friends were choosing early graduation, but Christy had two credits left. So while her friends were finishing early, she had to continue on. One evening as she was practicing her dance routines in the red room, she said, with tears streaming down her face, "It's just not fair; I want early graduation."

Then it hit me! Teresa had graduated early—not from high school but from life. She had crammed and worked overtime, undergoing the discipline of illness, and now she had graduated before the rest of us. I began to imagine the new body that would house her precious spirit; it would be more beautiful than before. In scripture King David sinned with Bathsheba, had her husband killed, had an illegitimate child, and then lost that son at birth. David said, "Someday I will go to him, but he cannot come back to me" (2 Sm 12:23, NCV). That scripture gave me a measure of comfort, for though I hated God, I was still reading His word.

Teresa's life had become a testimony to everything that was precious and beautiful. In reflection, I could see she truly was a martyred saint, with the same spirit as the St. Teresa I read about. She had become a martyr by the ravages of nature. Nothing could have been as cruel as what nature had done to her body. Her gifting was incredible; her insights and commitment to all that was good put her head and shoulders above her peers. She packed twenty years full of more dynamic living than many put into seventy years.

Visions

I was having periodic flashes of Teresa. I saw Jesus taking her to a barn full of horses, and He let her pick out her very own filly. On another occasion I saw Teresa sitting on a high stool painting a vast mural, even more ethereal than her earthly paintings. She appeared in perfect, glowing health with that sparkle in her eyes. Again I saw her in an arena training great white stallions. Were these imaginary wishes on my part? Or were they indeed glimpses into her new existence? I do not know, but my aching heart was lifted just a teeny tiny bit, and I was grateful.

A wife of one of Valley's pastors wrote me this:

The world unseen is all around, but sometimes we can see glimpses of its beauty. It is wrapped in mystery—but here and there we get a hint of things beyond the range—of hearing and seeing, something wonderful and strange.

When you least expect it you can sense or you can feel the presence of a loved one lost, a presence that is real—bringing you a blessing, and the heart is comforted, strengthened for the living of the days that lie ahead. Ask not how or where or why. Accept the peace it brings. Seek not for an explanation when an angel's wings brush you in a crowd, or when you catch a flower's sweet breath. Take it as a proof that love survives the change called death.

During this grief journey, I would try to sort things in Teresa's bedroom, but I could only lovingly fold her clothes and carefully put them back into their drawers. I tried to change the look of her bedroom, changing the bedspread, but on Don Ralph's short furlough from the service, he would say, "Please put her bedspread back on," and I did.

New Beginnings

I was able to begin saying, "Why not me?" I believe this was the beginning of healing for me. Tragedy produces pain: pain of the mind, pain of the heart, pain of the whole soul. It is a signal to find healing. Faith is sometimes doubt that takes courage. It can just be a coward moving forward. *Grief* is a love word! Don and I found that ignoring the grief did not make the pain go away. We found that talking and reflecting over and over helped. We found that we needed to stay away from people who tried to steal the grief from us, only crippling us further. I also decided to declare, quoting Job, "Though he slay me, yet will I trust in him" (Jb 13:15, KJV)!

There were still moments when I railed against God for allowing this dreaded disease to attack one of our jewels. I was still trying to make sense of this horrendous tragedy that had struck our lives. We were not well by any means. But I knew I had loved the Lord since I was two years of age, and He was the very source of my being. Where could I run, even though I felt abandoned by God?

Many times Don and I felt like ripping down the "House of Shekinah" sign, but the deep desire for the reality of that sign stayed us from rash actions. I believe one can be a person of faith and still doubt. There is so much we, being finite, cannot possibly understand. We often walked on two tracks—faith and doubt—imposed upon each other. Strong winds come and destroy the flimsy house of faith, and a new house of faith must be built. Would that ever happen?

Some of our would-be comforters wondered why we were so crushed. While we knew that others over the years had suffered tragedies that did not ease our pain. I looked at some of our friends whom I thought had no tragedies in their lives. It made me wonder what we had done wrong. I wondered if the charismatic fundamentalists were correct in their evaluation of us.

Though we were on our way to healing, we were not there yet! Don had not had as much time as I had to reflect, for he continued to teach day and night classes with no reprieve. He tried so hard to be a strong leader in our home, but he was dripping with grief.

CHAPTER 23

Tidal Wave of Grief

> Oh, do not hold us guilty for our former sins! Let
> your tenderhearted mercies meet our needs, for we
> are brought low to the dust. Help us, God of our
> salvation! Help us for the honor of your name.
> —Ps 79:8–9, TLB

Find a Cause

As I listened to the news about orphaned children being airlifted out of Korea due to the Korean War, I wondered if this was to be our new mission. Activity would be a way to hide. Didn't we need to find a reason for God to bless us again? Teresa had not been gone for a year yet, and I was still searching for some meaning to this whole tragedy. Hadn't I loved children with all my heart? This was the deception of finding a worthy mission. Wisdom was missing!

We approached Holt Agency in Eugene, Oregon, and were quickly approved to adopt a child. A darling little girl arrived by air, and we picked her up at the airport, but I never could bring myself to follow through with the adoption. Her deep-seated deprivation and needs, the lack in her reservoir, and the lack in my reservoir, left me further depleted. I saw the unhealthy dynamic damage our own young children. Her demands overruled the needs of those three little jewels we had already committed to and bonded with. I simply could not do it. I was totally unaware of how deeply wounded I was. Our attempt to abort the grief probably made us appear strong, but strong we were not!

Don and I felt the great weight of guilt, but we did not bond like we needed to in order to parent this little girl, so we had her moved to another family. Holt then sent us a little boy who needed major heart surgery because he had a severe heart valve leak. We were able to give him that the much-needed surgery by using our Kaiser coverage. We were glad to give a child the gift of health, but even this worthy mission did not mend our broken hearts. We did not bond with him either, or he with us. A new heart only increased his energy for tantrums and aggression.

Don and I had not recovered from our three-year battle, nor had we embraced our grief. We simply had no emotional reserve to embrace these children. Don was still teaching many classes as well as ministering part time. We had laid out $7,000 to bring these children to the United States, and the result was surely better lives and better health for them, but these attempts did nothing toward our healing. We were still too wounded to adequately care for these children.

Our whole family needed to recover from the three-year battle we had faced in order to be whole enough to nurture the three little ones already dropped into our lives to love and polish. What were we thinking? Through our guilt of not following through with the adoptions, we could only say, "Lord, bless these little ones and place them in homes where they can grow and develop into the people you want them to be. Forgive us for thinking we were strong and did not need to heal our family first and foremost!"

Christy and Michele were struggling with their own grief and needed the atmosphere in the home to be restored. Both girls so desperately needed a mom of sound mind. Why would we take on more responsibility with such a fragmented home? Subconsciously I had thought taking in more children would heal all our hurts and our marriage as well. Such was my irrational thinking in the midst of a journey back to wholeness.

One of our dear friends at Valley Presbyterian church was Gene Pong. He had grieved with us at the loss of our daughter. Not long after that, he and his wife came to us when she was diagnosed with lymphoma. We walked beside him in his own loss, but when he saw us struggling with some of our choices, he stated that our gifting was also our curse. How true! In other words our strength was also our weakness. My love for children crowded out wisdom. We were just trying to gain some kind of understanding of this horrible, unthinkable tragedy in our lives. We needed meaning more than life itself. We wanted to understand, but there was no understanding.

More Missions

A friend from Valley called and asked if we would take an AFS student for six months. Don Ralph had previously been chosen as an exchange student, so we did have interest in the program. Our friend was so insistent, explaining that they could find no one else, and they knew how good we were with young people. We succumbed to the pressure, but it was not a pleasant experience, for how can you celebrate with such grief hanging in the air? It seemed like people always wanted us to be the former people they had known.

Don's personal war was still raging—the one started by his relative's dastardly comment that everything had happened because Don had left the ministry. He had maintained a ministry on the college campus and had continued in church ministry on the side, but so subtle was his family's influence that he began to explore the possibility of having his ordination transferred to the Presbyterian Church. Consequently Don received his ordination in the Presbyterian Church (PCUSA), even though we had been assisting at Valley Presbyterian Church. We had been working with young adults and with new members, but Don did not have the credentials to be a teaching elder, as Presbyterian pastors are called.

Don was highly approved and endorsed, and he took an interim position in The Dalles, Oregon, for the summer months of 1975—although he still retained his teaching position at Portland Community College. The people in the church were lovely, and I suppose the experience was slightly healing, but that sword of Damocles was still hanging over our heads. We took the youth waterskiing and had the youth from Valley down to help with services, still trying our best to appear normal. People within the congregation told Don how much he helped the church.

When the church hired a dynamic young pastor, Don was called to take the Troutdale Presbyterian church as interim pastor. This was a fragmented group because their pastor had unexpectedly died: during a celebration at the church, the pastor was stricken with a heart attack and died on the spot. We were able to give adequate leadership even though Don was also maintaining his teaching career. It was a meaningful time, but we were still fragmented, and I am sure it showed. Don had not taken time to grieve properly with his busy schedule. He just kept going, all the while trying to be normal and give adequate leadership at the church and to his many classes in sociology.

Happy Times

Each week we would drive back and forth to Troutdale from our House of Shekinah. Thursdays, right after Don's last class of the day, we would jump in the car with very excited children to serve the Cherry Park Presbyterian Church. Christy and Michele were both still in high school and both working on weekends as well as wrestling with their own continual heartbreak. Don Ralph was in the Indian Ocean in a private maneuver, unable to tell us about the mission. The younger children thoroughly willingly shared in the experience. They loved it and made new friends. This church asked Don to become the full-time pastor, but he simply could not give up the security of his tenured teaching.

Don ministered at Cherry Park Presbyterian Church for five years. During this time, the church grew with young families, and we made many beautiful friends for life, but some of the elders wanted a pastor on-site giving full-time service.

While they were interviewing candidates, we took the opportunity to go to a Schuller seminar at the Crystal Cathedral in Garden Grove, California. It was wonderful to get away with our three younger children. We almost felt whole again. While there, I was walking across the beautiful campus, and it seemed Teresa said to me, "Mom, it makes me so happy to see you and Dad like this." I don't know the reality of that experience either, but I know it gave me a lilt in my heart. I believe it was the first time I had joy in my heart since Teresa's demise. Don and I had such fun with the young children, swimming in the motel pool at night in that wonderful, sunny California weather. It reminded me of how much I had loved Don when we were living in Southern California as newlyweds.

More Mistakes

But of course you cannot exist on the mountaintop for long, and we had to go back to our responsibilities at church, home, and college campus. While we served at the Cherry Park Presbyterian Church, a realtor joined the church with his young family. He was smooth talking, and we were friends. Our young children were friends. Don trusted him, so as Don was wrestling with what his relatives had said, this smooth-talking realtor encouraged him to take equity out of our home and purchase property in the gorge near Lateral Falls. This realtor told Don we could subdivide it, enabling us to make big money, so Don could go back into full-time ministry.

Don had too much security and benefits in teaching to give it up for a small church salary. He was making a good salary, and we were able to provide our children with the necessities of life. We did not want to deprive these younger children by having an inadequate income! But it seemed like the relator's reasoning made sense…maybe. Don decided he would pull out equity from our home in Beaverton to buy the gorge property. There was no wisdom involved! As Don was negotiating with the realtor, the Troutdale church hired a full-time minister.

Insanity Reigns

After Don's service at Cherry Park, we went back to church at Valley, and Don was made minister of visitation. He called on the newcomers, and then we would invite them to our home. The enlarged red room was the perfect place to entertain. The newcomers felt so welcome and were more than happy to join the church after such a "welcome to Valley" party. I loved entertaining these people, and there was a measure of peace and tranquility for me.

Our friends, the Hansens, whom we ministered with in Colfax, Washington, were now serving in Valley Presbyterian Church as pastor and wife. We felt we had come full circle, now both in Oregon. How we loved that family! When we returned to our home church in 1980, Don was serving as assistant to Jack Hansen at Valley Presbyterian Church. However, on occasion he would go out to a Presbyterian Church in Aloha, Oregon to teach Bible classes. The church was only about ten miles from our home, and a dear couple there, the Sloats, wanted him as their pastor. (The church had an older pastor who was about to retire after years of ministry.)

Colonel Sloat kept calling him with their request. Don knew it was a very sick and troubled church, and he wrestled with going there. But he concluded, as a sociologist, he could handle a troubled church. After all, sociologists know the dynamics of people and groups. He would know how to be tactful and discerning, he thought! He also believed a church could not possibly harm him; after losing a daughter, what could be worse?

The church elders said they were quite content with Don continuing to teach, as he had been doing. I did not want to go, but I consoled myself that nothing would change for the children and me. I still had the security of my House of Shekinah. I would be surrounded by memories Teresa had created. Even though I did not want to go to Aloha, my commitment to Don had always echoed Ruth's words to her mother-in-law, Naomi: "wither thou goest, I will go" (Ru 1:16, KJV).

Very soon after Don accepted the call, he was elected to go to general assembly in Atlanta. While he was there, the moderator of the Presbytery of the Cascades told him he could not have a church and continue teaching. The former leadership in the presbytery was happy to have a sociologist teacher serving as pastor. Don, who was still wounded and compliant, listened to this gentleman.

We had young children still at home who needed to have medical coverage and adequate provision. I was livid that Don was told he could no longer teach. But his parents had told him he had lost his daughter because he had left the ministry. When you are in grief, reason and common sense take a backseat to your actions. It was as if Don had become a mechanical robot with no wisdom, insight, or consideration of the ramifications of such a decision. Was he really going to pastor this troubled church and take early retirement from teaching? Bad choices seemed to create only more bad choices. The filters of decision making were clogged!

But believing the recent purchase of the gorge property ensured a good return. Don opted to take early retirement from teaching. After twenty years on a college campus, I am sure he was severely exhausted. How could he not be exhausted from his horrendous schedule of teaching, counseling, and working in a church on the weekends, along with fighting a battle for his daughter's life? Not only had he had not taken time to embrace his grief, but he had big-time burnout! He was in a total fog, having never taken time to embrace his grief.

Alligator Farm

Don had been convinced to take money out of our home and secure property in the gorge. But it turned out to be our alligator farm in the gorge, because it eventually ate us alive. For a time we did have fun going out there, cutting trees, and wading in the stream under the falls. Only momentarily did it seem to be a good decision, though. It was the lull before the tidal wave picked up speed. Deception is so subtle, especially when wrong decisions are made without wisdom kicking in! It turned out to be a disastrous move, one that we never fully recovered from. For what the realtor did not tell us was that the Columbia Gorge historical property could not be developed.

Our land was near Lateral Falls, and we were stuck with property that was a poor investment, plus we suffered the lost equity from our home. Furthermore,

Don had taken early retirement, according to the demands of the presbytery moderator, so now what could we do? The die was cast. The tidal wave only picked up speed from there on. This recent decision did not help our ailing marriage. Don, almost in puppet fashion, was being jerked around by everything and was not dealing with what should have been top priority: his wife and children. By retiring he lost medical coverage for our young children. With the bad investment, there was barely enough income to cover the family needs.

He tried to make adjustments to his decision. He thought if he sold our home and we moved to Aloha, we could start a new life. Of course that was erroneous reasoning, as we had been doing since we'd lost one of our jewels. We were truly in another zone of reality, for nothing made sense. Don sold our House of Shekinah to move out to the community where he was to be pastor. His was that if we left that house, maybe we would leave some of the pain. He was wrong!

There was a young military man in the Aloha congregation who came to Don for counseling. I believe he was seeking more of an endorsement than counseling, for he was having an affair with his neighbor. In Don's compassion he did not observe what a con artist this man was. The man also wanted to sell his home and was thinking Don would be a good prospect. So after selling our House of Shekinah, Don made an earnest money down payment on this gentleman's house.

I was shocked by having to leave our home. As I was reading my Bible and praying about it, the scripture Proverbs 6:3–4 (TLB) jumped out at me: "Quick! Get out of it if you possibly can! Swallow your pride; don't let embarrassment stand in the way. Go and beg to have your name erased." Everything was off track. I so wanted to go back to the fork in the road, where somehow we had taken a very wrong turn! Everything seemed so terribly wrong. Our lives and finances were bankrupt. I begged Don not to buy that house. But once again a decision had been made, and Don did not feel he could renege on it.

That home had no beauty, no anointing, and was full of pain and darkness. We sold it as soon as possible and floundered around before we found adequate housing. We found that bad choices were nearly impossible to undo. We felt like we were in a forest, with trees so thick we could not find our way out. Again it was a dear friend, Jack Hansen, who gave us some guidance in finding our way out of the maze. He had connections and directed us to a lovely rental. There was so much pain…Couldn't we just go back to our charmed life? We were ready for that midcourse correction. Would it ever come?

Eye-Openers

A few miracles and wake-up calls did appear here and there. One life-impacting event was our decision to lead a group of healthy-thinking people from the Aloha church to the Holy Land. We made plans with excitement in our hearts for this opportunity of a lifetime. Out of the country and away, there was some joy in our hearts. (We left our young children with my sister up in Seattle. We had left them there when we had taken Teresa and Don Ralph to ORU, and my sister was more than happy to have them again.)

It was a good trip. There were young people in the group, and they seemed to gravitate to us, which I loved. I had loved being involved with youth in my ministry. However, our decisions of the recent past cascaded in on us. While staying in a motel overlooking the Sea of Galilee, Don began weeping and could not stop. The depth to which we had fallen seemed to crush him.

As we continued from Jerusalem on down through the Sinai Desert, on our way to Egypt, I felt as though our souls were as barren as the desert itself. There were skeletons of armory vehicles lying about. As I looked out the windows of that travel bus, I viewed our family: desolate, broken, and abandoned…ruins strewn everywhere. In my barren condition, I so wanted the joy of our former life, the life where laughter and happiness rang through every experience. But the joy was not there. Must healing come so slowly? I discovered my wound that had closed over was not healed at all.

Chiseled

To say we were chiseled down to bedrock would be putting it mildly. Serving the church in Aloha was also like chiseling granite. It was such a sick church. The congregation ran the gamut from charismatic to extremely liberal and godless. There was mega turmoil within. I believe this was the first time, Don had not been a cherished pastor, so sick was the congregation. Did we think we were healthy enough to lead them?

One middle-aged leader, who said she'd had a hysterectomy, had a live-in boyfriend and now claimed she was pregnant—though she later stated she had lost the child. Her father, a pastor there, had been convicted of molesting children years before. Was sexual sin rampant everywhere? It seemed it was not only on campuses, within the charismatic movement, and in the new sensitivity gatherings, but here we were faced with it in a local church.

Even as a pastor's wife, I was approached for sexual favors when I attended a presbytery meeting Don and I were attending in Southern Oregon. The meeting was running long, and I was bored. I decided to take a stroll outside. While I was walking around in the parking lot, one of the presbytery leaders propositioned me. It reminded me of the time I was followed home from work in Aberdeen. I could not get back into the meeting fast enough. This was ridiculous! If I had reported it, what proof would I have? I was appalled. I strongly believed in fidelity to one's mate, and I was shocked by this gentleman's obvious intent. Did no one believe in sexual boundaries? Boundaries were being torn down all around us. My innocent values were being challenged. It seemed all our puritan values were being challenged.

The choir director told Don, "If we don't like you, we will get rid of you!" On another occasion we had a former neighbor boy of ours play the piano along with the organist. He was extremely gifted, and we thought it would be a treat for the people. Some of members of the congregation were blessed and said so, but the choir director told Don, "If you ever do that again, both the organist and I will walk out. You have no authority to bring someone in."

Some of the church leader's children were taking drugs during worship, and our children were subject to this kind of influence. What should we have done? The internal fighting among the church members had been great even before Don had accepted the call, and it seemed that some of the elders were always angry at Don. One incident really infuriated some of the elders: A new young couple had joined the church, but soon after they had joined, the husband took a trip to Southern California, and while he was there he committed suicide. The frantic wife called Don to perform his funeral, and Don opted to hold it in the church. Don encouraged the family and tried to get the elders to understand the duress this young man must have been under to take his life. At such a time, mercy—not judgment—is needed. The elders did not believe the man merited a Christian service or burial by the church. Don held firm, and the service was still held in the church. Don nurtured the family with love and mercy, and the disgruntled session members were not present.

On another occasion a teenager, Niki, was murdered by her boyfriend. The family of the victim had been our friends. Their youngest daughter and Danielle, who were in kindergarten together, were best friends. The family wanted Don to do Niki's service. They asked him to baptize her after that horrendous crime. She had not been baptized in life, and her parents wanted the ceremony of baptism for their dead daughter. They needed this satisfaction with all their hearts. The

Presbyterian Church does not hold baptizing the dead as a tenet; Presbyterians do not perform last rites, as the Catholics do. However, Don did not care; he wanted to honor the grieving family's request. He knew the pain far too well!

So on a very solemn occasion, Don stepped into a local mortuary with Niki's family and lifted the white sheet that covered her bludgeoned body to give this darling girl the last rites. He placed his finger on her forehead, made the sign of the cross, and said he baptized her in the name of the Father, Son, and Holy Spirit. We knew all about the uncontrollable grief and disbelief that such a tragedy could happen to a beloved daughter, which the parents were experiencing.

Later, during the funeral service, the mother sat by her daughter's casket and caressed Niki's arms and legs. I could not do in my daughter's death what I had done in her life...but that mother did in her daughter's death what she could not do in her daughter's life. Niki's parents needed this macabre exercise to bring a measure of healing for their broken hearts. In life I had never left the side of Teresa's bed—caressing her, encouraging her, bathing her, praying for her—but at the time of her death I ran!

In spite of the negatives, the church did grow, and Don was able to bring in new people who became our forever friends. Don had such a way of relating to hurting people. How can you not relate when you have felt the searing pain of grief? His ministry was dynamic, but our personal lives continued to crumble, and we needed a midcourse correction! How does one self-correct when every choice seems to force one deeper into a chasm of despair?

With our house sales, we lost money and equity, and those decisions took us deeper into a cesspool of unhealthiness! Don thought he was doing everything right, only to regret his decisions later. How could everything be all right when every decision was wrong? If we were to survive, we had to begin again. We tried to remember that *grief* is a love word. My love for Don had tarnished, but it had not died. We were determined to check the compass and make a midcourse correction...but we didn't know exactly what we should do. We were stuck and growing more stuck by the year. The corrosive effects of the five past years had made Don more vulnerable and emotionally crushed than ever...and we had thought nothing could hurt us further after losing a daughter!

CHAPTER 24

Life Experience Changes Theology

> There is only one corner of the universe you can be
> certain of improving, and that's your own self.
> —Aldous Huxley

> A journey of a thousand miles begins with a single step.
> —Lao Tzu

Limited Knowledge

Perhaps occasionally—even often—in this dark place, Don and I had longing in our hearts for a return to simple black-and-white theology, where every aspect of life is addressed within the walls of that accepted theology. But life, theology, and spirituality are always fluid. Therefore we could not remain within closed walls of belief. Coming out of our dysfunctional backgrounds into establishing our own celebrant family unit, I was determined to control my environment with positive thinking and actions. My immediate family would live to its full potential of gifting and contribute to the betterment of society.

My early Sunday school training had guided me into a trusting faith in my Heavenly Father. I accepted the theology that to walk humbly before God, follow the Ten Commandments, and follow Jesus Christ and His teachings would bring ultimately successful living and protection. I lived in a small circle of life, insulated from the greater picture of unanswerable pain and suffering in our world village. I certainly was aware of pain in the larger picture, but it did not affect my little world. I had peripheral knowledge of the martyrs of the past, of early pioneer tragedies, and of the pain of war and losses, but somehow it did not penetrate my exclusive rights to protection.

I had combined a little modern psychology with a little current theology to determine my own theology and destiny. And for many years, it seemed this theology was accurate. Furthermore I must surely have had some inside knowledge, for my life merited notice from all those around me. I had a perfect husband and four children, and I was declaring and determined to be polishing jewels for the Kingdom of God. Who could question my theology of life? God surely looked upon me with favor to grant me these precious jewels to polish. I had prayed early on that if God needed to teach me something, He could do anything—except touch these gifted children.

Naïveté

As I described earlier, when Teresa was stricken with leukemia, though the shock was unbearable, Don and I still maintained that God would heal her, and we would testify to the power of God. As we battled the disease, Teresa gave witness to her love of Jesus. We read books on healing, tried every suggested remedy, fasted, prayed, and enlisted multiple groups of people to pray with us. We determined we would write a book together, giving God the glory for *Miracles Take Work*.

The nature of the disease is elusive, and one could surmise that a miracle has taken place only to be gravely disappointed when the disease reoccurs. A three-year battle ensued, and we never once gave in to the gnawing subconscious belief that we might lose the fight against this deadly disease. I knew Job had stated, "What I feared has come upon me…" (Jb 3:25, NIV). However, I merely pushed those disturbing thoughts aside. In reality, according to Dr. Glass, Teresa's disease followed the typical process of the disease. The difference was her vigorous fight to overcome it. He said usually patients last eight to eleven months without treatment and one year to one and one-half years with treatment. Further, remissions usually last less than one year. We were able to have an additional one and one-half years with our jewel.

Overshadowed

There was always such a sense of God's presence throughout the three-year battle. Much of the time, it seemed we had protection in the curtained sanctuary of God. When our daughter finally succumbed to leukemia, our whole family was left in a shambles of disbelief and pain. Nature had become our enemy and had resulted in twentieth-century martyrdom. In our case nature was as real as any flesh-and-blood enemy. The disparity between those who lived but were throwing away their lives on things like shooting up with drugs and a talented girl with not enough hours to achieve and celebrate life became glaring. But hadn't she said, "I'd go through it again for Jesus"? Death, our greatest unconquerable enemy, is insurmountable. It defies, it separates, it shatters dreams, it cuts short relationships, and it puts a veil between generations, people, and friends. Our roots seemed too shallow at the time to survive such a crushing blow.

Our family was too devastated, disillusioned, and exhausted to consider much theology. But in order to enter into a healing process, we either had to walk back through our gathered information that had led us to our present philosophical and theological views—tossing and sorting those views—or walk on in disbelief and bitterness, perhaps even throwing away all beliefs and values. Bitterness can be a cover for immediate and devastating sorrow. We had internalized some of the current evangelical (charismatic) thought of the day. At that moment in time, our destiny had to be transformed and altered and new thoughts embraced. We knew we had to develop a new theology from this life experience, for our present belief was shattered into a million pieces.

It was not a quick or casual process. Years had been involved in gathering beliefs and views. I had to see that Teresa's babyhood gave way to childhood, childhood gave way to youth, and the rest of the stages of development were compacted into her early graduation to another stage of existence, about, we could only speculate. It became my detour into radically questioning God's sovereignty that has led me into a deeper appreciation of that very sovereignty. The scriptures tell us "Eye has not seen, nor ear heard, nor have entered into the heart of man the things which God has prepared for those who love Him" (1 Cor 2:9, NKJV). Our vision is limited to this stage of existence. We do not see the whole picture or know the last chapter!

Slowly, Surely

I discovered that wholeness can be achieved out of great tragedy. Tremendous victory of spirit is possible only in the face of tremendous battle. As recorded in Job 13:15, "Though he slay me, yet will I trust in him." That finally became my scripture. I spent many hours and days and even months screaming at God. I told Him I hated Him, though I also said I did not even believe in Him. Uncaring people declared I had a rebellious spirit or that I had lost my faith.

Even worse, they were pouring thoughtless statements like salt into our wounds. But I screamed, "Why me?" until I came to say, "Why not me?"

As I began reading some of those who have endured great sufferings—such as Dietrich Bonhoeffer and, recently, Stewart Alsop—I was able to understand life on a different level intellectually, emotionally, and spiritually. Bonhoeffer wrote this:

> Nothing can fill the gap when we are away from those we love, and it would be wrong to try and find anything. We must simply hold out and win through. That sounds very hard at first, but at the same time it is a great consolation, since leaving the gap unfilled preserves the bonds between us. It is nonsense to say that God fills the gap; he does not fill it, but keeps it empty so that our communion with one another may be kept alive, even at the cost of pain.

When I read of the deeds and sufferings of the saints, I could perceive Teresa as a saint for what she endured.

I saw that I must create a new language and a new way of thinking in order to reveal again the secrets of truth. Even cripples and fragmented humanity possess an inner wholeness. All humans, I believe, desire to walk in perfection and wholeness. In some cases, if that is not achieved they either place blame on themselves or turn their backs totally on God and deny any existence of a loving Heavenly Father Creator. I did not want that to be our story.

We are finite humans with all the foibles possible. When I did something my mother did not approve of, she would say, "I never thought you would do that." That is probably where some of my desire for perfection came. But perfection is not possible for the human being! Too many past experiences are coded in the heart and need to be healed and removed. This coding often rises to the surface and renders us immobile and unable to function at maximum capacity. I so wanted to be free from the negative imprinting from the distant and immediate past.

Grief Does Not Care

Within the confines of our depth of grief, Don and I cared nothing for correctness of theology. We just wanted some answers to hold us together. I came to a personal awareness that we do live in an imperfect world, with imperfect humans. It is a conundrum: we look at the inequitable injustices of life and see they can bring a broader scope of belief and faith. Crises can either shatter one's faith altogether or strengthen it. This awareness brought paramount insight as I walked this lonely journey to wholeness. I began to place myself alongside all those who have suffered great pain throughout the ages rather than living in my presumably safe and secure, sheltered place in history. To try to take control of one's own life takes one out of the realm of the human and tries to put one into God's position of sovereignty.

Don and I had taken some of the charismatic thought of the day as our own—specifically that we had the power to control healing if we never allowed negative possibilities to enter our thoughts and just spoke healing. These beliefs also included that God wants only good to happen in our lives. I knew I had to adopt a new theological transformation, and it would not be an easy or a quick process. Over and over, through several years, I had to embrace my new understanding about Teresa's whole life and demise. We became grateful for the theology of the communion of the saints. And as we studied this concept further, we realized our bond with Teresa remains unbroken. The scripture in Hebrews 12:1 tells us there is a great cloud of witnesses who are cheering us on this part of our eternal journey.

Eternal Time Line

I believe that most of us forget we are on an eternal time line. Wholeness can be achieved out of great tragedy. Tremendous victory of spirit is possible only in the face of tremendous battle. I began reading anything I could get my hands on to find peace for our tragedy. Bonhoeffer, in discussing modern martyrdom and quoting Baumgarten (1912–89), wrote these words: "there are times in which lectures and publications no longer suffice to communicate the necessary truth." Bonhoeffer's confinement in prison caused a refinement of his personal theology. When life and experience deny everything we have learned and believed and our spirits are pressed to the max, it makes us unload our extra theological baggage and get down to the raw truth.

So as I accepted the fact that we are a world full of imperfect humans who face injustices, I broadened my scope and took a quantum leap of faith. All my family and I had faced could shatter all belief or bring me to a deeper appreciation of all humankind and our struggles to make peace with our Creator. I did not want my faith shattered and thrown on the dung heap! So my search began. It does help to hear about other people's pain, difficulty, persecution, and affliction, because we can then recognize that in our struggles, we are not alone in history.

Out of this desperate time of pain came a genuine growth of belief and hope. To keep one's sanity—and mine was nearly lost—the mind must still hold on to a hope of redemption and restoration. We cannot put God into a man-made form. We cannot make him our sugar daddy or our heavenly Santa Claus! We try to make God anthropomorphic, but He is not.

I hold to the belief, and hope that perhaps in another realm, we might be reunited with our daughter. I must hold that hope, along with my doubt, to maintain my sanity. I seize the courage to hang on to that hope. I have to put my faith in a broader scope, and my journey of faith had to become more fluid. But we all, as fellow human beings on this journey of life, maybe on an eternal time line, must be free to challenge and change our own theologies. We all need freedom to search and find workable faith out of our most painful experiences.

Religious systems of the past have viewed the realities of the world from their narrow views, excluding all other possibilities. It is my opinion that religious beliefs affect all aspects of life. Some religious systems want to lock you in; what they proclaim is sacred, and you are to shun what these systems think is secular. In the innocence of my youth, I believed all of life was sacred, so while I wrestled with guilt in the realm of Christian service, my aspirations for an exciting life still took precedence. Previous generations of varied religious and politic beliefs and practices handed me much baggage. I believe this imprinting at an early age can severely influence and handicap one's lifelong values and ethics—that is unless somewhere and somehow the cycle can be broken. One cannot minimize religious influence, as well as biological and environmental determinism, in the formation of the personality. All of this imprinting can create a cognitive dissonance and conflict within an individual's personality. I was no exception to all of these factors and influences at a very young age. With my strong will and the toxic imprinting, I am thankful for the positive counter influences that helped me filter the religious system in later years.

The evangelical charismatics did not give me the freedom to explore my own theology, but I seized it, knowing if I did not change my beliefs, I too would perish. Our charismatic friends totally dropped my family and I, for they thought we had lost a daughter's healing because of our disbelief, sin in our lives, or lack of faith. It was our dear liberal friends who just came with food, love, embracing arms, and healing words and led us back to redemption. Our life terrain had changed.

CHAPTER 25

Salt or Healing Balm: A More Excellent Way

> Nevertheless, that time of darkness and
> despair will not go on forever.
> —Is 9:1, NLT

> Share each other's troubles and problems…
> —Gal 6:2, TLB

Freedom at Last

From our experience we learned over and over that there is a more excellent way to minister to the grieving than many of the devastating clichés we encountered. In the process of healing, I realized most individuals were trying only to bring relief, and their ignorance resulted in more damage than healing. So many factors enter into one's philosophy and its expression. In hindsight I feel enriched to have grown through the negative experiences. Those encounters have become useful tools—examples of what not to do.

So many of us become like mechanical robots, never aware of our influence and power for healing or destruction. We have solidified our personalities as we have grown up, and our personalities have become locked-in like rock. We live in oblivion, never unlocking our hearts to reality. I honestly do not believe most thoughtless clichés are meant to harm, and our experience was not an isolated one.

Many writers, including Rabbi Harold Kushner, have written books, such as *Why Bad Things Happen to Good People*. Kushner addresses the unexplainable events that happen to some of the best and most holy people. I found great comfort in these books and learned that nasty things can happen to good people and good things can happen to nasty people. My family and I were classic examples. We were good people with a nearly perfect family. Of course we probably all have a little bit of nasty and a little bit of good residing within us!

Eyes Opened

Much of our horror and grief defied explanation or pat answers, but we screamed for understanding and compassion. I believe we take a great risk when we believe we can analyze a tragedy and place judgment. All the grieving want is compassion and understanding. Our lives had been so idealistic, but those in the fundamentalist community could assume only that there had to have been great sin in our lives.

Down through history the concept of God has been so distorted. Instead of appearing as a loving God, He is often portrayed as a cruel taskmaster, whipping his children into shape. I, for one, cannot serve a God who would inflict the ravages of leukemia on one of his children, but the fact that our world has fallen from grace gives me hope that the redemption of mankind has not yet taken place.

The aftermath of tragedy can be as devastating as the tragedy itself. This is especially true if grief is not dealt with, as in our case. Aborting the grief of loss became like aborting a pregnancy. It needs to be carried to full term, or psychological damage results. If grief is not resolved and embraced, many mental and physical maladies can surface—as well as a plethora of poor choices. Don and I were trying to repress our chronic grief, and we could not. Each experience of grief must be framed and hung, but it must not be painted over and over. It took us years to heal and recover mentally, emotionally, physically, and spiritually. We go backward periodically, but we continue to move forward knowing the last chapter of our lives is yet to be written. We have moments of insight and joy as we remember the twenty incredible years we spent with our daughter.

Love and Mercy

Though I thought I could never possibly recover, eventually deep-down wells of my soul began to bubble to life. The pain was no less, but joy accompanied it.

I have come to see the incredible resilience of the soul of humankind if it's put into an incubator of love. I believe in my search for wholeness, I have touched the heart of God. It is with this recognition that those of us who have suffered great loss can become conduits of God's compassion and mercy. Unfortunately our society places too much value on carrying on, doing well, or coping after loss. Grief is a process and not an event.

Still Our Daughter

I now see that a relationship that was supposedly broken by death is not really broken. That relationship is kept alive with gratitude for the time and experiences shared with our loved ones. Remembering and celebrating the joy of a life helps heal the broken heart. I know beyond the shadow of a doubt that the value of one child can never be replaced by another. I have learned to celebrate the doctrine of the communion of the saints, for this keeps the bonds of love open and alive. I have to take hope in the scripture "for we know that when this earthly tent we live in is taken down (that is, when we die and leave this earthly body), —when we die and leave these bodies—we will have a house in heaven, an eternal body made for us by God himself and not by human hands" (2 Cor 5:1).

Father Forgive

I want to repeat it again and again: I have come to believe that thoughtless clichés are not meant to wound or harm but are spoken with good intent and out of ignorance. Each person comes from a different paradigm. When I read Mark 12:31, it says, "Love thy neighbor as thyself." It does not say, "Judge thy neighbor"! I have learned that grief is a part of life—the other side of joy. "All of life is suffering" is a noble truth in Buddhist teaching. One can be as refined as pure gold through suffering and grief—in our case both through the tragedy and through the aftermath of that tragedy. Grief is not a problem to be cured but embraced. The human spirit has an incredible ability to bounce back from the depths of despair. Though limping, there can be joy again. I was able to say with Christ, "Father, forgive them, for they know not what they do." I could not hold people accountable for the pain they inflicted on our hearts.

The life terrain changes as we age, and we must adapt to the new changes and find meaning in that new terrain. Each life is a book with unfinished chapters. I learned that denying and repressing our wounds only made those wounds infected. My family and I needed the incubator of love to cleanse out the deep pain and wounds of our souls. Those who said our family's tragedy happened so we could minister to others were partially correct—although I would never say that to a grieving person. I learned that *holy listening* to the wounded and brokenhearted is all you can do. There is great joy in companioning those in deep sorrow and loss.

The root word of the word *religion* is *religio*, which means "to bind together." For me this has dynamic significance. At a time when shattering loss incapacitates, religion can be a healing factor. The injured and wounded need that healing. But this type of healing can take place only through the ultimate love of Christ—through us, the conduits of that love. I believe Christ's wounds are humanity's source of healing, and, likewise, our wounds can become the source for others' healing as well. This is a universal creed and truth that surpasses ethnic, cultural, philosophical, and religious boundaries. It is for humanity a light in the darkness. Crucifixion is always public, but resurrection comes silently, early in the morning!

POSTSCRIPT

Kyrie Eleison—Lord, Have Mercy

> Have you never heard? Have you never understood? The Lord
> is the everlasting God, the Creator of all the earth. He never
> grows weak or weary. No one can measure the depths of his
> understanding. He gives power to the weak and strength to
> the powerless. But those who trust in the Lord will find new
> strength. They will soar high on wings like eagles. They will
> run and not grow weary. They will walk and not faint.
> —Is 40:28–31, NLT

New Lessons

Sometime after our loss, while we were still recovering, Suzanne New—the choir director who had sung at Teresa's memorial and the dear who had brought us a huge bag of carrots and garlic—was having the Valley Choir sing a requiem Mass just before Easter. I joined the choir for that Mass. We practiced for hours before the performance and were almost too exhausted to sing when it was time to perform, but all the practice had locked the words securely in my mind and heart. As I sang those words over and over, a healing began to rise in my heart: Kyrie eleison—Lord have mercy. Christ said on the cross, "Father, forgive them, for they know not what they do" (Luke 23:24, KJV). Isn't it all about the mercy of God in the end?

Don and I came to more fully see how we had been put in an unholy vise—maybe as martyrs ourselves—alongside Teresa. For when a child dies, the whole family dies little by little. We had to forgive those who had so painfully wounded us and forgive ourselves for the poor choices that further crippled us and pro-hibited us from getting well. We had not asked for anyone to fix us, change us, or give us advice, but in our vulnerability all of these things happened. There was too much salt and not enough balm. No matter what the ethnic, cultural or religious background each of us comes from, pain is pain, loss is loss, and grief is grief!

There was no emotional help available when we so desperately needed it. At the time we were stricken with our unbelievable loss, much of the prevalent theology, in and out of the church, suggested that pain and suffering were the direct results of sin in one's life. We noted this belief was present especially in those who had not yet had personal experiences with loss. Too many in our cul-ture try to ignore pain and suffering altogether. As was true with us, most would rather remain in denial than face the possibility of loss in their own lives. Thus many of us abort all signs of grief. Don and I were in that vast majority of people who would rather remain in denial and believe that bad things happen only to other people.

We were broken, and we did not know where to turn. I concluded that the ultimate ministry is to become a conduit of God's mercy and love. We remem-bered mostly the bad comments and adverse behavior rather than basking only in our deep friendships. So, creeping and crawling, we started the process of going from brokenness to healing. In the dark streets of the mind, former hurts reside and remain, but we tried to stay off those streets and move forward. We bumped along the corridors of our past life. We were blinded and could not see the whole tapestry of our lives, but we hoped it was woven together with God's grace and mercy. We knew we were blessed in so many areas. We realized we must embrace the grief that had so crippled us. Grief that is not embraced can and does result in many pathological ailments. We were no exception.

It was not hard to miss that too many religious systems remain on a super-ficial level, not touching the depths of real personal need. Our human dilemma gives us more connectedness to each other than the forms and beliefs we share. Doctrines have locked personalities into walls of contempt for each other's doc-trinal views. Being doctrinally correct is more important to many people than meeting the needs of those in pain.

It is my belief that every pew, cathedral, and hospital bed holds a broken heart from one event or another. Often we see beautifully coiffed and jeweled women and men with spit and polish in church, but their souls may nevertheless be bleeding internally. From all outward appearances, we would assume they have it all together, and all is well with their souls. Not necessarily so! Outward appearance does not always disclose the bleeding heart within. As Don and I reflected on our past, we saw that most of the people with barbs were only trying to protect the fences surrounding their beliefs and fears. They were afraid our grief might invade their holy ground. To them we were not acting as good Christians should in our grief.

I wonder if, in many churches, we do not put on facades of perfection. The church has promoted this appearance in its attempt to follow the perfection of Christ. We have not truly embraced what it means to be human but see our brokenness and weakness as failures. Our High Priest, Christ, understands our weaknesses, for He faced all of the same temptations we do, yet He did not sin. "So let us come boldly to the throne of our gracious God. There we will receive his mercy, and we will find grace to help us when we need it most" (Heb 4:16, NLT).

After years of trying to gain some semblance of mental and physical health after our walking through the valley of death, I was able to complete my degree in philosophy and religion as well as receive a pastoral care certificate. These achievements were so very healing—maybe it was just the fact that my mind had to be on achieving another dream! It also helped me learn so much about other religions as well with how to more effectively walk beside those who are grieving or wounded. My family and I were all going through a metamorphosis—a painful and healing journey. In the midst of tragic loss and grief, one is very vulnerable to words and actions. Out of my family's personal experience with grief, we have been able to walk with others as they go through their journeys of grief, and we have discovered there are much better ways to journey alongside those in despair.

Recovery is possible, though none of us can believe it is at the time of loss. Words and actions can bring either life or further death to the individual grieving, making the recovery time lengthier or even impossible. Words and actions can aid in the journey to faith and hope, or they can further throw someone into despair and hopelessness. I learned from my studies and personal experience that to minister to and aid in the healing of the bereaved and brokenhearted, one must transcend philosophical, religious, and ethnic boundaries. This is not easy, for most people maintain their religious training and beliefs from the past. When hearts are broken beyond repair, there needs to be help given related to issues of death and dying. If this is lacking, many of us try to abort all signs of grief.

If there is no liberation from the toxic imprinting of the past, there can be no healing. Even though many people throw out their faith in grief, our spirits still cry out for a Sovereign Deity to come fill the God space. We cry out to have the vast arena of pain canceled and filled with joy once again. All of life must reside in the realm of sacred and not secular versus sacred.

Our family learned that the road to wholeness often runs right through the garbage dump! Bitter and harsh words, put-downs, and invalidation stick like pieces of shrapnel in one's brain—never to be forgotten. It is difficult for the grieving to recover, but pain always brings a message. Accept it with gratitude. Rather than saying, "Why me?" change the question to "why not me?"

But experientially that will take time. Remember too that anger intensifies the pain, so to ignore pain is to drive it deeper. Tragedy always produces pain— pain of mind, pain of the heart, and pain of the whole soul, but deep pain can be a wake-up call to newness of life. For me it was a call to a higher realm of living. It is a butterfly emerging from a cocoon covering over grief, complacency, and a protected, callused personality. It is a signal to find healing. Pain can become a metamorphosis to new freedom and new beginnings. A more real self can emerge. A broken vessel releases the fragrance of what is contained within. A closed and sealed vessel cannot. My prayer became, "Dear Lord, help us to extend mercy to all!" This, in part, is what our journey through grief has taught us.

Kyrie Eleison—Lord, Have Mercy

This dates back to pre-Christian liturgies, apostolic times. It evolved
into a mass in Rome, used as a chant—a liturgical exclamation.
Kyrie eleison, Christe eleison: Lord, have mercy, Christ have mercy.
Kyrie eleison: Lord, have mercy.
Alto e glorioso Dio: Most high and glorious God,
Illumina le tenebre del cuore mio: Illuminate the darkness of my heart
E dammi fede retta: And grant us an upright faith,
E carita perfetta, speranza certa: Perfect love and certain hope,
Umilta profonda: Profound humility,
Saggezza e conoseimento: And wisdom and understanding,

O Signore, affinche io facci: O Lord that I might follow
IL tuo santo e ver a
ace commandamento: Your holy and true commandment.
Kyrie eleison: Lord, have mercy.

Epilogue

This book has swirled around in my head for almost forty years. Much water has passed under the bridge and many events—good and bad—have transpired. Removing my protective mask, I have told my story—mainly for my children, who have endured tragedy and its aftermath, if not in person then as observers at the edge of each event.

Our family was not without problems, but in comparison to much of society, it was a joyous and happy family. To us it was ideal—that is until one of our children…jewels, in our eyes…lost a three-year battle with leukemia. During that battle my husband and I often talked to our daughter about writing a book entitled *Miracles Take Work*, for we overturned every stone in our search for a miracle. When in the end we lost the battle, our world crashed, and we were to find little help either spiritually or scientifically within our culture. Many of those who suffer massive loss seem to exit from life itself! We are a classic example.

Though much of our journey was filled with charm and goodness, it was walking through the valley of death that taught us the most, enhanced our ability to minister to others, and allowed us to embrace the mercy of God for ourselves and others. We truly were chiseled by life at every turn and in every chapter of our lives.

It is my desire, in putting down our journey, that my children and others will more fully understand what happens when one tries to abort grief. In this painful journey, Don and I have met many others who have dropped out of life and have tried to abort their own grief. For me, my theology was transformed; our lives have taken on a new dimension in every way, for we know there is a better day coming.

Finally, I hope our lives have proven God is faithful in all of life. He redeems us from our bad, unknowing choices. Often we do the wrong thing for the right reasons, and it takes time to undo some choices—sometimes half a lifetime. But our last chapters are yet to be written.

Don and I have had the privilege to lead a fantastic church near Mt. Hood that is filled with the most loving people anywhere. We were able to assist fifty-plus church and community friends make their transitions into the next world in the twelve years we served there. My phobias were dissipated as we stood with them and they took their last breath. Those friends are eternal.

My heart was further opened to what Christ said were the greatest commandments when we led a trip to Egypt. Our guide was a devote Muslim, a most godly and kind man, Ahmed. It brought to memory those two greatest commandments—that is to love God with all your heart and love your neighbor as yourself. I found myself overcome with such an intense love for this man half-way around the world, of a different faith, yet my neighbor. He, too, is our eternal friend.

Don and I were able to lead many trips abroad, and I was able to complete my bachelor's degree in philosophy and religion at the age of sixty-eight—plus securing a certificate in pastoral care that has enabled me to journey with even more compassion. Our remaining children and grandchildren have made our hearts dance. Don Ralph retired as a lieutenant colonel from the marines and is Aviation Director at Eastern Kentucky University. Christy earned a degree from Pacific Lutheran University in Tacoma, Washington—the same university Raju graduated from. She has been our artist, leveler and prayer warrior. Michele graduated from Portland State University and was a manager for a Nautilus Club for many years while raising three successful children. Raju and his family still grace our lives. Raju, now retired from DuPont, has gone back to India and other places to minister and to train indigenous workers for gospel work.

Our three younger children have given Don and I such joy and healing. Cean is Head master and Sexton of a local cemetery. He has always loved the funeral business with a passion. Danielle, the daughter most like Teresa, has had the same love of horses. It has led her and her husband, a fire chief, to a farm, where they raise many more animals and three adorable children. Jason, a high degree black belt, is living in Southern California and working in a prestigious job while raising two of our adorable grandchildren. Jason is the one who selected the title of this book—most appropriate.

Our children have provided us with their wonderful spouses and grandchildren—even great-grandchildren. The children are our legacy of pride, and we know from this vantage point how we are indeed blessed in so many areas of our lives. I had always believed that is was parents who taught and guided their children, but have found that it is those children who have taught us so very much about life. Our hearts have healed, though the tragedy seems to have happened, in emotion, only yesterday for us all. And yes, the smoke of battle has cleared, and we are still standing in the shadow of the Cross. Though we know we are on the downside of our years on Earth, our faith is intact! Our riches are the friends we have collected over the years.

To our children—our jewels and legacy—grandchildren, great-grandchildren, and dear friends: we dedicate *Our Story* to you.

http://www.shekinahmoments.com
ruthygibbs@gmail.com

Please feel free to add your comments. To anyone in grief, I would love to talk to you.

A percent of the price of each book sold will go to St. Jude's to care for children suffering from the dreaded disease cancer. Thank you for sharing our story.

GLOSSARY

Advent Christian: The denomination calls itself First-Day Adventists. It was started by William Miller in Salem, Massachusetts, in the year 1860. In 1831 Miller started proclaiming that Christ would return in the year 1844. Thousands of followers sold all their possessions. They were called Millerites. Then one of Miller's disciples said the date was to be in 1854.

One of the basic beliefs of this denomination is soul sleeping. (See definition of *soul sleeping* below.) At the resurrection the godly will rise to immortality, and the wicked will be burned up for eternal extinction. In 2006 the denomination had about the same membership number—25,000—that it did in 1925.

Alcan Highway: A highway built during World War II connecting the contiguous United States to Alaska through Canada. It was completed in 1944.

Anthropomorphic: Reducing God to the form and attributes of man.

Azacitidine: One of the first drugs used to treat leukemia.

Biola: A university in Southern California once associated with the Baptist denomination. They now have several campuses and no denominational affiliation.

Bobbsey Twins: A series of books about the adventures of the Bobbsey twins, written by Laura Lee Hope from 1909 to 1979, often written by ghostwriters. These were children's books popular during the 1930s and 1940s.

Bums: (homeless people) in the 1950s: Went from house to house asking for help rather than standing on street corners with signs.

Carl Rogers: Started an offshoot group related to the sensitivity groups that were sweeping the land in the 1960s. This type of group ran through the YMCA and churches and even started appearing in grade schools.

Colfax: A small rural town in the Palouse area of Whitman County, Washington. Surrounding the wealthy community and farmland there are beautifully rolling hills that make this community so inviting. Added to Colfax's present population of 3,300 are the thousands more who live on ranches and in other towns and communities scattered over the rolling Palouse hills—people who look to this resourceful trade center and seat of government for security. They all know the vital role this friendly city plays in their daily lives. All depend in whole or in part upon Colfax's varied services as well as its cultural and religious life disparity, which are entirely distinct or separate from each other.

Cytosine: A drug to eradicate the duplication of leukemia cells.

Dysfunctional: Abnormal or impaired functioning.

Father Bennett: An Episcopal minister who initially preached a sermon about the underground movement of the Pentecostal speaking in tongues, sharing how he was involved and how he too had spoken in tongues. The story hit the news media, and as a result many Christians joined the movement, which caused much division within the mainline denominations, bringing both new life and damage to the Christian community.

Free Methodist: An ultraconservative part of the Methodist church.

Fundamentalist: A movement marked by rigid adherence to basic principles, with only one authority, as interpreted by the leaders.

Gamma Globulin: Given to strengthen the immunity system; given to Teresa in the first two weeks of her life, after she had contracted measles. Much later, I researched why a newborn would be given this gamma globulin. At the time I was too young and inexperienced to ask questions.

Head Start: A program started under the auspices of the Office of Economic Opportunity for poor children who needed a jump-start to enter public schools.

Hurlbut's Story of the Bible: Written in 1932 simply to tell the stories of the Bible.

Imprinting: To fix firmly in the mind without personal choice.

John Birch Society: A political advocacy group that supports anticommunism and limited government. It has been described as radical right. The John Birch Society was established in California in 1958.

Kathryn Kuhlman: Started holding miraculous healing meetings throughout the world in the 1960s and '70s. Kathryn was a part of the charismatic movement.

Leukemia: When abnormal white blood cells proliferate in the bone marrow, crowding out the ability to produce normal blood cells. It invades other organs of the body as well.

Mesa Verde: Cliff dwellings developed in AD 400, mostly built out of sandstone. Archaeology students are often taken there for discovery opportunities. Mesa Verde is located in Southern Colorado.

Metamorphosis: A major change in the appearance or character of someone or something.

Miracle: An interruption in the course of nature beyond the natural laws of science.

Missionary: A missionary is one who goes out to recruit for and share a belief or religion.

Northwest Christian University: Affiliated with the Disciples of Christ and Church of Christ denominations; located in Eugene, Oregon.

Office of Economic Opportunity: Developed in 1964 during Lyndon Johnson's presidency as part of the war on poverty, with social and economic initiatives.

Paradigm: A theory or a group of ideas about how something should be done, made, or thought about.

Ouija board: A game enlisting spirits to answer questions with the use of a pointer, which supposedly spells out the answers on a board. The pointer is held in the players' hands, and the spirits move it around on an alphabet on the board.

Red-light district: A section of a city or town reserved for the use of prostitution.

Redemption: the act of saving people from sin and evil. The word is sometimes used as buying back or redeeming a prior owned item.

Room 101: A torture chamber referred to in George Orwell's book *1984*. Prisoners were subjected to their worst nightmares in this chamber.

Sacred: worthy of religious worship: very holy

Secular: Worldly rather than holy and spiritual.

Soul sleeping: The belief that when one dies, there is no afterlife; the soul is nothing more than breath. Soul sleeping is a concept taken from the Psalms.

The Sound of Music: A musical produced on Broadway and in film in the 1960s. The Sound of Music is a story about the von Trapp family that took place in Austria around 1938.

The Three Faces of Eve: A book and a movie done on a woman who developed multiple personalities due to various traumas in her life.

Transcendence: the quality or state of being transcendent. I used this word as transcending the cares and realities of human frailties.

Youth for Christ: a movement started in the 1940's. Billy Graham, became YFC's first full-time staff member. The movement under Billy Graham's leadership spread like wild fire in many communities.

BIBLIOGRAPHY

Alsop, Stewart. *Stay of Execution: A Sort of Memoir*. New York: J. Lippincott Co., 1973.

Bateson, Mary Catherine. *Peripheral Visions*. New York: Harper Collins, 1994.

Hurlbut, Charles C. *Hurlbut's Story of the Bible*. Philadelphia, Pa.: Universal Book and Bible House, 1932.

Hurnard, Hannah. *Hinds' Feet on High Places*. Old Tappan, New Jersey: Spire Books, 1968.

King, Marie Gentert, ed. *Foxe's Book of Martyrs*. Old Tappan, New Jersey: Spire Books, 1968.

Kübler-Ross, Elisabeth. *On Death and Dying*. New York: Macmillan Publishing Co., 1969.

Kushner, Harold S. *When Bad Things Happen to Good People*. New York: Schocken Books, 1981.

Lewis, C. S. *A Grief Observed*. New York: The Seabury Press, 1971.

Marquis, Don. *archy and mehitabel*. New York: Doubleday, Page & Co., 1927.

Nouwen, Henri J. *The Wounded Healer*. New York: Image Books Doubleday, 1972.

Osteen, John H. *There Is a Miracle in Your Mouth*. Houston, Texas: John H. Osteen, 1971.

Sanford, Agnes. *The Healing Light*. Lake Mary, New Jersey: Charisma Books, 1972.

Schiff, Harriet Sarnoff. *The Bereaved Parent*. New York: Crown Publishers, Inc., 1977.

Shoemaker, Helen. *I Stand by the Door*. New York: Harper & Row Publishers, 1967.

The Holy Bible, New Living Translation, Wheaton, Illinois, Tyndale House Publishers, Inc. 1996.

The Holy Bible, New King James Version, New York, New York: Thomas Nelson, Inc. 1982.

The Holy Bible, New International Version, New York, New York: Zondervan Bible Publishers, 1978.

The Holy Bible, King James Version, Iowa Falls, Iowa: Riverside Book and Bible House, 1971.

The Holy Bible, Living Bible Version, Wheaton, Illinois: Tyndale House Publishers, Inc., 1996.

The Holy Bible, New International Version, Grand Rapid, Michigan: Zondervan Publishers, 1979.

The Holy Bible, New Century Version, New York, New York: Thomas Nelson, Inc. 1991

Wiersbe, Warren W. *Why Us? When Bad Things Happen to God's People*. Old Tappan, New Jersey: Fleming H. Revell Company, 1984.

Made in the USA
Lexington, KY
19 November 2019